Companies With a Conscience

Companies With a Conscience

Intimate Portraits of Twelve Firms That Make a Difference

Updated and Revised

Mary Scott and Howard Rothman

A CITADEL PRESS BOOK
Published by Carol Publishing Group

A Citadel Press Book
Published by Carol Publishing Group
Citadel Press is a registered trademark of Carol Communications, Inc.
Editorial Offices: 600 Madison Avenue, New York, N.Y. 10022
Sales & Distribution Offices: 120 Enterprise Avenue, Secaucus, N.J. 07094
In Canada: Canadian Manda Group, P.O. Box 920, Station U, Toronto, Ontario M8Z 5P9
Queries regarding rights and permissions should be addressed to
Carol Publishing Group, 600 Madison Avenue, New York, N.Y. 10022

Carol Publishing Group books are available at special discounts
for bulk purchases, for sales promotions, fund raising, or
educational purposes. Special editions can be created to specifications.
For details, contact: Special Sales Department, Carol Publishing
Group, 120 Enterprise Avenue, Secaucus, N.J. 07094

Manufactured in the United States of America
10 9 8 7 6 5 4 3 2 1

Library of Congress Cataloging-in-Publication Data

Scott, Mary (Mary Barbara)
     Companies with a conscience : intimate portraits of twelve firms that make a difference
/ by Mary Scott and Howard Rothman.
        p.   cm.
     Updated paperback ed.
     "A Citadel Press book."
     ISBN 0-8065-1502-3 (pbk.)
     1. Social responsibility of business—United States—Case studies.   2. Business
enterprises—United States—Case studies.   I. Rothman, Howard.   II. Title.
HD60.5.U5S36   1994   93-45776
658.4'08—dc20   CIP

TO OUR FAMILIES, WITH LOVE

Contents

	Introduction	3
1.	Teatime, Nineties Style	9
2.	From Welfare to Working	22
3.	One Step Ahead	35
4.	Ice Cream & Integrity	46
5.	Banking on the Community	62
6.	Selling What Comes Naturally	76
7.	Baking, Building, and Benefiting	91
8.	Rolling Along	103
9.	Less Is More	118
10.	Grateful—and Generous	135
11.	Back to the Land	151
12.	The Spirit of Esprit	166
13.	The Additional Enlightened	180
14.	Lessons of Conscientious Leadership	206

Preface

A new kind of company is surfacing in America. The growing need to care for our planet and its diminishing resources and the heartfelt desire by many up-and-coming firms now able—and willing—to contribute to their communities are combining to spawn a new era of socially responsible business. The "Companies With a Conscience" have arrived.

Profitable, alternatively conceived endeavors have sprung up in industries as diverse as banking and rock and roll. Often quirky but always quality driven, these companies succeeded through the early nineties as many of their less-than-conscientious peers fell victim to recession or scandal. This book—almost two years in the making—presents a close-up look at the companies and the people who compose the nucleus of this conscientious corporate movement. A dozen enterprises from across the United States are introduced in portraits that reveal both an uncanny flair for business and an uncommon commitment to people.

As the nineties wear on, it becomes increasingly apparent that business in general can no longer function or be judged solely on the basis of fiscal nets and grosses. A positive impact on employees, customers, and the community at large has assumed an equal or even greater significance in the overall picture. Today's bottom line emcompasses more than just dollars and cents, and corporations of all sizes and philosophical orientations are beginning to recognize this.

Companies With a Conscience: Intimate Portraits of Twelve Firms That Make a Difference looks closely at companies that have supported this concept since their inception. Each is captured in a profile that is based on the recollections and analyses of its founding entrepreneur and other major players. The vision, principles, and practical applications that led to annual sales of $100 million or more are explained by those who know them best. Supporting characters—those not integral to the formation and basic structuring of these enterprises—offer their opinions and comments on a first-name-only basis.

Companies With a Conscience examines the alternative route that these twelve companies—and several dozen more, in shortened form—have taken to success. It is for everyone who has adopted a conscientious life-style of their own. Business owners, corporate leaders, department managers, and most especially, members of the general public who deal with these companies and their employees every day will find the material intriguing and inspiring.

Acknowledgments

As we worked on *Companies With a Conscience,* we learned that our greatest source of information was the people we know—our family, our friends, and our colleagues. They sent us newspaper and magazine clippings, called us with ideas, and made countless suggestions that were invaluable to the project. The genuine interest and input of these people helped make *Companies With a Conscience* happen.

In particular we would like to thank Lee Holden, Linda Schwartz, Deb Nastaj, John Kirk, Lew Goodman, Jim Brown, Mark Horton, Megan Topping, Missy Park, Owen Dempsey, Brian Hanson, Mark Skinner, Brigitte Coutu, Fred Droz, Jeff Uhrlaub, Rod Walker, Jacqueline Harp, Meg Lukens, Nell Newman, Paige Springer, Donita Rapp, Pam Cole, Ann Krcik, Justis Fennell, Cynthia Sharp, Suzanne Nakasian, Kathy Randall, David Creek, Cameron Sears, Queenie Taylor, Bill Werlin, Barbara Geehan, Lisa Geil, Andrea Gabbard, Molly Mattaliano, Clare Hertel, Bob Woodward, Megan Montgomery, Bruce Hamilton, Una Baker, Kay Kinsella, Cynthia and Dick Randall, Paul Morton, Diane Frazier, David Knight, and everyone else who has been supportive.

Thanks to Mary Louise Scott, John Arndt, Adrian Barrett, Meredith Miller, and Parry Burnhap. And a special thanks for their ideas, editing, and invaluable input to Tom Scott, John Scott, and Pat Rothman.

Thanks to our agents, Richard Curtis and Katherine Almy, for taking on our project. Finally, we would like to acknowledge Hillel Black and especially Denise O'Sullivan for their talented editing and never-ending enthusiasm for *Companies With a Conscience.*

Companies With a Conscience

Introduction

In October 1993, more than six hundred like-minded business people, members of a group called Businesses for Social Responsibility, met for a two-day conference in Washington, D.C. President Bill Clinton was one of the first speakers to address the group. "I have admiration for this organization," he said. "I believe the purpose of policy is to help the American people live up to the fullest of their God-given potential, and help them live together in strength and harmony, and to fulfill their responsibility, as well as their dreams.

"That obligation can be met in different ways, in different times," he continued. "Sometimes the history of the nation can only be met by a willingness to undertake the rigors of profound change. I believe this is the time."

A new energy, a new motivation, and a new drive is sweeping business in America in the 1990s. Since the original printing of the hardcover edition of *Companies With A Conscience* in December, 1992, there's been an outburst of the newest generation of caring capitalism. An increasing number of university business schools and undergraduate programs are adopting business ethics programs; regional and national business groups are forming to address issues of social responsibility; an increasing number of businesses are adopting environmental and social programs; and we have an administration that salutes businesses as agents for change.

It's much easier now, in hindsight, to explain why we wrote *Companies With a Conscience* than it was to articulate the fine points of

3

the project when it first came up early in 1991. At that time, the two of us began talking about the way corporate America seemed to be resetting its moral compass. We marveled at how the greed-is-good, house-of-cards economic engineering of the eighties was no longer in favor. And how the Michael Milkens, Charles Keatings, and Gordon Gekkos of our world—real-life Wall Street money men and cinematic West Coast power brokers alike—were suddenly and decisively out of fashion.

Because our professional and writing careers had been spent concentrating on topics like progressive business management and our personal lives had been marked by a long-standing commitment to a variety of social causes, we were more than a little interested in the trend. We decided to find out just what was going on.

From the start, evidence of this newfound ethical standard appeared everywhere. Companies like Apple Computer and Wal-Mart were actively encouraging their employees and customers to recycle. Campbell Soup and H. J. Heinz were among those offering on-site day-care programs. Avon Products and General Mills were developing policies to help female and minority workers. Coca-Cola and 3M were investing heavily in community outreach efforts.

We also discovered that the environment really had taken center stage and that corporations of all persuasions were jumping over one another to initiate "green" policies. Candice Bergen told us how US Sprint was pledging a portion of its receipts to environmental groups. The WD-40 Co. announced a "Preserve Our Parks" foundation to be funded with proceeds from the sale of its household lubricant. Even General Motors released a packet of information called General Motors and the Environment.

We knew something important had begun to happen when McDonald's Corp. announced a far-reaching plan to eliminate polystyrene sandwich boxes, introduce recycled paper bags, and implement large-scale food- and paper-waste composting as a means of dramatically reducing trash at its eighty-five hundred fast-food franchises. We also remained skeptical until we learned more.

What we eventually found was a still small—but steadily growing—movement toward "caring capitalism," as one of its major proponents describes it. The basic tenet is that business doesn't have to be a negative force in society and businesspeople don't have to be the "bad guys." We determined that enterprises that buy into this concept are part of an increasing network of companies with a conscience. We decided to find out exactly who these companies were. And just what they were doing that was so memorable from a business, and socially responsible, point of view.

Although giants like Wal-Mart, Heinz, 3M, and McDonald's receive the bulk of publicity for their actions in this area, we quickly discovered that smaller, often-unknown companies really were the leaders in the nascent movement toward corporate responsibility. What's more, we also discovered that many of the small- and mid-sized firms were actually making a regular and substantial profit. Armed with statistics that told us some 1.3 million new businesses—primarily in this category—had opened their doors in 1991 alone, we felt that an examination of such leading-edge entrepreneurial efforts would offer the most in the way of lessons and appeal.

Even with that much of a background, our search still took us in some unexpected directions. We met regular people from Long Island who crank out the world's finest premium ice cream and a Buddhist abbot from Yonkers who bakes incredibly popular gourmet desserts. There were health-food aficionados in the shoe, grocery, and clothing businesses. Tea makers and welfare recipients existed side by side. So did bankers and rock and rollers.

The short-term result of our search is the collection of profiles contained in the following pages of *Companies With a Conscience: Intimate Portraits of Twelve Firms That Make a Difference,* a book that identifies and then examines a dozen socially responsible—and successful—businesses in America. These are the firms that are changing not only the way they do business but the way it is conducted by all of us. And they are the firms that treat all people within their influence—employees, customers, and residents of their communities—with the utmost respect, without losing their focus on the bottom line.

As we moved more deeply into the subject, we encountered a lot of businesspeople interested in the way our leading-edge companies were combining a commitment to the planet with one for the balance sheet. We noted the mushrooming number of business schools requiring classes on environmental or ethical issues for an M.B.A.

degree. And we watched as companies like IBM and Coors began supporting major conferences on business ethics for their peers across the United States.

So how did we choose the companies we eventually decided to include? We started by talking to people at a few of the benchmark businesses we already knew about. Ben & Jerry's Homemade—founded by two Long Island ice cream men—was a natural because of its major social agenda; Patagonia and Celestial Seasonings were two others we were aware of right from the start. Workers at these companies told us about employees at others, who recommended people elsewhere, who knew somebody worth interviewing at still another firm. Eventually, we researched hundreds of businesses and spoke with dozens of business leaders and business educators.

We then established a firm list of criteria for potential candidates, two of which were most critical.

First, we wanted only companies with a proven record of conscientious business practices over a significant period of time. While the McDonald's Corp.'s recent environmentally based actions are certainly laudatory, we sought businesses that were longtime leaders in this area rather than merely followers. We looked, therefore, for corporate structures that contained a well-articulated social mission interwoven into their basic fabric.

And we wanted only companies that had been consistently profitable over this same time, with all indications of continued success. So we looked for a clearly defined economic program as well. It was easy to find superb examples of conscientious nonprofits, along with well-meaning, new for-profits that were poised to advance from fledgling to full-fledged. But we wanted companies that could truly serve as viable role models for the corporate America that is taking shape in the nineties. For that we needed businesses that proved you could have your cake and eat it, too.

Sometimes our search provided some unexpected insights. Always it offered an intriguing look into the many different ways that businesses are choosing to demonstrate their combined social dedication and fiscal commitment. One constant we uncovered among prospective subjects was an entrepreneurial bent; another was a general reluctance to "blow their own horns" by even participating in a project of this nature. But all of this ran second to a genuine desire to serve as a role model to other companies interested in adopting such a route to responsibility and success. All of the companies we selected were therefore happy to provide us with the access and information we needed to help inspire others with their stories.

We eventually settled on the twelve firms profiled in the following pages and believe our choices are interesting as well as informative. Some of the companies carry names known to the general public, for example, Birkenstock and Ben & Jerry's. Others, such as Quickie Designs and America Works, serve a much more specialized audience.

But all of these businesses are included enthusiastically because they fulfill our criteria as well, or better, than any of the other candidates.

Still, we were not entirely satisfied. There were so many more companies doing good work, so many more profitable efforts worthy of attention. What to do? We eventually decided on an additional chapter, which briefly describes a number of the other interesting businesses we encountered along the way with conscientious programs and responsible practices. We have still left out more than we'd like.

We also included a final chapter in which we distill the factors common to these companies with a conscience and note characteristics that make them the companies they are. Foremost among these, as we've already suggested, is a concern for people. The way each enterprise exhibits it, though, is always somewhat different.

Other recurring traits—and the way these businesses go about helping their various communities—are less easy to categorize. Most are deeply dedicated to environmental issues. Many give away money. Some only employ the people they are trying to help. Others continuously sponsor a wide array of fund-raising events. Taken individually, they represent the cream of the creative crop in today's new business world. Taken as a whole, they offer tremendous insight into the wide-ranging ways that companies can earn money while making the world a better place.

In the months that passed since *Companies With A Conscience* first appeared, businesses profiled within its pages continued to prove that their success—due largely to the incorporation of these trains into their cultures—is no fluke. Alfalfa's Markets, for example, evolved from three stores to six. Celestial Seasonings went public and completed a very well-received stock offering. Ben & Jerry's flourished; America Works expanded; Quickie Designs branched into related new endeavors. And, bringing this back to where we started, President Clinton introduced legislation to create community development banks around the U.S. using South Shore Bank as a model.

We sincerely hope these profiles inspire others to take up the cause of "caring capitalism," the phrase created and exemplified by Ben Cohen and Jerry Greenfield of Ben & Jerry's. Those we met along the way certainly affected us deeply. So we, too, have decided to help and are donating 5 percent of our profits from this project to a selection of social and environmental causes.

1

Teatime, Nineties Style

Company name: Celestial Seasonings Inc.
Type of business: herbal tea producer
Location: Boulder, Colorado
Number of employees: 216
Year founded: 1969

"Mo's back!"

That simple exclamation, and the excitement surrounding it, meant more to America's leading herbal tea company than anything else in its corporate history. The summer of 1991 marked the trumpeted return of Mo Siegel—founding herb picker, self-taught marketing genius, and idea man extraordinaire—to the $54 million company he had founded in 1969 at the age of twenty. Now, at forty-one, the still-boyish-looking "philosopher/businessman" was ending a five-year retirement to lead his Boulder, Colorado–based Celestial Seasonings Inc. into the next century. Everyone, from the customers who took a personal interest in his company to the executive who stepped aside for his return, was ecstatic.

And rightly so. Although wildly successful virtually from its inception, Celestial had reached a critical juncture. Years of consistent growth put it solidly atop the domestic herbal tea market, responsible for more sales than all of its competitors combined. Some forty of its distinctive tea flavors could be found in grocery outlets and health-food stores throughout the United States and in several countries overseas. Farmers around the world were carefully—and exclusively—cultivating $5 million worth of herb crops every year to its exacting standards. A series of innovative environmental measures, both internal and external, helped make the company as popular as its product.

Still, all was not well. An ill-fated marriage with Kraft, the food-industry giant that bought Celestial in 1984, proved more disastrous than anyone imagined and ended in an expensive divorce just four years later. The resulting bills put a serious strain on the tea company's cash flow, and fiscal fallout threatened to overshadow all of Celestial's good works. It put a definite damper on things at the firm's sprawling plant in the shadow of the Rocky Mountains.

But then Mo was back, and it was almost as if he had never left. Economic damage from the leveraged buy-out (LBO) that allowed Celestial to retake itself from Kraft was not going to just disappear. But the enthusiasm and risk taking and seat-of-the-pants decision making that made the company an iconoclastic beacon returned with its well-known founder. Everyone from tea baggers to the company's president could feel it. And Siegel—who once tramped through the mountains on herb-picking expeditions, sewed muslin tea bags, helped design Celestial's unique packaging, and sold finished products to local health-food stores—felt it, too.

"The LBO has been hard on the company. It made us private, but it stung," the soft-spoken Siegel said a few months after his return. "Now we're going to bring about some pretty dramatic changes. We're going to introduce a plethora of new products. We're going to redo our boxes and upgrade our art. We're going to be better." He stops, clasps his hands together, and looks a visitor straight in the eye. "Really," he adds, "I'm pretty pumped."

Siegel, combining a people-oriented counterculture heritage with an energetic all-business approach, does seem exactly the right sort of executive to bring about such improvements at Celestial Seasonings. He is—those who know him agree—a hands-on manager who immerses himself in everything, from advertising plans to tea recipes. But all of his movements are driven by a genuine affection for both his company and his employees, as well as for a product that he honestly believes is good for the world and for his customers. His approach, therefore, is to once again rededicate the company to the good-for-the-earth philosophy under which it was founded—and under which it flourished.

"I've always been a very value driven person, and I want a certain set of values in this company that are immovable: quality of the product, love of the consumers, giving the best we can give to the world, taking care of our people," he explains. "My idea is to build a company, with dedicated people, who love their work and want to put out the best tea in the world."

That, he adds, and a business that eventually reaches a half-billion dollars in sales. "I have what you call the fire in the belly," Siegel says.

Cup of Tea?

Everyone at Celestial, it seems, asks visitors, upon their arrival, if they'd like a cup of tea. Coffee and soda pop are rarely mentioned. Here, instead, it is Red Zinger or Chamomile? Peppermint or Sleepytime? Cinnamon Vienna or Mandarin Orange Spice? Distinctive names for distinctive teas, poured with pride and enjoyed across the board.

Barney Feinblum is no exception, at least as far as the offering of tea is concerned. In other areas, however, his is quite a different story. Hired by Celestial in 1976, when he was just twenty-eight, Feinblum still favors the type of casual clothing—jeans, open-collared shirts, and hiking boots—that remain the chosen attire for most everyone in the company but Mo Siegel, who usually is the only one in the entire building with a necktie. But Feinblum's appearance and quickness to pour a cup of tea can be somewhat deceiving. As president and chief executive officer (CEO), he is in charge of Celestial's daily workings. And he was also the person most responsible for keeping the company on track during its brief but very unhappy alliance with Kraft.

"Business has to reflect the values of society," says Feinblum, who was elevated from vice-president of finance to president of the company when Siegel retired in 1986. "You don't have to be a dirtball to succeed."

Feinblum, a native of New York, chose to live in the Rocky Mountain West when he was studying for an MBA at the University of Colorado at Boulder. While working for Samsonite Corp., the Denver-based luggage maker, he was offered a job as production manager at Celestial. Although the position paid just $225 a week—two-thirds of his then current salary—Feinblum jumped at the chance to work at a firm that had no dress codes, no reserved parking spaces, and no artificial symbols of status or class like most of the rest of corporate America.

Instead, when Feinblum arrived, Celestial reflected the values imbued by Siegel, who gathered wild herbs in the mountains outside Aspen during the company's first year of operation. The following year, Siegel's friend Wyck Hay joined him. They, along with various relatives and friends, moved their base of operations to Boulder and picked enough herbs to produce five hundred pounds of their first blend, which they called Mo's 36 Herb tea. The group packaged the product in ten thousand hand-sewn muslin bags and sold it successfully through a Boulder health-food store.

Hay's brother John joined the company in 1971, and he and Siegel became copresidents. They capitalized their enterprise with $800, realized from the sale of Hay's Datsun 240Z, and established a production facility in an old barn outside of town. Owing to his personality and flair, Siegel took up Celestial's public relations, operations, and marketing arms and quickly became the company's most visible public figure. John Hay assumed responsibility for sales and finance, performing those vital duties competently, albeit in the background. Wyck Hay took over Celestial's art and advertising division until he left the firm in 1976.

As herbal teas caught the fancy of more and more Americans, Celestial remained on the fledgling industry's cutting edge. Sales outlets were expanded to stores throughout Colorado, New Mexico, and the East Coast. The partners stopped picking herbs themselves and pioneered a development and importation network in locales like Guatemala and China. Celestial committed to using only the highest-quality products and began working with growers around the world to ensure that its supplies of exotic ingredients, such as hibiscus flowers and lemon grass, remained both consistent and up to its exacting standards. The results—then and now—help the company retain its deserved reputation for excellence.

"The Celestial name is known worldwide for high integrity and trust," says Kay Wright, the company's botanicals purchasing manager. Wright, who travels the globe to oversee production, meets personally with farmers to explain Celestial's philosophy and ensure that crops meet its needs; in return, she and the company offer dependable employment opportunities and natural crop-management techniques to Third and Fourth World growers in as many as thirty-five different countries. "The growers call us picky and fussy, but they know that if they produce a quality product, we'll stick with them. They trust us," she adds, "and they want to work with us."

Local employees always have, too, and people with all sorts of backgrounds flocked to the rapidly expanding tea maker during the 1970s. There they found a benevolent employer who really cared for their needs: Free family-style hot lunches were served daily, employees were presented with bonus checks on their birthdays, and a stock-ownership plan gave everyone a stake in the company. In addition, Celestial offered rapid advancement opportunities to all of its competent workers. Wright, for instance, had degrees in anthropology and English when she was hired in 1975 to straighten files; a year later, she was buying domestic herbs, and when the chief herb buyer resigned shortly thereafter, she moved into one of the company's most interesting jobs—one she is proud to hold to this day.

Consumers and their environment also were treated with the utmost respect. All-natural ingredients, grown without pesticides, always composed the entire formulation for each of Celestial's various teas. Wasteful packaging components—such as individual foil envelopes, strings, tags, and staples—never were found on any of the company's products. And additional healthful activities were promoted to the public, primarily cycling, which got its foremost U.S. race in 1975 when the firm created the reknowned Red Zinger Bicycle Classic.

Barney Feinblum was one of the many young workers initially attracted by this commitment to corporate responsibility, personal growth, and employee camaraderie. He also grew with Celestial. The company took off in both name recognition and sales. Feinblum was among those who helped ensure that, throughout it all, the firm remained a great place to work.

Above the desks of Feinblum and a few other executives, in fact, a large poster outlining Celestial Seasonings' formalized corporate "Beliefs" says as much about the company, its workers, and its product as anything ever written about the firm. Among the numerous points is a telling section on employees, which concludes: "We believe in hiring above-average people who have a 'hands-on' approach to work and a quest for excellent results. In exchange, we are committed to the development of our good people by identifying, cultivating, training, rewarding, retaining, and promoting those individuals who are committed to moving our organization forward."

"The family feeling keeps people here," agrees an employee named Kathy, who was hired to brew tea, part-time, for consumer testing panels. Six years later, as part of the company's Consumer Services Division, she was overseeing the personalized responses sent to each of the twenty-three thousand callers and letter writers who contact Celestial each year. "Everyone—employees and customers—is treated fairly," she says. "Without them, we wouldn't have a company."

And that, most observers agree, is the primary reason the ill-fated partnership with Kraft seriously threatened to undermine one of the nation's most conscientious companies.

The Cheese Stands Alone

Mo Siegel initially felt the deal could work, and to this day he still believes it could have benefited both Celestial and Kraft. Besides, Siegel was beginning to burn out on a business that had consumed a large part of his adult life, and he honestly felt it was time to move on. "I started this company when I was twenty, and I just had enough," he says today. "I wanted two things: I wanted cash, and I wanted to know that my company was in good hands. And, at the time, Kraft looked like a great home for Celestial."

By the late 1970s, Siegel also realized that his firm was in need of a fiscal transfusion. Supermarkets had started selling the company's teas—taking them mainstream and away from the exclusive domain of health-food stores—but the rising sales that followed were not matched by corresponding increases in profits. At the same time, the cyclical nature of the herbal tea business, in which three-quarters of all products are consumed in winter, left an ever-larger hole in the firm's cash flow during the warmer months. A ten-member strategic planning team, created by Siegel and including Feinblum, searched desperately for ways to end the company's consistent inability to get on its financial feet and fund necessary growth.

When, out of the blue, General Mills offered to purchase Celestial for $8.3 million in 1979, the idea of a buy-out was first broached. But Feinblum, by then vice-president of finance, convinced the firm's principals to explore other options. One was a proposed public stock offering that unfortunately failed before it got off the ground. By that time, however, the company's two copresidents also found they no longer could work together, even though they remained close personal friends. So when Siegel and Hay became acquainted with H. Keith Ridgway—a senior Kraft executive regularly in Boulder to visit his son living there—the two companies began talking about a way to merge their enterprises and allow Celestial's founders to gracefully exit the stage.

The deal, as they always do, took much longer to consummate than anyone suspected. But by the time Celestial finally became a part of Kraft's Retail Food Group in July 1984, the price tag had also grown far beyond original expectations: Kraft eventually paid a reported $40 million for the tea maker and additionally shelled out about $4 million more to purchase employee stock. When every worker then received a check equal to approximately one year's salary, most of them thought, like Siegel, that the match was made in heaven.

At first, it appeared as if this were true. In addition to the sorely needed capital that Celestial required to finance increased production, Kraft provided market-research expertise and doubled its new acquisition's annual advertising budget from $2 million to $4 million in 1985. Soon Celestial also doubled its share of the booming herbal tea market and moved ahead of all its competitors.

Almost as quickly, however, negative signs also appeared. Kraft gave new products a series of generic names like "Celestial Seasonings Herb & Spice Cooking Blend," which served to quickly alienate those employees and consumers who had grown accustomed to teas called Red Zinger and Morning Thunder. The new parent company also moved slowly and cautiously in both research and development, halting the risk-taking entrepreneurship that had marked Celestial's operation since its founding.

"It was frustrating because we couldn't implement changes fast enough and Kraft didn't understand why we had to make changes that we knew we had to make," says Trish Flaster, hired as Celestial's botanist just two years before the acquisition. "Mixing up a blend of tea is nothing like making mayonnaise," she continues. "Mayonnaise has a recipe, and you use exactly the same ingredients each time. But botanical ingredients change every single time you order them because of different climactic influences—the rains, the soils. Batches have to be adjusted every time. You have to be flexible, and Kraft wasn't."

Feinblum, one of the few Celestial officials who opposed the deal from the outset, watched in horror as his small, innovative company began to change. Kraft was building market share, to be sure, but it also was spending large sums of money on ill-conceived spin-off ventures like salad dressings and spices, none of which ever got out of the test phase. It also poured millions into a national TV ad campaign that featured actress Mariette Hartley and got Celestial's name in front of the public but turned off many longtime customers who despised the company's new middle-of-the-road direction.

Siegel remained with Celestial until 1986, when he left with the announced aim of pursuing philanthropic ventures and traveling the world. He selected Feinblum as his successor and was at first turned down flat. Feinblum says now that he wanted to open a sprout farm rather than work for a Fortune 500 company, but he eventually decided that the experience could be beneficial, and so he accepted the position as Celestial's new president and CEO.

Feinblum, however, began to regret his decision almost immediately. Ridgway, the Kraft executive who befriended Siegel and Hay, retired; in his absence, Kraft demanded even more accounting and tighter control. The parent also proposed that drug testing be implented at the Boulder plant, which Feinblum and others there vehemently opposed. (The issue was eventually dropped.) And when the division in which Celestial had been placed fell behind in its profitability, Kraft shifted the tea company to yet another corporate arm, where it became even more isolated and more ripe for meddling by its absentee management.

By mid-1987, Feinblum was actively exploring ways to get Celestial back from Kraft. He first presented the idea of an LBO to officials of the parent company that fall, offering around $40 million to seal the deal. Kraft informed him that the tea maker was not for sale.

Kraft then added the final insult to its brief but injurious term of ownership. Less than three months after Feinblum was told that he couldn't buy the company, Kraft announced that it was selling the Boulder firm, after all: to Thomas J. Lipton, Inc. When word got out that Celestial might now be owned by its archrival—and rumors began to spread that the Boulder operation would then be shuttered and moved to Englewood Cliffs, N.J.—the frustration turned to anger.

Suggesting that this proposed deal would be in violation of federal antitrust laws, Celestial officials were certain that the sale would be rejected by the Federal Trade Commission (FTC); neither the FTC nor the U.S. Justice Department, however, accepted their argument. But another competitor—R. C. Bigelow Inc., the manufacturer of Constant Comment teas—brought suit to block the proposed sale in 1988, claiming that the deal would create a company controlling more than 80 percent of the specialty tea market. The U.S. Court of Appeals in its home state of Connecticut agreed and enjoined the merger.

Desperate now to put together some sort of deal, Kraft then allowed Feinblum to make a new offer. The Celestial president contacted Vestar Capital Partners, Inc., a New York–based investment firm, and hurriedly put together a $60 million LBO proposal. With Kraft itself now under the gun—it had unexpectedly become the subject of a hostile takeover attempt by Philp Morris Companies, Inc.—the deal was quickly sealed. And on November 2, 1988, Celestial Seasonings regained its independence. "We now call that our Independence Day," says a former employee of the firm.

A New Beginning

Despite the financial hardships brought about by the LBO, Celestial immediately pressed on. One of its first actions was to create a board of directors. Mo Siegel was invited to join, and he accepted. A second major act was the groundbreaking for a new corporate headquarters on ninety-one acres of vacant land on the outskirts of Boulder. This sprawling two-story plant-and-office complex, which opened in 1990, consolidated all operations that had previously taken place in seven different Boulder-area buildings. It also came to symbolize the break with Kraft more graphically than anything else that transpired after the buyback.

"It was very important when we designed this building to maintain the culture of our company, which was 'We're all in this together,'" says Feinblum. "There isn't an office and a factory; here we come together physically. When we worked for Kraft and I went up to their headquarters in Illinois, the intimidation process started the minute I got out of the elevator," he continues. "Status symbols—like different-colored badges to establish a hierarchy—were everywhere. But there is no need for that at Celestial; it's very important to let people here know that they can communicate with anybody on any subject."

Part of that is manifested in the building's spacious dining room, which is a contemporary manifestation of the free-meal program that the company ran in its earliest days. While the assorted healthful products in this cafeteria now cost money, they are priced very low. And the resultant program—which Celestial subsidizes to the tune of about $75,000 a year—does help employees come together on a daily basis and foster the concept of free corporate speech.

"There really is an open-door policy here," notes one longtime employee. "You need to go through the chain of command for some things because your supervisor needs to know what is going on. But if that doesn't work or if you get frustrated by the system, you can ask anybody and everybody at the top for an hour of their time. And they'll give it to you."

Besides its beneficial impact on employees, this policy can bring about significant and needed change at Celestial. John Odbert, former vice-president of human resources and now a long-term management consultant for the firm, recalls the time a janitor suggested that owning its own trucks—rather than hiring common carriers to move herbs in from the coasts and finished teas out from the plant—would save the company money. His supervisors listened carefully and agreed. They bought the vehicles, hired the drivers, and placed the janitor in charge of the new department. "For a lot of people, this has been a real shot in the arm, careerwise," Odbert notes.

Such corporate thinking has also led to the development of an impressive internal environmental program. Coordinated by an employee committee formed just before Earth Day, 1989, and now overseen by botanist Flaster, it includes the regular recycling of various products used in tea production (like paper, aluminum, glass, cardboard, and burlap). In addition, it calls for recycled office paper products to be purchased whenever possible; caused personal recycling bins to be placed beside all desks; suggested that used plant materials, such as the fiber barrels in which some herbs arrive, be offered to schools and community groups before they are simply discarded; encouraged double-sided copying; and eliminated all cardboard and plastic from the cafeteria.

Not surprisingly, Celestial's consumer products are made with predominantly recycled and good-for-the-earth materials, too. All packages, for instance, are 100 percent recycled paperboard. The freshness of tea bags is assured by natural-colored, unbleached, waxed inner box liners. And Celestial became the first company to use only oxygen-bleached tea bags instead of the standard chlorine-bleached versions that add dioxin—one of the world's most toxic man-made chemicals—to the water supply. "That's something we're very proud of, because no one else offered that option until we forced the industry to make oxygen-bleached tea bags for us," Flaster notes. "Now everyone has fallen in line. It's pretty impressive."

Celestial has, furthermore, recommitted itself to the sport of bicycling, an activity that first became closely associated with the company in the mid-1970s. And it continues to spearhead such community efforts as the seven-year-old Best Buddy Bear program, which provides every police officer, firefighter, and paramedic in Colorado with a Sleepytime teddy bear to help them comfort any traumatized youngsters they encounter in their work.

"Of the things we've done, that is what we're most proud of," Feinblum says of the teddy bear program, which has never been widely publicized and remains largely unknown except to those who participate in it or benefit from it. "Like all of the extra efforts we make, we did it because we thought it was a good thing to do," he continues. "Our profit benefit is nonexistent, and even if it costs us a little money, so what? We've always tried to be good corporate citizens."

Now, though, Celestial is also trying to regain the good corporate positioning that it lost on Independence Day.

The Prodigal Returns

Mo Siegel is in Celestial's lunchroom, deciding between a breaded whitefish platter and a sloppy joe sandwich. Two cafeteria workers are trying to get him to choose the fish; Siegel is leaning toward the sandwich. "I'm into healthy things, but I probably don't eat as much health food as some people think I do," he says. "I'm more into exercise and vitamins."

At the urging of his employees, Siegel reluctantly selects the fish. While his plate is being prepared, he roots through a box containing the latest entries in an ongoing employee poll designed to help the firm select a name for its newest tea. And before he carries his food tray to the register, another worker approaches him with the prototypes for two new tea boxes. "No, no," he says gently while paying for his food. "They don't say 'herbal tea' anywhere. They have to say 'herbal tea.'"

Siegel, a self-described philosopher/businessman, enthusiastically dropped out of the corporate world in 1986 to pursue the first part of this sobriquet and just as energetically reentered it five years later because he couldn't give up the second. "After about a year, I missed the people, and I missed being in a company. I like companies, and the bigger they are, the better," he says earnestly. "I left this company because I thought I could go off and do public service for the rest of my life. I came back because I found out I couldn't."

To fill the void that developed during his absence, Siegel started Earth Wise Inc., which designs and manufactures a variety of "environmentally friendly" household cleaning products as well as trash bags made from 100 percent recycled plastic. Much like his teas, Siegel's new offerings do what they promise to do for a competitive price and without harming the earth or its people. And, again like his teas, their recycled and recyclable packaging features interesting, bold artwork and intriguing philosophical quotations. By mid-1991, his new venture employed five and was recording annual sales of $1 million.

When Siegel came back to Celestial as chairman and CEO, the tea company also agreed to take Earth Wise under its wing. "Strategically, we might not have gone out and bought a soap company," says Feinblum, who stayed on as president and assumed the additional title of COO upon Siegel's return. "But I think it fits. Our customers view us as makers of good-for-the-world products, and so people who are Celestial customers are likely to be Earth Wise customers as well. It's a concept of selling our customers more of the products that they use."

Celestial had tried to introduce related new products before, including a number of hair-care items and the spice and salad dressing lines envisioned by Kraft. These failed, Feinblum believes, not because the products were bad but because the strategies to create and introduce them were not executed properly. But as the small and independent entity it once again is, he adds, Celestial can and will attempt to initiate such projects in the future. Until the LBO's fallout is contained, however, its ability to do so remains limited.

Still, Celestial is consistently moving ahead with a large assortment of new tea products. A gourmet tea line of traditional black teas, several organically grown blends, numerous naturally decaffeinated flavors, larger family-sized packages, and various iced herb teas all have been introduced in recent years. And while about 80 percent of the company's beverage products are now sold in supermarkets, it continues testing new herbal blends like Mama Bear's Cold Care and Bengal Spice in the outlets that started it all: health-food stores.

While much at Celestial has changed over the years, it seems, much also remains the same. And Mo Siegel's triumphant return only serves to underscore that point.

"When I started this company, I said I'd like to take it to $100 million as soon as possible," he says. "My hardest time was in the beginning, because even though I was young, I never wanted to have a little company. Then, like now, I wanted to see us have good values, be a really good-for-the-world company, and be big. But I know that getting big is difficult. Getting big is work."

Fortunately for Celestial Seasonings, Mo Siegel is back. And once again he's willing to work as hard as it takes to achieve his formidable goals. This time, however, Siegel has a big advantage: The right people and the right structure are already in place.

2

From Welfare to Working

Company name: America Works, Inc.
Type of business: employment agency
Locations: New York, New York, Hartford,
Connecticut, and Indianapolis, Indiana
Year founded: 1984

Dawn, a native of New York's South Bronx, had never been to Wall Street. A single mother to a three-year-old son, she was living at her mother's South Bronx apartment and relying solely on public assistance. When she visited Manhattan's downtown concrete canyon for the first time to interview for a secretarial position with a prestigious law firm, she didn't know what to expect. "I was scared," the twenty-three-year-old woman says. "I had graduated from high school and a business trade school, but when I had my son, I couldn't keep up with a job. Then," she adds, "when I was ready, I couldn't find one. I was depressed and anxious."

Then Dawn learned about America Works. "My friends told me about this agency that works with single mothers on welfare, and I called them right away," says the professionally dressed and well-groomed woman, seated in the conference room at the law office where she has now worked for seven months. After being placed on a three-month waiting list, Dawn entered the downtown office and classrooms of America Works. She went through its one-week pre-employment session and three-to-five-week business lab and with the company's help eventually landed the job as assistant to a lawyer specializing in immigration law.

"It's been amazing," says Dawn. "I've learned so much, and I'm able to take care of myself and my son and be on my own. My life belongs to me."

Dawn's story may sound unique, but she is just one of more than twenty-five hundred former welfare recipients in Connecticut and New York who has been taken off the public doles because of America Works. The company, a profitable employment agency with offices in Hartford, Connecticut, and Manhattan, takes in $4 million annually by finding jobs in the private sector for more than 550 welfare recipients each year. It attracts these job candidates through word-of-mouth testimonials, active recruiting, direct-mail solicitations, classified ads, and the extensive television and newspaper coverage it receives. After training its resultant clients, or "job applicants," in basic office procedures and helping them polish their typing, filing, and related skills, the company seeks entry-level, private-sector jobs for them. At the same time, an aggressive sales staff reaches out to potential employers who are looking for secretaries, receptionists, telemarketers, and food handlers.

Once a match is made, the newly hired employees work on a trial basis for four months. America Works pays them a modest hourly wage, while billing the employer a small markup to cover wages, benefits, and monitoring expenses. Typically, the cost to employers during this period is about a dollar an hour less than the ordinary payroll cost for that position. The employee, meanwhile, also receives reduced welfare benefits during this period.

If the tryout proves successful, the employee then goes on the company's payroll at its going rate, and the welfare payments stop. If they stay on the job for a year, their employer can also qualify for a federal tax credit amounting to more than $1,000.

America Works, on the other hand, makes its money from the state and from the companies that hire its clients. Each time one of these clients is fully weaned from welfare, the company charges the state. In Connecticut the charge is $4,000; in New York it is $5,300.

A recent New York study estimated that the cost of keeping a mother and two children on welfare for one year is a total of $23,900 (which includes an $11,000 administration cost, a cash grant, Medicaid, and food stamps). The state's return on investment to America Works is almost five to one. "For $5,300, we guarantee the state doesn't have to pay $24,000," says Peter Cove, founder of America Works. Cove started the company in 1985, and he now runs it with his wife, sociologist Lee Bowes, who serves as chief executive officer (CEO). "I've always been involved in community action programs," says the fifty-one-year-old Cove, an enthusiastic dark-haired man who favors bow ties. "I was at the University of Wisconsin in 1963 when the country was going through a great deal of turmoil," he says. "Kennedy was shot, and the civil rights movement was in full swing. This undoubtedly influenced what I've devoted my career to."

A veteran of several nonprofit efforts, including Pres. Lyndon Johnson's War on Poverty, Cove eventually took over Massachusetts-based Transitional Employment Enterprises (TEE), a not-for-profit agency funded in part by the Ford Foundation. "TEE was the prototype for this kind of activity and proved to me that 'supported work' for the disadvantaged could work and that it could move to the private sector," Cove says in his Lower Manhattan office. "It was at this point of my career that I began to understand my own mission," he continues. "I learned that what is important in a person's life is work and employment; work is therapy, and helping to provide a job is perhaps the central and most important thing I or society could do for a person. I also learned that the majority of people on public assistance would rather be working. And that's what America is all about."

In the Beginning

After eight years with TEE, Cove was anxious to take his concept on the road. "The only way to grow and expand was with capital, which was needed to fuel the expansion," he says. With $1 million from his own savings and various bank loans, Cove left TEE and launched America Works.

There were three motivating factors in the decision, Cove explains. "First, I wanted to spread what we were doing, and you can't grow a not-for-profit organization, because you need capital to expand," he says. "Second, I wanted to accumulate money for myself. And third, I knew we had operated TEE as a business and that it was possible to do the same thing on a for-profit basis."

Although the company now enjoys growth and profitability, its first several years were filled with what Cove considers some "great learning experiences." Leaving Bowes to run TEE, Cove set up shop at America Works. His first client was the state of Ohio, whose governor had been aware of Cove's success in Boston and advanced him some money to cover opening expenses. "I set up two offices, found people to run them in both Cleveland and Dayton, and got America Works rolling," Cove recalls.

Though he successfully placed welfare recipients in full-time jobs, Cove and America Works had a short-lived stay in Ohio. "We were creamed politically," he says. "We were brought in by the governor, who pushed us past the state's welfare department. I think the perception that we were outsiders and the fact we were a for-profit company made us very threatening. We pulled out after two years."

Yet Cove did learn a valuable lesson from this initial experience. "How you are born politically speaks more to the success of a program than whether or not the program is any good," he says. "How we are perceived by the local government is a great predictor of whether or not we are successful."

Luckily, the company experienced a far more positive response in Connecticut. A program already existed there to get welfare dependents, primarily mothers, into the work force. Seeing the success at TEE, several key state officials and the welfare commissioner brought America Works to Hartford. "We didn't have protection in Ohio; in Connecticut we had a lot of support from the various government layers. This allowed us to establish the company to do something new and what was not done before. Since then, we have been able to survive and succeed with a solid program, even in tough economic times," says Cove.

Today America Works's Hartford office employs eight full-time people and annually places 150 welfare recipients in private-sector jobs.

In 1988, America Works was invited to New York to salvage a similar, but unsuccessful, job placement program. "The state recognized that we had the management capacity to rescue this, and we did," Cove notes. At this point, Bowes became the head of the company, running both the Hartford and New York offices. But as their company evolved, so did their problems. There was an ever-growing need for increased capital. "We were mucking around back then and needed more money," says Cove. Fortunately, though, in 1987 they had created a partnership with Abe Levoitz, a retired tallow manufacturer from Boston, who became a partner providing a significant capital infusion.

"Besides the needed capital, Abe has given us a business sense and expertise that we didn't have before. And it was invaluable," says Bowes. "While Peter and I were a bit expansive, Abe is the one who pulled in the reins. He got us going on daily, weekly, and monthly accountings, so we knew where we stood every day. He further demonstrated the need to emphasize that we are paid only for proven placements."

Both Cove and Bowes believe that the three very unique and different perspectives on their business have contributed to the company's success. "We all have our strengths, and we all have very different outlooks on many different things. Peter is the visionary, I run the day-to-day operations, and Abe makes sure it all balances out. The tri-leadership has made a big difference," says Bowes.

How It Works

America Works's New York office hums with activity. On any given day, dozens of clients, or job candidates, as well as the eighteen-person in-house staff, moves about the classroom, work lab, telemarketing headquarters, sales department, and conference room that constitute the company offices. Still, Bowes and Cove describe their organization as being very personal. "We don't have a lot of layers, even though at any one time eighty to one hundred workers are on our payroll, plus our own staff," says Bowes.

The company is divided into five divisions: Preemployment, Business Lab, Sales, Job Match, and Corporate Representatives. Duties are well-divided, though the interaction between workers is apparent—and vital—to the company's ongoing success.

The process starts in Preemployment, where job candidates spend their first week. In this orientation class, they are introduced to both America Works and to what is expected of them once they walk out its doors.

In a long, narrow classroom, Paula, a single mother with a three-year-old son, is an instructor, mentor, and inspiration to the eighteen primarily African-American and Hispanic women in attendance. "The whole purpose of the preemployment week is to prepare our candidates for interviews," she says. "We work on math and English skills. Half the battle," she adds, "is to get the women to effectively express themselves."

According to Paula, a former schoolteacher who was once on welfare herself, many of the candidates have completed high school or received an equivalency diploma; others dropped out after the ninth or tenth grades. Many are single mothers; some have out-of-work husbands. "A sign of the times," says Paula.

"On Mondays we talk about public assistance programs and what they were originally designed for," Paula says. "Most participants doubt the system; they don't understand that it is there to provide the tools for them to pick themselves up and go on." Yet, according to Paula, many of the candidates have been welfare recipients for many years. Some come from families in which multiple generations have survived only on public assistance. "A woman here recently told me she was a fourth-generation welfare recipient," Paula adds. "No one in her family had taken care of themselves in decades. Recently, her son made reference to her 'never being able to work.' She felt ashamed and decided to give America Works a try. Within two months she landed a job with a bank."

Much of the candidates' initial days are spent preparing for the Thursday meeting with the company's sales force. There each job candidate must individually address the group. They provide their name, background, education, work experience, and goals. And then, in the days leading up to the presentation, the candidates practice.

"My name is Vinceer," says a woman with a quiet voice. "I live in the Bronx and went to the American Business Institute. I know how to type, file, and use Word Perfect. I had a job at Burger King and made manager. My goals are to get a job, be a better parent, and lose weight. I would like to have a house and a car and for my children to be beautiful people." She tries to sit down but is called back to stand in front of the group.

"So, what did we think of her presentation?" booms Paula.

The women in the class respond. "She looked down too much," says one. "I couldn't hear her very well," exclaims another. "You should never wear leather to an interview," a third comments. "She seems sad," notes one more.

After hearing the appraisal, Paula summarizes the reaction. "Never, ever, apologize for yourself," she says. "If there is one thing you need to relay it is that you are proud. That what you've done in your life is fine. And you need to let people know that no matter what your experience, even if it's been keeping a home, that's work, and you're worthy of more work."

Later, Paula explains both her thoughts and her own inspiration for initiating a new class of women through the orientation procedure each week. "They've been living dark lives, wondering from one day to the next how to make ends meet," she says. "They've had their downs. I feel that if in this time I have a chance to influence and to help build their self-confidence, then I have to give it my all," she says. "We make the best of any situation, and we laugh and joke a lot. I know what it is like to be on welfare, and I know what it's like to get off of it. So they understand me."

The encouragement Paula delivers to her classes is a reflection of the enthusiasm she receives from America Works management. "Everyone here is wonderful, and I've received nothing but support from Peter and Lee," says Paula. "There is always another challenge, and I like that. Lee has just asked me to start a speakers' series so we can invite experts on health and life insurance, financial planners, and others to come in and speak with the classes." Paula is obviously as happy with this as her students are with the help and direction she offers them.

Practical Knowledge

Electric typewriters buzz and rows of computers hum as participants in the Business Lab—the second stop for all applicants—brush up on the skills required to fill the entry-level positions they strive for. All candidates must come to the workshop from 9:00 A.M. to 4:00 P.M. daily, Monday through Friday.

Maria runs the Business Lab, where the day is divided between classroom workshops and independent training. "They come here to practice their clerical skills, and they must treat it as a job," says the spirited six-year America Works veteran. "They don't get a paycheck for coming here, and they work independently on improving their skills. They must sign in. And it's also a time for candidates to work with the Job Match representative and to be on call to go out on interviews."

Pansy, a thirty-five-year-old single mother of four, is about to become a grandmother for the second time. Until a year ago she was an office manager for a real estate company; then her employer went out of business. Now hoping to reenter the workplace, Pansy sits at a computer honing her word processing skills. She is called out of the lab by Risa, a corporate representative, who tells her about an interview for a receptionist position at a lingerie company.

At a small table in the hallway, Risa further explains that the prospective employer is a small, family-owned manufacturer. She describes to Pansy the woman who will interview her. Then Risa and Pansy practice a mock interview. Following the ten-minute session, Risa reviews Pansy's performance—her eye contact, her voice, her grammar—and mentions the importance of asking questions about the company and the available position.

In this, as in all settings, job candidates are treated with the greatest amount of professionalism and courtesy by all America Works employees.

"Our candidates are very valuable to us in many ways," says Risa, who has worked at America Works for four years. "We expect them to look and act professionally at all times and to do a good job in representing us. It's essential that they are treated with both respect and compassion."

Connecting the applicant with the right position—called Job Match—is a job left to Don, a middle-aged man who had previously worked for ITT for more than twenty-four years. "After an early retirement two years ago, I immediately came to work here," he says. "I taught for quite a while and now find lots of joy in placing our candidates. We have a seventy percent success rate."

Though the three-week Business Lab and Job Match are integral components of the America Works formula, Cove believes that the company's equal emphasis on sales, marketing, and on-site follow-up is what distinguishes it from other employee placement firms. "When you look at where the money is spent at most government-sponsored employment programs, you see it goes primarily to training and education, to supporting the candidates with counseling, teachers, and classroom training. We are not as training oriented," says Cove. "Rather, we believe in on-the-job support.

"Our candidates have dignity," he adds. "Most of them have been in classrooms for way too long, and they've been failed by the education and training systems. Our belief is that people need jobs, not training."

Accordingly, America Works has installed a complete post-job support program. A major part of it involves bimonthly visits by America Works corporate representatives during the four-month trial period.

"We're here to deal with the issues that may keep our people from doing a good job," explains Phil, a fast-talking, all-smiles America Works employee. On any given day, Phil visits up to ten different offices to check on America Works employees. "I'm there to interact both with the supervisors and with our workers," he says. "If there are day-care problems or employees are late or there is an abusive mate at home, we can interact. Any situations that need outside help, we're there to support them."

It is precisely backing of this type that keeps many company clients returning to America Works. "We do not hire these people for any philanthropic reasons, only because it makes great business sense," says Lauren, office manager of the downtown Manhattan law firm where two America Works clients currently are employed. "These are incredibly tough positions to fill. You run an ad in the paper and get five hundred resumes. With America Works, there is a prescreening process that makes it easier for us. Then," she continues, "there is the four-month trial period, and Phil is here to interact with the workers, so I can express my concerns with him rather than confront the workers directly. He must have a magical touch with them, too," she notes. "He's solved every single problem. And we've hired all our candidates after the tryout is over. Denise is the best receptionist we've ever had, and Dawn is becoming a better legal assistant every day. It's wonderful to watch them grow."

To Phil, working with both the employers and the America Works personnel is personally and professionally fulfilling. "To help give these people the opportunity to contribute and make a difference, well, that is what it's all about," he says.

Selling the Program

Rob worked for several years at one of New York City's top-name employment agencies before he started as a salesperson with America Works. After no less than five interviews with Bowes, Cove, and other personnel, he was hired on as the fifth full-time salesperson.

"A strong sales effort is essential to our success," explains Bowes. "We don't have anything to do with job development, so we call cold, contact every company we know, and sell our service." Bowes further emphasizes the point that "selling means you don't give it away. Our attitude is not 'take our poor welfare recipients, please.' Rather, we sell something they need and are willing to pay for." Once a sales call is made, a company that is interested in the service places a job order listing the requirements and requesting an interview with candidates who qualify for a particular position.

Rob, who has worked with America Works for two years, enjoys promoting his firm. It is also immediately obvious to everyone that he is a polished salesperson. Meeting with the human resources director of a public transportation agency, he efficiently and thoroughly reviews all the particulars: that there is a trial period; that the company pays America Works, which then pays the candidate's salary during this period; that a corporate representative who will visit regularly is available to help manage the new worker. In addition, he notes that a thorough Job Match program ensures that all candidates sent for interviews meet all company requirements. Then Rob discusses tax benefits and the fact that his company will handle all necessary paperwork and cut through any red tape.

The most interesting part of Rob's sales pitch, however, is what he doesn't say: the words "welfare" and "public assistance" never come out of his mouth.

"No, it's certainly not part of the pitch, because it has very little relevance to the outcome," Rob explains after a meeting where he received two job orders. "We're selling a service here, and we stand behind it. We certainly don't deny the fact that our clients are on welfare, but we know we are working with people who truly want to work. That makes all the difference."

Interestingly, Rob's own mother was on welfare for several years when he was a child. "Sure, I know what it's like," he says. "I know being on welfare doesn't have to be such a stigma and that most people on welfare don't want to be. Understanding this helps me do my job."

America Works relies primarily on cold calls to companies throughout its base cities to sell its service, and part of its sales program includes a telemarketing effort. Though the company's emphasis until now has been on midsized law firms, publishing houses, insurance agencies, and the like, Bowes now wants to see it move on to some major corporations. At this point, however, they are meeting resistance.

"Yes, we are definitely different from other employment agencies," she says. "The whole four-month trial period, plus working with welfare payments and eventually rolling salaries over to your own payroll, can be confusing. Human resources people are either very open and willing to give us a try, or they just don't want to deal with anything that is at all different." In addition, limitations are placed on America Works by the government agencies that pay out benefits. Still, the company is not daunted. "We have state government contracts that we always fulfill," says Cove. "And with ten percent of the country's welfare population in New York alone, as well as a continuing need for good entry-level workers, we know there is plenty of room for growth."

This growth is a major focus of the firm, too. While Bowes tends to much of the day-to-day operations, Cove is involved with opening additional America Works offices in other cities. "We have the model, and it has proven to be successful," explains Cove, who most recently opened an office in Indianapolis. "We are different from government agencies that train and place welfare recipients in jobs. We're unique in that we only charge the government when we successfully employ a former welfare recipient. And the worker is employed seven months prior to receiving the full fee.

Yet there are problems with moving to other locations. "First of all, we are outsiders, and local governments aren't used to working with new people from beyond their jurisdiction. Secondly," Cove says, "we are a for-profit company, and that doesn't sit well with many people; they don't trust our motives. This is common when the private sector works with the government. We're an idea that is ahead of our time."

People Are the Key

America Works's success is largely the result of a strong and caring staff. Bowes feels that the selection of a diversified and thoughtful group of employees is essential to the growth and development of the company. "We are proud of our staff; everyone works well together, and in that sense it makes it very enjoyable," Bowes says. "I typically want to have a mixed staff, both racially and ethically, and an age balance so that we don't have one predominant group. I need extremely intelligent employees. Past job experience, on the other hand, is not as critical. What's important to me and what I look for when I hire employees is a strong self-awareness; how attentive they are of their own selves. And I also pay strict attention to the analytical skills that help them understand other people. They are therefore bound by life awareness and come here in the morning happy to be here."

The obvious enthusiasm of the workers tends to be a motivating factor for both Bowes and Cove. Furthermore, Cove receives inspiration from the fact that an antiestablishment person like himself can prove there is something more to business than the conventional wisdom of corporate America. "I want to show that there is a different way of doing things," he says. "What I love about us being a private company is that our philosophy is not just a theory; it's real, it exists, and it's successful. We are demonstrating something here."

The New York operation typifies this. In 1988, the company placed 125 former welfare recipients in private positions; today it is up to 300 per year. Ninety percent of these workers remain at their jobs one year after they are hired, and a recent New York audit revealed that 80 percent of the employees are with the same companies after two and a half years.

Still, both Bowes and Cove admit that to start an America Works at this point would prove to be quite costly. "To get this going in any market now would cost a minimum of $250,000. The first year, we don't make any money; in the second year we may break even; and in the third year we can do well," Cove says. "We have to make the initial investment, and because of the way we are paid—after the person has been employed for so many months—the payoff doesn't come until quite a bit later."

Bowes and Cove "mucked around in our business for a long time" and do not hesitate to offer a number of the ideas that eventually helped make their business successful.

First of all, Bowes says, trust your instincts and make rational judgments. Second—but just as critically—if you are not a "businessperson" per se, make sure you enlist the help of a savvy investor or have a dedicated partner with a financial stake in the company. "When Abe joined us, it was as if we both got the equivalent of MBAs," says Cove. "He understood better than I the importance of the performance-based contract. He knew how to take that concept and make it right, make it profitable.

Finally, notes Bowes, "when you start a business, you have to have the right people in the right places. That is an essential ingredient."

As America Works seeks out future growth opportunities both within Connecticut, New York, and Indianapolis, as well as in other cities throughout the country, it can be further inspired by the people it employs and helps. People, in fact, like Dawn, who secured a job on Wall Street the first time she ever set foot there. In a letter she sent to America Works following her successful job search, she wrote, "Thanks to all of you, and especially Peter and Lee, for giving me the opportunity. My son and I both thank you from the bottom of our hearts."

Bowes and Cove may not say it in so many words, but it is apparent that such reactions are the real motivation behind America Works.

3

One Step Ahead

Company name: Birkenstock Footprint Sandals, Inc.
Type of business: wholesale distributor
Location: Novato, California
Number of employees: 130
Year founded: 1967

Back in 1989, a member of the in-house marketing department at
Birkenstock Footprint Sandals approached her superior with a somewhat radical suggestion. The employee, Diana, recognized that Birkenstock already was embracing many of the conscientious business
practices championed by its German-based parent company. She
knew, for instance, that the Novato, California, distributor of cork-
heeled sandals had always used only recycled cardboard materials for
its shoe boxes. But Diana believed her company could do more.
Much more. So she told her manager how she felt.

Rather than being patronized or ignored, as she might have been
in another multi-million-dollar enterprise, Diana was encouraged to
take her idea and expand upon it. With her manager's approval, she
formed a twelve-member in-house "eco task force" comprised of representatives drawn from a variety of Birkenstock departments. Its initial purpose was to study and draft suggestions on how the company,
its dealers, and even neighboring businesses could improve recycling

efforts and decrease the amount of energy resources used in day-to-day operations.

The task force soon proved so successful that Birkenstock allowed its members to spend one hour per week of company time on ecological projects. In fact, members felt so good about their accomplishments that they volunteered their lunch hours for meetings in order to spend the extra company-donated time on actual projects. Since its formation, the task force has made significant accomplishments. They include collecting materials for an in-house library; compiling resources from which they could purchase nontoxic, earth-friendly products; and producing a newsletter that reports on environmental activities at the company.

In addition to influencing Birkenstock's environmental direction, the group has also helped shape the community in which it operates. For example, Diane, who still leads the task force, now also meets monthly with representatives of other Novato-area businesses to share ideas on sources for recycled paper, low-energy light bulbs, and other conservation-minded products and concepts.

While such activity by employees and encouragement from management may be unusual at other firms, at Birkenstock it is mainstream. Since it was launched in 1967 by owner and president Margot Fraser, the company has exemplified a business that views people—employees, dealers, and customers—as its greatest asset. Even after its consistent growth, moving to new corporate offices in early 1992 that house 125 workers, the firm continues to focus on its people. Employees are encouraged to expand beyond their day-to-day duties and contribute ideas concerning areas in which they have a particular interest. Sharing in the total effort remains as important as sharing in the rewards.

"We recognize that people have a need to contribute, to feel enthusiastic about what they are doing, and we try to create an atmosphere where this happens," says Mary Jones, who, as a part-time bookkeeper, was the company's first employee and is now its sole vice-president. As her duties expanded over the years to include primary human resource responsibilities at Birkenstock, Jones now finds herself counseling other employees on workplace situations and ways in which they can use their talents better. "I'm really here to help out, to motivate, and to encourage workers to constantly strive for higher and greater situations," Jones says.

The people-oriented philosophy, Jones explains, follows that of the company's founder and president, Margot Fraser. Another example of this, she says, involves a woman named Kerry who used to work in accounts receivable.

"Kerry reported to me," Jones recalls, "and several years ago she came to me and said, 'Mary, I really think your correspondences could use some help.' I had no idea she liked writing, but I said, 'Sure, please take a look.' I saw she was a beautiful writer, and then she told me she always dreamed of being a writer. She started writing my letters, and Margot gave her her own letters to write. She was doing all this in addition to her accounting job, but like a lot of people here, she reached the point when she had to move one way or another. She chose to become our full-time company writer. "But really," Jones adds, "it sincerely started with her saying what she dreamed and being in a position where she could fulfill that goal."

Different From the Start

The dreams of Margot Fraser, now sixty-three, never included owning and operating a company that distributes more than a million pairs of sandals a year, but she ended up with one, anyway. It all started with an innocent vacation trip to her native homeland in 1966.

"I was living in California, and my husband and I took our annual trip to Germany," says Fraser, who at the time suffered from chronic foot problems. "Every year while in Germany I bought a new pair of shoes that were good for the feet, since they were unavailable in the United States. At a health spa in Bavaria, I saw my first pair of Birkenstocks." She bought them, took them home, and was quickly hooked.

After three months of wearing the chunky sandals, Fraser noticed a dramatic change. "I looked down at my feet and said, 'My God, my toes have straightened out!'" she recalls with a laugh. "At that time some of my friends wanted to get pairs, so I wrote to the company and ordered several." But Fraser was still a housewife, with no thought of getting into the shoe business. "I was a former dress designer and much more interested in the arts than in business," she says.

Even if she had been interested right from the start, Fraser still faced a formidable obstacle that might have scared her off. In those days, Birkenstock was a brand-new product—even in Germany, where the Birkenstock family had been making custom shoes for more than two hundred years. It was not until Karl Birkenstock entered the business in 1954 that the idea of mass-producing anatomically correct shoes was conceived. In 1964, a year before Fraser's trip to Bavaria, Karl's dream finally took shape with the creation of a single-strap sandal designed for postoperative wear. This sandal was just beginning to gain a following in Germany when Fraser bought her first pair.

Fraser's involvement, though, was motivated by more than pure profit. She wanted to sell Birkenstock sandals simply because she hoped to provide comfortable, beneficial footwear for women who suffered through the day's fashionable but tight high-heeled shoes. "I immediately thought of other women when I started wearing my own Birkenstocks," she says. "They had suffered long enough in pointy shoes!"

Despite Fraser's enthusiasm for sharing this discovery, her first foray into the shoe market was a failure. "I brought the shoes to two California shoe stores, one in Berkeley and one in Santa Cruz, in 1966," she says. "Both owners looked at me and said, 'Women will never wear those things!' Interestingly," she adds, "both eventually signed on and are now very strong dealers."

After these initial visits to shoe stores, Fraser turned instead to friends who were connected with the health-food industry. They advised her to show the Birkenstocks at an upcoming trade show in San Francisco. She took their advice and set up a minimal display. "There we were with only a table, a tablecloth, and a few sandals displayed on top," she remembers. "What happened was women began buying one pair at a time, mostly for themselves." But something else happened, too: Slowly and surely, the company began developing a following in the industry. Fraser now believes that this initial entry into the health-food market was critical to her eventual success.

"Health-food-store owners are dedicated people," she says. "They also have a clientele they can talk to easily, and they recommend products. But this was an effective entry into business. Remember, I was quite naive. If I had grown too fast, I wouldn't have known what to do."

If the Shoe Fits . . .

In those initial years during the late 1960s and early 1970s, Birkenstock experienced limited sales, and growth was very slow. "I would buy a few dozen pairs at a time from Germany and sell them to my tiny network of health-food stores," says Fraser. But it was during those early times that she also cultivated her refreshingly compassionate philosophy toward business and developed the people-oriented practices that later would serve her so well.

"I started selling Birkenstocks from the closet of my college dorm in 1972," says Melanie Grimes, one of Fraser's early vendors. "When I eventually opened a store of my own and ordered eighty-seven pairs of shoes, the shipment arrived with a letter from Margot saying, 'If the shoes are not for you and your customers, please send them back for a full refund.' That letter is still on the wall." Grimes now owns three Birkenstock licensed stores in the Seattle area, and she likes to keep reminding Fraser of that long-ago promise. "I keep threatening to send back my entire shipment," she says.

Grimes also remembers her initial business relationship with Fraser as being both supportive and nurturing. "When I was planning on opening my first store," she says, "I was choosing between two locations. One was in town on a busy street. The other was way out of town, in the back of a friend's health-food store. When I asked for Margot's advice, she said, 'Go where you are happy, because if you are happy, you will sell shoes.'"

Grimes decided to join her friend at the out-of-the-way health-food store, a decision she now considers vital to her eventual success. "I would have been overwhelmed at the Main Street location," she admits. "At the health-food store, I was small. Yet I grew at a rate I could handle."

Margot Fraser's business grew slowly, too, and she believes it helped her mature at a manageable rate. "I was very, very unknowledgeable about business," she says. "I didn't realize it took money to make money. I didn't understand about financing, didn't make projections or sales reports. I was just trying to get women into Birkenstocks."

Previously, Fraser had worked as a dress designer for a Canadian manufacturer, and that, more than anything else, helped her form the pro-people views that would ultimately shape her firm. "It was there that I experienced many of the frustrating aspects of being an employee," she notes of her stint at the dress operation. "I was doing design, but I didn't know a thing about the rest of the company. I was in my own bubble."

It was Fraser's initial decision to sell exclusively through health-food stores—"where," she now says, "people were tripping over vitamins while testing out shoes"—and the fact that she was importing rather than manufacturing shoes that allowed the self-professed housewife with sore feet to launch a business that in 1991 grew from $20 million to $38 million in annual sales. Yet it was her sincere concern both for the people who worked for her and for those who bought her product that created the growing legion of loyal dealers and customers springing up around the country.

In 1973, shoe-store owners approached Fraser asking to see, and carry, her line. In addition, a number of entrepreneurs opened "concept stores" shortly thereafter, presenting the sandals in a highlighted position as the primary product they offered.

But even after broadening her dealer network to include these mass-market options, Fraser never lost sight of the basic ideas and philosophies that had taken her so far. "We attracted a number of bright, motivated people who perhaps felt they didn't fit into the established corporate world and wanted to start their own business," she says. "This was a way to earn a living while also providing a beneficial service." She readily accepted these new dealers and enthusiastically invited them to grow along with her company. And by the early 1990s, Fraser's distributorship had blossomed to more than seventy-three independently owned "concept stores" and fifteen hundred dealers throughout the United States. Correspondingly, her line grew from one style in one color to more than 150 styles and several colors. Fraser's biannual trips overseas helped her develop her ideas and subsequent proposals related to the German manufacturer. All of this has resulted in vastly improved sales figures every year. From

1989 to 1992, sales increased by at least 30 percent each year.

Additionally, the Birkenstock shoe line has now gained unprecedented acceptance from trend-setting celebrities; its passionate supporters include well-known names like singer Madonna and actor Harrison Ford, also Chelsea Clinton, Michelle Pfeiffer, and Norman Schwarzkopf. It has become the subject of numerous articles in *Time, Newsweek,* and *Forbes* magazines, as well as in newspapers throughout the country, both for its new found fashion acceptance and because it alleviates chronic foot pain. And while "Birkies" often are still associated with proponents of the alternative life-styles adopted by their original wearers, the shoe has also developed a strong following among mainstream Americans and is worn by men and women from all walks of life.

The Conscience Remains

Today Birkenstock exhibits many traits that qualify it as one of America's most socially and environmentally responsible companies. For example, it donates a percentage of its annual profits to a variety of community causes, mostly concentrating on local efforts near the firm's Marin County headquarters. Fraser and her staff feel it is important to give something to the area in which they live and conduct business. Recipients of these donations to date include the Marin Conservation League, the Marin Agricultural Trust, the Environmental Action Committee of West Marin, and the Marine Mammal Center. The company also grants larger donations to various social efforts, such as Canine Companions for Independence, a national organization that provides trained assistance dogs to people with disabilities.

An atmosphere that encourages internal communication as well as employee appreciation is emphasized in the company's offices. This, staff members agree, has been evident and integral to the operation since its founding. "When I started out and hired Mary Jones as the part-time bookkeeper," says Fraser. "I said to her, 'Look, this is what we want to achieve. Now, how do you think we do it?' I learned much later that this is called participation management."

Now Jones is responsible for human resources. This position, she believes, is unique and carries with it a special imperative. "Being

Margot's first employee, I think I know what her philosophy of caring for people is all about," Jones says. "I'm the one to ensure that it all happens." Such thinking also guarantees that the company's overriding people orientation will continue even when Fraser eventually decides it is time to step down.

The enthusiasm and motivation that such attitudes engender in the work force is evident to all of the company's dealers and to other businesses with which it comes in contact. Once, a representative of the telephone company came to the firm's offices to help teach positive phone skills to members of the customer service department. "He was amazed at how enthusiastic everyone was," Jones says. "Normally, he said, he is called in after numerous complaints, and his clinic is regarded as a punishment. Therefore, those who undergo it are defensive and not so anxious to learn. But we don't look at clinics that way." Jones says. "We are constantly trying to encourage and motivate, and any and all training is appreciated."

This positive attitude is in evidence throughout the company and even has a central role in its employee handbook. Rather than the negative "don't do this, don't do that" tone common in such volumes, Birkenstock's handbook emphasizes the firm's belief in individual growth.

One passage reads:

> Birkenstock has a strong commitment to staff development. We want to help you succeed. We also encourage you to strive for your own individual growth and advancement in the company. You are encouraged to plan a growth program for yourself, take responsibility for it, and work closely with your manager and the personnel department on monitoring your growth. Decide what your own talents and abilities are and what can be accomplished as a result. Decide on the skill you must develop to achieve your goals.

To further advance this cause, Birkenstock constantly invites consultants and experts to come in-house and present seminars and workshops to its employees. Also, the company reimburses its workers for tuition fees resulting from professional seminars and college classes.

Communication Is Key

Stemming from Fraser's prior experience at the Canadian dress manufacturer, Birkenstock has developed as a company that emphasizes communication among employees and between departments. "It was easy when we were a small group and we could all sit in the same conference room," says Fraser. But as the company grew and its departments became more segmented, it became obvious that new methods were needed. Once a month, therefore, the company hosts brown-bag luncheons that take place either in its large showroom/conference area or on an outside deck overlooking a wooded area. One department, such as advertising or shipping or the special eco task force, will update the others on current activities they are working on.

"It's the awareness of knowing exactly what is going on throughout the company that keeps us on our toes," says Matt, who works in Birkenstock's shipping department. "There are twenty-two of us responsible for shipping more than a million pairs of shoes a year. It could be tiring and thankless work, but because we are included in so many parts of the business, we feel we're really an important part of the whole picture."

One way the company staff does not communicate, however, is through written memos. In an age when many employees elsewhere rely on the memo as the sole means for getting across an important point to an often unresponsive recipient, this is refreshing indeed. A rare memo at Birkenstock tells employees how their communications should be handled instead:

- Broadcast your announcements in person, via computer message, and via voice mail broadcasts when appropriate. In other words, if everyone doesn't need to have a written copy, don't give them one!
- Try to use everything at least twice! Use the back of the computer paper as scrap paper. Be creative and find new uses for things.
- Don't use Post-its! You can usually write right on the document!

This focus on communicating in person also goes further to include management's sharing projected sales and profits for the year with everyone in the company. At the beginning of each fiscal year, all employees meet and discuss the figures. "A lot of people on the outside are surprised that we would share our goals with every worker, ranging from our shipping clerks to receptionists," says Jones. "But we realize that it is up to everyone to realize these goals, and we want them to be with us from the beginning."

Moreover, openly communicating the company's overall goals is a motivator throughout the work force. "Everyone feels that we are in on what was always a big secret. Once we learn what the company-wide goals are, each department works on an action plan on how to achieve those projections. We are all in on it," says Suzanne, an employee in the payroll department.

In addition, Birkenstock believes in paying for productivity. For years, the company determined its compensation packages by informally canvassing neighboring businesses and others in the industry. As sales grew, however, Fraser and her managers realized there was a need to hire consultants to help them determine pay structures for their various levels. "We look at our location, our industry, and our position," says Jones. "If there is a job we feel is especially important to us, then we will provide extra compensation." Among those positions considered essential is that of warehouse shipping clerk, and Birkenstock pays above the industry norm for it. "They are our vital link between the company and the customer," Jones explains.

Upper-management salaries also are essentially in line with comparable positions at other local industries. Despite the firm's increasing sales and the company's solid growth, its directors and managers, including Mary Jones and Margot Fraser, receive fair but not excessive salaries. "We want to make sure managers aren't making enormous amounts of money," says Jones. "We are competitive for the job they are doing; we are fair for the market rate."

Even more importantly, perhaps, upper management does not receive the type of perks—like car and clothing allowances—that tend to alienate rank-and-file employees. Companywide bonuses, though, are another matter. "Once in a while we will get an extra fifty dollars in our paycheck; yet that is the same fifty dollars for everyone here. Beyond the salaries and incentive bonuses, there are no extra benefits for upper management," Jones notes.

This approach has not prevented the company from hiring and

retaining highly qualified and motivated people. According to Jones, only one manager left the firm between 1985 to 1990.

The pension and profit-sharing program was launched in 1978 and has proven to be another real motivator to the work force. Employees are fully vested in seven years, and they are now also eligible for new incentives based on the company's profits. It is this type of policy, where individual achievement and corporate generosity take center stage, that has been the key to Birkenstock's growth, maturation, and ultimate success. Since Margot Fraser initially discovered that first pair of sandals in Bavaria some three decades ago, she and her staff have developed a company that communicates with each other and those they do business with on a continuing basis. Because of that, as well as an excellent product that virtually speaks for itself, Birkenstock truly has remained a step ahead of its competition.

4

Ice Cream & Integrity

Company name: Ben & Jerry's Homemade Inc.
Type of business: premium ice cream and frozen
yogurt maker
Location: Waterbury, Springfield, Rockingham,
St. Alban's, Vermont
Number of employees: 600
Year founded: 1978

It is seven-thirty on an unseasonably warm November morning in
Vermont, and Ben Cohen wants orange juice. The kitchen in a
quaint country inn where he has scheduled a breakfast meeting is not
yet open for business, so Cohen decides to fend for himself. He
searches through a few cabinets until he finds a glass, then roots
through a walk-in refrigerator for the juice. "I need liquids," he says
with a husky laugh. "Now."

Cohen, wearing scruffy sneakers and a T-shirt plastered with the
image of a smiling sun, looks like the kind of guy who always pours
his own beverages—and helps his breakfast companions do the same.
He does not look like the cofounder and chief executive officer (CEO)
of a $135 million food company that employs 600 people and draws
more visitors than any other tourist attraction in the Green Mountain

State. He also doesn't look like half the team that oversees ninety retail franchises and company-owned stores in three countries as well as a fledgling manufacturing and retailing operation in the Soviet Union.

Cohen still looks—with the exception of a little gray in his beard—and acts much as he did when he and partner Jerry Greenfield first opened an ice cream shop in an abandoned Vermont gas station in 1978. Then both twenty-eight, they vowed to stay in business for one year. Their now phenomenally popular and successful company, Ben & Jerry's Homemade Inc., may have grown by leaps and bounds since that time, but Jerry and Ben themselves have remained true to their roots.

Cohen and Greenfield have created one of the most impressive examples of corporate responsibility that the business world has ever seen. At the same time their company was achieving an almost mythical status in the minds of ice cream lovers everywhere, the boyhood friends managed to keep treating their employees like family, purchase as many ingredients as possible from suppliers that adhere to their principles and philosophies, and support worthy causes and organizations in both their home state and around the world. They even created a nonprofit foundation to give away a full 7.5 percent of their company's pretax profits each year.

As becomes apparent to everyone they meet, Ben and Jerry also remained surprisingly free of pretensions. They're still "regular" guys who haven't strayed one iota from their sixties roots as they set about the task of building a very nineties company. Their hair may be a little sparser than it used to be, but it's never been trimmed to fit the standard corporate mold, and neither have they.

Their company has been faced with challenges and problems, though. Like any growing business, theirs has certainly had its ups and downs. But as an example of caring capitalism—as the duo refers to their overall corporate philosophy—Ben & Jerry's is hard to beat. The company produces an excellent product, helps its suppliers, aids its community, and supports its workers. It is precisely what it purports to be.

The same can be said about Jerry and Ben. The only thing different about the two old friends today, in fact, is their ability to now help more of the causes that they and their colleagues deem worthy of support. Unlike most of their peers in corporate America, their willingness and enthusiasm for such philanthropy never faded.

"In the past, people who consciously decided to go into business usually did so because they saw it as a way to make a lot of money. People who were motivated by social and humanitarian values tended not to go into business because they saw business as valueless," Cohen says, settling into his breakfast meeting with a glass of fresh orange juice. "But some of these people with strong social and humanitarian values—like Jerry and me—got into business by accident and were not sorted through that grid. So, through some quirk of fate, instead of ending up in a nonprofit social service agency, we happen to be trapped in a for-profit business."

Cohen laughs heartily once again and reiterates two quotes that his company has lived by since its first anniversary—which they commemorated by giving away free ice cream cones. One was from Jerry: "If it's not fun, why do it?" The other was from Ben: "Business has a responsibility to give back to the community." And even when it was hard to do so, Cohen now recalls, the two have diligently adhered to both of these tenets.

"I think it's always difficult to do anything right," he muses aloud. "It's like that song by Jethro Tull, 'Nothing is easy.' If what you are trying to do is produce the highest-quality ice cream, that's difficult. If you're trying to make a lot of money, that's difficult. And if you're trying to run your business in a way that benefits the community, that's difficult, too. But I don't think any of those things are difficult to the point of not being possible," he adds. "I think it's really just a matter of priorities."

At Home in Vermont

The town of Waterbury is just a blip on Vermont's Interstate 89, nestled in a scenic valley about halfway between the state's capital and its largest city. Despite its prime location, Waterbury has been essentially unremarkable for most of its lengthy history. It is home to a few shops and restaurants, a couple of country inns, the Vermont state police, and some spectacular views. But it wasn't until the arrival of Ben and Jerry—and the decision to locate their main ice cream plant as well as their corporate offices in this community of about eight thousand—that Waterbury really showed up on the map.

The 43,000-square-foot plant began operating in 1985, and faithful ice cream lovers from around the world have been flocking to it ever since. Suprised company officials admitted 41,000 visitors during the first six months after they opened their doors to tourists, but they got over their shock by 1991, when an even larger number walked through the plant every month during peak season. Some 220,000 took the tour that year, making Ben & Jerry's Homemade the number-one tourist attraction in this very tourist oriented state.

But visits were not the only thing that skyrocketed between the mid- and late 1980s. An employee named Mary, who had driven a Ben & Jerry's ice cream truck in 1982 and was later hired to organize the new tour program, recalls that there were only forty-two employees at the company when she came on board in 1986. The year before, sales were just $9 million. But the company then embarked on a rapid nationwide expansion, thanks to funds raised through a special stock offering open only to Vermont residents and a second traditional option for investors across the country. The employee ranks and the corporate revenues were soon to increase tenfold.

All of the activity that brought about such growth, however, was accomplished without the company's altering any of its counterculture business practices: Tons of ice cream and lots of money were still given away, traditional advertising was never employed, and a unique management style remained in force. Longtime employees, such as Mary—as well as newcomers like a woman named Sarah, who started in the gift shop in late 1990—attribute this to the purposeful vision of Cohen and Greenfield, who never deviated from the unorthodox path that they chose long before.

"For a while we were growing at about a hundred percent a year," recalls Cohen, who freely admits to being troubled by a pace that would delight most other business leaders. "Our outside sales were expanding faster than our internal organization and our infrastructure. We knew we were growing too fast. So we made a very conscious decision to slow our outward growth and devote a large amount of energy and resources to improving the quality of our organization— the way we work together as a team and the way we develop each of our employees."

The company, he continues, dramatically changed the way it did business—something that Ben & Jerry's remained able to do because of the way it was structured. Movement into new markets was slowed; expansion of franchised "scoop shops" was curtailed. These actions put the company back on track, Cohen notes, and growth then continued as an organized juggernaut that shows no sign of abating as the nineties wear on.

But none of this is really surprising when one considers the history of the company and the background of its founders, two boyhood friends from Merrick, New York. They first bonded together as outsiders (and lovers of food) in the seventh grade, when they couldn't run track as well as the others in their junior high school class. Neither could find their niche as young adults, either—Greenfield tried his hand as a lab technician while hoping to get into medical school; Cohen studied pottery, drove a taxi, and taught crafts—and their drift to Vermont was as aimless as their career paths.

But then serendipity: The two discovered a correspondence course in ice cream making that was offered by Penn State and only cost five dollars. They took it, Greenfield and Cohen often say, because they could afford it and because they liked ice cream. And after achieving a perfect score on the open-book final exam, the duo took a $12,000 investment ($4,000 of which was borrowed) and in 1978 opened their first scoop shop in the college town of Burlington.

Financial success didn't come overnight—it actually took about five years before the young company turned a profit—but notoriety was theirs right from the start. It came in part from their strongly flavored homemade concoctions with unusual names. For example, Dastardly Mash and New York Super Fudge Chunk. But it also came in part from the two owners, who endeared themselves to locals by working hard and plastering their images on the pint containers of their product that they soon began selling throughout the winter in order to keep the business going.

The Seeds of Giving

In the summer of 1991, Ben & Jerry's sponsored free "One World, One Heart" festivals in Chicago, San Francisco, and Stowe, Vermont.

Each included performances by such popular musicians as Dr. John, David Bromberg, John Prine, and Carlos Santana. Each included family-oriented activities like Dye Your Own Tie Dye T-shirts and Ben & Jerry's New Vaudeville Light Circus Bus. Each included presentations by a group called 20/20 Vision, which aims to cut military spending and meet environmental and human needs, as well as free ice cream cones for attendees who wrote postcards or made videos on-site for their congressional representatives.

Each also included the dumping of a billion seeds of grass on festival grounds to point out the excesses of the U.S. military budget by illustrating how much a billion of something really is.

By all accounts, the festivals were a huge success. As many as 100,000 people attended in each location. Hundreds of shirts were tie dyed, and performances on the circus bus were viewed by hundreds more. Thousands of postcards and video messages were sent to Washington, and tons of grass seeds were scooped into recycled paper bags by festival goers who could not help but think about the relationship they had to the billions of dollars spent annually on America's war-making machinery.

"One of the nice things about becoming bigger is that you can throw bigger parties," Jerry and Ben said in the flier announcing each event. "This festival is a time to play and celebrate together—it's also an opportunity to take the first step in a sustained effort at working together for a more just world."

But this message and the medium that carried it were only the latest manifestations of a concern for their environment that Greenfield and Cohen have been espousing since their company's beginnings.

"When we first started, our only goal was to have our homemade ice cream parlor on the corner; we didn't plan on being anything larger than that," Cohen remembers. "And while we had strong feelings about wanting to be a business that benefited the community, we didn't know what that meant at the time. So on our first anniversary, we gave out free cones to everybody to celebrate our first year in business and our amazement that we hadn't gone bankrupt yet."

As the company evolved, so did Ben and Jerry's commitment to their constituents. They continued their annual cone giveaways and instituted free summer movies and a yearly fall festival. But, Cohen notes, "these things just came about organically. The movie series came about because we were located at a gas station that had a big white wall next to it and we figured it was a great place to put up chairs where the cars used to go. And after our first summer, we really wanted to thank our customers for patronizing us and allowing us to survive, so we started our Fall Down festivals, which were family days of fun and games held in the park across the street from our shop."

In addition, the company began donating a lot of ice cream to a variety of local community organizations. But it wasn't really difficult yet to juggle business and social concerns, because the company wasn't even making a profit.

Ben & Jerry's eventually reached the point where its balance sheets were written in black ink; however, in 1981 it opened its first franchise, and by 1983 it was distributing ice cream outside of Vermont. Fred "Chico" Lager, a local nightclub owner, was brought in as president. And the company was giving away more and more ice cream and money. Everything, in fact, looked terrific—for a while.

"Originally, Jerry and I were ice cream men working in this ice cream shop," Cohen says. "But then the business started to become more of a business, and we had a bunch of employees and were spending our time talking on the phone and writing letters and memos and hiring and firing. We turned to each other and realized we were no longer ice cream men; we were businessmen. Our immediate reaction was to sell the business, because we didn't want to be businessmen. But then I ran into this old restaurateur down in Brattleboro, and he convinced me to keep the business. He said that if there was something I didn't like, I should just change it. That really hadn't occurred to me before."

They decided to raise capital for expansion in a novel way: by offering residents of their adopted state a chance to buy a piece of their company. In 1984, they sponsored the first-ever Vermont in-state public stock offering with a low minimum buy of $126 to allow everyone in who wanted a chance to participate. The sale was advertised in the front section of local newspapers, and it eventually raised $750,000—enough to finance construction of their Waterbury plant. A traditional nationwide public offering in 1985 permitted the expansion to continue, and their evolving commitment to social issues also continued as their financial resources grew.

A Foundation for Success

"We knew the main thing business does is make money, and if we were going to give back to the community, we had to give away a whole bunch of money," Cohen says. "So that's what we started to do."

To keep this commitment viable—and to appease the legions of new stockholders who sometimes wanted Ben & Jerry's run more like the public company that it had become—the partners created the nonprofit Ben & Jerry's Foundation in 1985. Initially established through a donation of company stock, the foundation was designed to "support projects which are models for social change; projects infused with a spirit of generosity and hopefulness; projects which enhance people's quality of life; and projects which exhibit creative problem solving."

Some of the causes Ben and Jerry support are the Devastators, an all-children's Afro-Latin percussion band that works to combat drug abuse, AIDS, and homelessness; the Heifer Project, which provides agricultural animals to impoverished communities; Boston's Women's Institute for Housing and Economic Development; and the Worker Owned Network of Athens, Georgia.

Each year since, the company has kept the foundation alive by donating to it 7.5 percent of Ben & Jerry's pretax profits. Grant proposals are solicited that relate to children and families, disadvantaged groups, and the environment.

That, however, is only the beginning of the company's philanthropic efforts. A special Employee Community Fund—financed by half of all revenue taken in from the one dollar charged to each adult who takes the plant tour—is granted to nonprofit community and statewide groups in Vermont. Funding decisions are made by voluntary employee committees, and recipients range from the Association of Vermont Recyclers to a group of woodworkers who produce toys for underprivileged local youngsters.

Factory seconds are also either given away to community organizations in the state, donated to food banks, or sold by special arrangement in Vermont stores—with a portion of that income also donated to community organizations, such as libraries, recreation centers, and local fire and rescue squads. In 1990, these payments totaled nearly $210,000. According to estimates from an employee named Eloise, who handles the community relations program, the company gave away about eight thousand gallons of free ice cream in 1991 to approximately one thousand Vermont organizations that simply requested it.

"Every day I come to work I feel I'm making the world a better place," says plant manager Don "Mac" MacLaughlin. His sentiments, in one form or another, are commonly echoed at every level in the company.

Despite such solidly based good feelings and the charitable activity on which they are based, Jerry, Ben, and others in the company felt they weren't doing enough. So in 1988 they wrote a Statement of Mission that dedicated the firm "to the creation and demonstration of a new corporate concept of linked prosperity." It consisted of three interrelated parts: a product mission ("to make, distribute and sell the finest-quality all-natural ice cream. . . ."), a social mission ("to operate the company in a way that actively recognizes the central role that business plays in the structure of society by initiating innovative ways to improve the quality of life. . . ."), and an economic mission ("to operate the company on a sound financial basis. . . .").

But this, it seems, was still not enough for Ben & Jerry's. For even with this new mission and a foundation giving away maybe $300,000 a year, the partners noticed that they were flooded with requests for assistance that they simply could not fill.

"All of them were worthy causes," Cohen recalls, "and we realized we were never going to solve all the problems that we were looking to solve. Our contributions were just a drop in the bucket. We started thinking about why there were all these social needs that went unmet, and it didn't take long to realize that it was because 40 percent of the national budget was going to the military. So we came to the conclusion that if we were really going to help the community and meet these social needs, we had to use our power as a business to direct money out of the military and into human and environmental needs."

Fortuitously, at just about that time, the company was coming out with a chocolate-covered ice cream bar on a stick. It decided to call the product a Peace Pop and use the packaging to talk to customers about a new organization that Ben & Jerry's was helping to found called One Percent for Peace. The group would actively promote the idea of redirecting 1 percent of the U.S. military budget to peaceful and humanitarian activities, and the Peace Pop would represent the first attempt by Ben & Jerry's to use its packaging to advance a social cause.

The company has continued with this theme ever since, too, attaching various messages onto its pints—such as those about the disappearance of America's family farms and the destruction of the world's rain forests. And this led quite naturally into another innovative area that Ben & Jerry's has successfully pioneered: that of purchasing its raw materials in a way that aids both the environment and the individual causes it chooses to support.

Blueberries, Peaches, Nuts, and Brownies

Few people outside of Maine know that the state's Passamaquoddy Indians, a group that has long been excluded from economic prosperity, works hard at the business of harvesting and processing wild blueberries on their reservation. Ben & Jerry's found out, however, and in the summer of 1990 the company contracted to buy $330,000 worth of fresh berries for use in its Wild Maine Blueberry ice cream from them.

At the same time, Ben & Jerry's was buying Brazil and cashew nuts from the Amazon rain forest for its Rainforest Crunch ice cream, brownies prepared by homeless employees of Greyston Bakery for Chocolate Fudge Brownie ice cream, peaches grown by African-American farmers in Georgia for Fresh Georgia Peach ice cream, and dairy ingredients from the five-hundred-member St. Albans Cooperative in Vermont for every one of its products. Developing such relationships with suppliers that address unmet social needs has become just another aspect of Ben & Jerry's ongoing mission and another way to meet its unique "two-part bottom line."

"This act—just consciously sourcing our ingredients, even though it might cost us more than somewhere else—ends up bringing about a more positive benefit than probably all of the money that we give away through our foundation," Cohen believes.

"We now do this on every level," he continues, "because we made it an integral part of our bottom line. We tried to figure out why business tends to be valueless and uncaring and in the worst situations actually harmful to the community and exploitative to its workers and its environment. And we found that this is because the success of business is measured solely by the traditional bottom line—that is, by how much money is left at the end of the year."

So Jerry and Ben decided to change the way their company measured success. They developed an alternative "two-part bottom line" that assesses the year by how much money is left over as well as by how much the company has helped the community. It didn't work right away; managers felt that the two goals were mutually exclusive. But the founders convinced them to simply add a new variable to their purchasing decisions and taught them to pick vendors according to three factors (social benefit, price, and quality) rather than the usual two (price and quality).

And once they began, the task became easier. Along with food products, Ben & Jerry's applied this philosophy to the millions of dollars of office and building supplies it regularly purchased. It switched to an insurance company and a credit-card issuer that place their premiums and profits in low-income housing and other similar investments. And it initiated proactive programs, like one in Newark, New Jersey, where Ben & Jerry's ice cream carts are operated by a foundation that runs a food bank and works with homeless people.

"Just by choosing these vendors, we're benefiting those other causes," Cohen explains. "Our goal is to integrate a concern for the community in all of our day-to-day business decisions. So far, we've been successful in maybe ten to twenty-five percent, so we've got a ways to go. But the trend is there; each year we find more and more ways to integrate this concern into our activities."

This move, not surprisingly, is also manifested in the company's resource-management efforts. Its environmental programs manager leads companywide efforts to raise awareness of recycling options and find markets for recyclable materials. Its art department works with suppliers that use recycled paper and soybean-based inks. Solid waste, such as cardboard and plastic pails, are reused whenever possible. And the company has even developed an incredible Solar Aquatics Greenhouse at its main plant that successfully purifies the waste from dairy production by means of a natural ecosystem of flowers, fish, and compost.

Ben & Jerry's also concentrates on the direct development of a variety of social and family activities, such as its free summer festivals. Other sponsorships of this nature include the Giraffe Project, which identifies and supports people who "stick their necks out" by doing exceptional things for their communities; the annual Halloween parade in New York's Greenwich Village, which distributes proceeds to various causes; free performances of the *Nutcracker Suite* for needy youngsters in several cities; and traveling voter-registration drives.

These projects not only extend Ben & Jerry's considerable social reach still farther; they also serve as the primary marketing tool for a company that never places traditional advertising in traditional media. "Rather than spending $35,000 on a full-page glossy ad, we'd rather do something that our public will enjoy," says Holly Alves, the marketing director. This concept must work, too: Consumers across the country clamor for the product, and more than fifteen thousand unsolicited job applications are received at the firm's headquarters each year.

Working for a Living

In the main plant, Peter, the company's flavor designer, toils in a room labeled "alchemy lab"; his business card officially proclaims him "primal ice cream therapist." The cabinets in his work space are tagged "sour things," "sinful things," "magical elixir," "secret stuff," "cold metallic things," and "I don't know."

Full-color life-sized cutouts of James Dean, John Wayne, and other movie stars, each wearing the pastel hair covering that is required headgear in all food-preparation areas, adorn numerous offices throughout the organization. White trash cans, emblazoned with the black markings of dairy cows, are everywhere. Wild and crazy artwork personalizes practically every work area. And if all that weren't enough, an officially designated group called the Joy Gang regularly sponsors a variety of companywide events, including a miniature car derby and an Elvis look-alike contest.

Alves remembers how this penchant for institutionalized fun once left her with some explaining to do. Shortly after she joined the company in 1990, her mother came up to Vermont from her home on Philadelphia's Main Line to see Alves in her new surroundings. Ironically, it was on the same day that sixties activist/prankster Wavy Gravy was visiting the plant to announce a new flavor named in his honor. The guest of honor was dressed, as usual, in a tie-dyed clown outfit; employees were acting even loonier than usual, and many were walking around with paper bags on their heads. "My mother was wondering what I had gotten myself into," Alves recalls.

Alves, too, wondered at first whether she made the right decision to leave a six-figure salary and a penthouse on San Francisco's Russian Hill for a lower-paying position and a smaller house in the hills of Vermont. "I was nervous that the company wouldn't be what it was supposed to be," she says. "But I was pleasantly surprised to find that it was."

Not everyone fits into the wacky atmosphere and liberal philosophy promoted by Ben and Jerry, of course, and those who don't tend to exit quickly. Overall, however, the turnover rate is only 8 percent, and most of those who stay are passionately committed to the founders' ideas and ideals.

Not surprisingly, the company also treats its primarily young work force quite well. Usual benefits, like health, dental, and life insurance, are supplemented by progressive programs, such as maternity and paternity leaves, stock-purchase options, educational assistance, profit sharing based on longevity, free membership at health clubs, wellness programs (cholesterol, blood pressure, smoking cessation, and substance-abuse counseling), and on-site educational seminars (writing skills, management, and financial advice). Even more unique is the domestic-partner coverage, which extends applicable benefits to nonmarried and homosexual partners of employees. And then there is the right to take home up to three free pints of ice cream every day.

Still, according to an employee named Carol in the benefits administration department, "the philosophy and social mission helps keep people more than the benefits."

One area that has occasionally proven a problem in recent years, however, is the company's salary structure. Ben & Jerry's works on a so-called compressed salary ratio, which means that the highest-paid employee can not make more than seven times the lowest full-time wage. The range was recently increased from its previous five-to-one ratio, but this policy—a visible extension of the "linked prosperity" philosophy—has caused several high-level job candidates to turn down employment offers.

Still, Ben & Jerry's appears to be a truly great place to work. People are committed to the company and to each other. And for those who come on board, the salary program that caps even Jerry and Ben's annual at less than $120,000 each is no deterrent.

"Money's not always the issue," notes plant manager Mac Mac-Laughlin, a former pro football player with fourteen years of management experience who bypassed several higher-paying offers when he chose to accept the job at Ben & Jerry's. "Sometimes in life you have to give something back."

Planning for the Future

At first glance, Ben & Jerry's looks a lot like other midsized companies. A communications coordinator keeps the burgeoning employee base informed about comings and goings. A manager of investor relations deals with Wall Street's growing interest. A human resources director manages personnel operations and employee development, while a quality assurance director plans and implements a company-wide program in quality control. But the similarities stop there. Look deeper and Ben & Jerry's structure is all its own.

The quality assurance director, for example, developed a Ben & Jerry's version of the currently popular Total Quality Management program that implores workers to "keep that euphoric feeling" by doing the "ten steps of the Improvement Boogie." The human resources director is a self-proclaimed jack-of-all-trades who arrived as a consultant in 1984, moves into jobs where he is needed, and wouldn't stick around if the company wasn't committed to its social mission. And the manager of investor relations, who grew up in Vermont and has a primary background in agriculture, rarely travels to New York, because "we don't want to hype the stock."

And then there is the communications coordinator. Part of her increasingly difficult job is to publish a monthly newsletter that informs the expanding work force about items of interest while also striving to be as irreverent and as entertaining as everything else the company does. The publication reports on important activities (e.g., the free summer festivals) and interesting phenomenon (the tattoos of employees). And sometimes it is dedicated to a seminal corporate event, such as the December 1990 retirement of popular company president "Chico" Lager. (This tribute included sarcastic reminiscences, old photos, and a series of artist's renderings detailing Lager's dramatic hair loss during his tenure.)

Keeping this type of wild and crazy attitude alive in a company growing as fast as this one is no easy task, but Ben and Jerry are both working hard to ensure that it is retained. Unless they are traveling, they come into the office every day. Cohen has moved into the media forefront as the official spokesperson and marketing guru. Greenfield has solidified his position as an employee cheerleader and is apt to be found on the plant floor in the middle of the night, working with the late shift as it packages ice cream on the assembly line.

Changes, though, are part of the game. New president Chuck Lacy has brought continuity to the organization (he was promoted from within) and solidified its professional direction, even if he doesn't have the emotional persona and acknowledged wit of his predecessor. The nationwide movement toward healthier, low-fat food prompted the introduction of several frozen yogurt flavors. And while the firm has barely adjusted to the opening of a second plant in Springfield, Vermont, and the relocation of its support offices to a building a few miles away from the main Waterbury plant, more construction is afoot: a $3 million distribution center was recently built in Rockingham and a $12 million manufacturing facility is planned for the town of St. Albans.

Financial gains continue at an almost staggering pace, too, despite the company's conscious effort to slow its growth. Sales increased 23 percent in 1989, 32 percent in 1990, and 30 percent in 1991, while Ben & Jerry's share of the national premium ice cream market grew from 23 percent to more than 31 percent during that time. And now that the company has moved its products into most major supermarket chains throughout the United States, future expansion will stem from the introduction of new products and their increased presence in independent grocery outlets across the country.

Moreover, the social side of Ben & Jerry's remains inseparable from the business side. Controversial stands are as common as ever: In 1990 alone the company officially opposed licensing of the Seabrook nuclear power plant in New Hampshire and military action in the Persian Gulf while supporting work-place rights for AIDS sufferers and a boycott of Salvadoran coffee. And the company's success, despite this penchant for unconventionality, continues to illustrate that even public corporations can make a profit while helping their communities.

Ben Cohen speaks of all this proudly, if not with more than a bit of awe, as he wraps up his early breakfast meeting on that uncommonly warm November morning in Vermont. It is time to point his well-worn sneakers toward company headquarters, where a meeting is scheduled for Ben & Jerry's board of directors. (Cohen is chairperson; Greenfield is assistant secretary.)

"When we started out, our only goal was to remain in business for a year at the old ice cream shop in that Burlington gas station," he notes, slipping on his jacket and heading toward the door. "We never had any idea that it would evolve into this."

5

Banking on the Community

Company name: Shorebank Corporation
Type of business: bank holding company
Location: Chicago, Illinois
Number of employees: 350
Year founded: 1973

From Chicago's Stony Island Avenue, at a point about nine miles south of the city's fabled Loop, you can see both the promise and the peril of urban America in the 1990s. On one side of the wide asphalt strip is South Shore, a neighborhood brimming with rehabilitated apartments, neat single-family homes, clean streets, and hope. On the other is Woodlawn, a section filled with burned-out buildings, debris-strewn lots, graffiti-scarred walls, and general despair. Stony Island serves to separate physically these two adjoining neighborhoods in the heart of America's third largest city, but in reality they are worlds apart. The difference between them is the Shorebank Corporation.

Formed in 1973, when South Shore and Woodlawn were experiencing equally the early stages of urban decline, Shorebank is an unusual kind of community development organization. With a bank at its core and a group of nonbankers at its helm, it is a multifaceted for-profit business created specifically to bolster the fortunes of South Shore. By most measures—and particularly in contrast to the deterioration that ultimately destroyed Woodlawn—it is a remarkable success.

Since its establishment, South Shore property values have risen far more rapidly than those in other city neighborhoods like Austin and East Side. Unusual coalitions of "housing entrepreneurs" renovated thousands of rental units in hundreds of buildings. New shopping centers and other buildings sprang up for the first time in decades. Thousands of local residents benefited from educational and job-placement programs; dozens of new businesses received organizational support. And the Shorebank Corporation—which has since replicated some of these programs in areas like Michigan and Missouri—is turning the kind of profit that satisfies both banking regulators and its investors.

In addition, after years of futilely trying to convince others of the merits of its methods, Shorebank's successes are finally being recognized. The corporation's ideals and activities were thoroughly described in "Community Capitalism," a 1988 sociological evaluation by University of Chicago professor Richard P. Taub. But the bank didn't receive much national attention until 1992. During that year's presidential campaign its goals and practices were repeatedly praised by Democratic candidate Bill Clinton (who, as governor of Arkansas, helped bring Shorebank and its concept to rural parts of his state). After the spring Los Angeles riots Shorebank was often cited as *the* model for effectively distributing loans for small business development and residential rehabilitation.

Such accomplishments and recognition, however, did not come easily. Money managers, developers, and even neighborhood residents were openly skeptical—if not downright hostile—when Shorebank's founders purchased a failing local bank and announced plans to use it as the centerpiece for an ambitious program of community redevelopment. The commercial revitalization that they originally targeted never has matched the neighborhood's residential rehabilitation. And achieving profitability was a mighty struggle for the first six years.

But with the help of dedicated employees, flexible managers, innovative programs, and a little old-fashioned luck, Shorebank has become *the* role model for socially responsible corporations–a growing segment of the business world that did not even exist when its founders entered South Shore some two decades ago.

"We wanted to create an institution that would do something like what we are doing now," says Ronald Grzywinski, chairman of Shorebank's board and the individual most responsible for its formation and development. "We had an idea. We had a vision. We knew that there had to be a better way to rebuild the cities of America for the benefit of the people who lived there."

The route taken by Grzywinski and the three other members of Shorebank's management team—Mary Houghton, Milton Davis, and James Fletcher—was to form a bank holding company specifically designed to revive its neighborhood by reinstalling credit, rehabilitating self-confidence, and reestablishing a functioning market economy. It does so by operating a bank, a real estate development subsidiary, a Minority Enterprise Small Business Investment Company, a nonprofit affiliate that creates housing and jobs, and a consulting arm that advises other public and private companies involved in economic development.

These efforts have proved so successful that Shorebank eventually expanded into the huge Austin neighborhood on Chicago's west side and developed or helped run a variety of related programs in rural Arkansas, Michigan's Upper Peninsula, Kansas City, and even Poland and Bangladesh.

Its roots remain in South Shore, though, and looking around that neighborhood today, it is not hard to find reasons for the continuing optimism expressed by Shorebank officials. From Jackson Park on the north to Eighty-third Street on the south and from Lake Michigan on the east to Stony Island Avenue on the west, South Shore's two and a half square miles and sixty-one thousand residents stand as a continuing testament to their vision.

The Roots of Rehabilitation

People at Shorebank like to tell the story of a former electric company employee who had a vision of his own. One of the first South Shore residents to take advantage of the new lending policies introduced by

Grzywinski and his cohorts, the man raised enough money to buy a delapidated forty-four-unit apartment house for $55,000. He fixed it up, leased it out, and sold it nine years later for $450,000. By 1991, at the age of sixty-eight, he owned seven more refurbished buildings and had become very wealthy.

His success inspired others, like the manager of a dry-cleaning business who bought a small apartment with money lent by Shorebank. The man repaired it, rented it, bought a second and a third. He eventually owned about fifty units and quit his dry-cleaning job in order to begin rehabilitating apartments full-time.

These impressive stories are hardly unique. Hundreds of "housing entrepreneurs," like the electric company employee and the dry-cleaning manager, are responsible for renovating more than seven thousand rental units since 1973. As they, with Shorebank's help, raise their own standards of living, they also make their community a better place.

Neither Grzywinski, Houghton, Davis, nor Fletcher seems surprised that this radical idea for urban improvement—born out of the social and civil rights movements of the sixties—works so well in the nineties. A team of complementary talents with a unified view, the foursome realized more than two decades ago that traditional nonprofit and government efforts were severely limited in their ability to handle complex urban woes. Though only in their thirties at the time, they understood that a new kind of for-profit attack with a social-worker orientation might be better.

Such thinking came about naturally. Grzywinski was a businessman before moving into banking, where he pioneered the community-oriented approach later embraced by Shorebank. Mary Houghton held a master's degree from the Johns Hopkins School of Advanced International Studies when she joined up with Grzywinski and the others. Milton Davis, a civil rights activist and chairman of the Chicago chapter of CORE (the Congress on Racial Equality), was on the faculty of the Graduate School of Business at the University of Chicago. James Fletcher was a former grade-school teacher, a veteran of Chicago's War on Poverty, and the assistant director of the federal Community Action Program.

The four, who lived near each other and often traveled in the same circles, joined forces to create their new kind of bank in the late sixties. To this day, none likes being referred to as a "banker." They see themselves instead as social reformers who operate their bank as a vehicle for societal change. And they believe this idea developed and flourished precisely because they were not "bankers" in the traditional sense.

"We were all working with various community-based organizations, and those organizations were trying to deal with a variety of problems in the neighborhoods in which they were located," Davis recalls. "But it was like an ant fighting an elephant because those organizations were always consumed with raising money to pay the rent, the light bill, and the staff. They simply had no time to deal with the problems they were confronting in the neighborhoods, and so there was no way those problems could ever be adequately addressed. We were convinced that we ought to take a look at designing an organization that would have a fighting chance of dealing with those problems."

The actual concept originated with Grzywinski, who grew up in a Polish-American neighborhood less than five miles from South Shore. After graduating from Chicago's Loyola University, he got a local job selling computers for IBM. He eventually left the corporate world to take a position with a bank in the nearby city of Lockport. After becoming president of that bank, he returned to his old neighborhood specifically to help organize a deal to buy a struggling bank in Hyde Park, an area just north of South Shore that was changing for the worse.

Under Grzywinski's supervision, this new Hyde Park Bank formed an Urban Development Division that made loans to minority entrepreneurs throughout Chicago. The program brought major deposits to the bank from government and private sources interested in furthering the Urban Development Division's goals and helped the bank itself return to profitability. It also attracted Davis, an African-American originally from Atlanta, Georgia, who was living in South Shore at the time; Houghton, a white program officer for the nonprofit Johnson Foundation who had recently relocated to Chicago; and Fletcher, an African American who had grown up in a public housing project five miles from South Shore.

The four learned the power of a bank as a development force, but they also discovered its limitations. Federal regulations at the time banned banks from most development-oriented activities, including the ownership of real estate that was not directly used by the institution. But Congress's approval of the 1970 amendments to the Bank Holding Company Act and the Federal Reserve's subsequent definition of newly permissible activities, erased that drawback. Bank holding companies were finally freed to invest in community development corporations—if their primary purpose was to benefit low- and moderate-income groups. Since that was precisely what the foursome wanted to do, they knew that a nontraditional banking structure could now best help them achieve their goals. They only needed an appropriate neighborhood in which to test their theories.

Shorebank Finds a Home

South Shore is one of those fiercely independent enclaves that gives Chicago its reputation as a city of neighborhoods. Built in 1893 to house railroad workers, it evolved into a middle-class bedroom community with large single-family homes, small brick bungalows, and street after street of multiunit apartment buildings.

Thanks in part to amenities like Jackson Park, a location along the Lake Michigan shoreline, and an easy commute to downtown, South Shore became one of the city's most desirable residential communities by the 1930s. Its main shopping district—Seventy-First Street— reflected this status, and residents of other southern sections traveled there by commuter train to browse through its high-fashion jewelry, clothing, and shoe stores. Local public schools also were first-rate, and their graduates often moved on to some of the best universities in the country.

By the 1950s, however, a major transformation was under way. Change rocked two nearby neighborhoods—Woodlawn and Hyde Park—as blacks increasingly moved in and whites moved out. People opted to live in newly constructed buildings within the city limits or in newly expanded suburbs to the south and west. Apartments in South Shore were not properly kept up, and single-family home values started to decline. Gradually, more and more longtime South Shore residents began to seek homes elsewhere.

As was the case in many urban areas throughout America, the situation only worsened as the years rolled by. Older apartment buildings deteriorated still further. Many were subdivided into smaller units, drawing poorer and poorer tenants. The number of welfare recipients mushroomed. Middle-class residents, both black and white, moved on when they could. Racial tensions increased. The Seventy-First Street shopping strip deteriorated. Crime rates soared. Property values in South Shore stagnated.

Within a few years, the neighborhood suffered an almost total decline. Most of the so-called experts declared its fate sealed. And in 1972 the area's primary financial institution, the South Shore National Bank, requested permission to relocate downtown.

Swayed by organized neighborhood opposition, the federal comptroller of the currency rejected the relocation application because the bank had "failed to show a persuasive reason for abandoning its service area." Ronald Grzywinski, who was seeking a neighborhood for his proposed banking-based development program, asked if the institution was for sale. He was told it was and that its book value was $3.2 million.

Grzywinski had left Hyde Park Bank in 1969 to develop a structure for his new community development effort. The resultant plan, which he completed with his three colleagues and the help of a few others, was initially called the Illinois Neighborhood Development Corporation. It was ready to go when the existing South Shore National Bank came on the market.

Raising the capital necessary to buy the bank was another story, however. The group sought its $3.2 million in units of $160,000, but, not surprisingly, its plan to purchase a failing bank in an economically depressed neighborhood for the purpose of testing a radical new idea had few takers. Over the next couple of months, in fact, only $800,000 was raised from a few individuals, a couple of foundations, and the United Church of Christ Board of Homeland Ministries. The other $2.4 million was secured through a loan guaranteed by Grzywinski and his wife.

On August 23, 1973—"vastly undercapitalized and seriously overleveraged," as its members now readily admit—the new management team took over South Shore Bank. Though it was faced with serious obstacles, the team decided to begin immediately the task for which it was formed.

"As we saw it, one of our chief purposes was to restore South

Shore's competitiveness by rebuilding the market forces disinvest-ment had destroyed," Grzywinski has written. "The neighborhood was far from hopeless. A lot of storefronts were boarded up, but not all. A dozen apartment buildings had been abandoned, but not more. The trouble was, every bank and savings and loan in town had red-lined South Shore, including the bank chartered to serve it—the South Shore National Bank. In the year before we bought the bank, it had made exactly two conventional home-mortgage loans for a total of $59,000."

Grzywinski and his colleagues aimed to change that. They planned to spark renewal by carefully—but deliberately—reinvesting all of their resources in just one targeted community: South Shore. Not many people had high expectations for their idea, but their convic-tion would prevail.

A Rocky Beginning

When South Shore's new owners took over in 1973, deposits were low. (They had, in fact, fallen from a peak of $80 million to about $42 million in little more than a decade.) Loan officers were reluctant to accept the new owners' liberalized lending criteria. The building itself had not been properly maintained for years. And its only parking lot was located across a busy street and out of sight, forcing customers to take a long and potentially dangerous walk in order to reach the bank.

"From the beginning, we envisioned that the bank would be the centerpiece," says James Fletcher, who now serves as its president. "But we bought a bank that was in trouble as opposed to buying a healthy bank, and that made a big difference." It meant that all of the affiliate activities they needed to proceed at full speed—the real estate development company, the minority investment company, the not-for-profit neighborhood advocate—would have to wait until the bank itself regained a solid financial footing. But, he adds, this didn't mean that all of Shorebank's community development efforts would have to be put on hold. So they set about the task of raising necessary capital.

The new owners felt they could do this by increasing deposits, which residents would be more willing to make once they understood their money was going only to development activity within their community. To further bolster this desirable deposit activity, they cut the minimum balance needed to open a savings account to one dollar, extended the bank's hours, reduced its service fees, and eliminated most paperwork. At the same time, they improved the bank's appearance, built a new parking lot directly across the street, and even constructed a drive-up teller facility a couple of blocks away.

Simultaneously, the bank overhauled its lending policy. From that point on, loan officers could only deny applications from South Shore residents—or from someone who wanted to buy a home or open a business in the community—after the applications were also rejected by the management committee. In addition, the bank began aggressively courting entrepreneurial borrowers, much like the owners had done with their urban development program at Hyde Park. Milton Davis—then president, now chairman, of the bank—and Grzywinski also visited an array of neighborhood organizations to explain Shorebank's programs and plans.

Unfortunately, as Grzywinski and the others now concede, not all of these moves met with success. Neighbors of the new drive-up facility disliked its potential to draw crime near their homes; others were angered that the bank tore down an apartment building to make way for its parking lot. Old loan officers never completely accepted the bank's new lending philosophy, and most were eventually replaced. Increasing the number of small savings accounts did not provide the capital Shorebank needed and actually lost money for the institution. But the biggest disappointment was the small-business-loan program.

"When we first got here," says Milton Davis, "we made noble efforts to make loans to all of the businesses along these streets. We lost every one of them. They just couldn't compete with the regional shopping malls, half an hour's drive from here, that have two hundred stores."

The managers refused to give up hope and fine-tuned their efforts. They appeased neighborhood groups opposed to their construction efforts as best they could. They raised savings-account fees in order to cover costs and decided to focus their lending efforts on South Shore's true strength—residential real estate.

Significantly, the program they formulated to fund that plan eventually turned their entire effort around. Called Development

Deposits, it is designed for outside depositors—from pension-fund managers to individual savers—who want to open a competitively structured account at Shore Bank because their funds will be used exclusively for development efforts within the Chicago neighborhood. Simple, yet radical, it reversed the usual banking practice of taking local deposits and then investing them in faraway projects.

"A community like South Shore, by definition, doesn't have the resources to fund long-term development operations," says Joan Shapiro, a South Shore senior vice-president in charge of this reverse-redlining program. "What happens in most cases is that you have a net outflow of investable resources from the low-income communities to the more affluent neighborhoods. Development Deposits brings outside resources into our service area."

Depositors have responded enthusiastically, with accounts opened by residents from all fifty states and seventeen other countries. And since the program's inception in 1974, their funds have helped Shorebank as well as South Shore. By early 1992 the Development Deposit portfolio reached about $120 million, or 60 percent of the bank's entire $230 million deposit base. "We'd be a very different bank without it," Shapiro says.

Not Business as Usual

Banks have received more than their share of public attention in recent years. Conflicts of interest, improper executive spending, discriminatory lending practices, federal takeovers, taxpayer bailouts. It's both a pleasure, and a surprise, to find one free from controversy—and one recording its seventeenth consecutive year of profitability in 1991 while lending money to South Shore residents who otherwise might not have obtained loans.

"People always ask me if that is risky. But where have the losses been in this industry in the last ten years?" Shapiro asks. "Not at a bank like South Shore. Our loan losses in 1991 were a little over six-tenths of one percent, the year before that they were forty-six hundredths of one percent, and the year before that forty-two hundredths of one percent. Who has really taken the risks?"

Most of the neighborhood-improvement loans originate in the bank's Development Division, which traces its roots to the Hyde Park

Bank Urban Development program. Shorebank's version was initially headed by Mary Houghton, who now serves as president of the corporation and executive vice-president of the bank. It is a vast improvement over the original because of the addition of Development Deposits and in its updated form has successfully funded small business development as well as multifamily housing rehabilitation, home improvement, community organization, and education.

"Since 1973, the bank and its affiliates have put $300 million into this neighborhood," says Milton Davis. "Most people would acknowledge that it's been this $300 million that has really made the difference in having this neighborhood be what it is today. And the prediction by a lot of people, especially the real estate arena, when we got here was that this neighborhood would go to abandonment and demolition in five years."

Shorebank has refurbished the area, he adds, without pushing low- and moderate-income residents out in favor of more well heeled newcomers. "That is the single thing I think most of us here are most proud of," Davis notes. "We have developed this neighborhood without gentrifying it. How? By developing or rehabilitating housing and then keeping the rents at a level that the people who already live here can afford."

By catching the neighborhood in the early stages of decline or when improvement was least expensive, Shorebank was able to both assist in a dramatic reversal of fortune and also maintain South Shore's viability for those earning $18,000 and less. It was also able to attract other investors, lenders, and developers, who now enter the neighborhood with projects of their own.

The Pieces Come Together

In 1978, Shorebank was fiscally able to begin adding the nonbank affiliates and subsidiaries that its originators envisioned. First came City Lands Corporation, a wholly owned residential and commercial real estate development subsidiary. This was followed by The Neighborhood Institute—the first tax-exempt affiliate ever formed by a bank holding company—which was created to tackle deep-seated housing and job problems. The Neighborhood Fund, a qualified

Minority Enterprise Small Business Investment Company, was created in 1979 to finance small-business loan requests that South Shore Bank could not approve. Shorebank Advisory Services, which acts as a consultant to both financial and nonfinancial institutions on issues like banking, economic development, and affordable housing, was authorized in 1987.

"From the beginning, we envisioned the bank as the centerpiece. But the bank, by regulation, can only do so much. It can only respond to people's requests. It can't cause things to happen," explains Jim Fletcher, who took part in Shorebank's initial planning but did not come over from Hyde Park until he accepted an offer to run The Neighborhood Institute when it was formed in 1978. "We needed action vehicles," he continues. "That's how we thought of the other pieces."

Over the years, the interrelationship between affiliates and subsidiaries has enabled Shorebank to put together a community revitalization program that works on many levels. Each organization in the corporation is responsible for impressive projects that help the others succeed.

Using a variety of funding methods, for example, City Lands rehabilitates large apartment houses, manages property, builds low- and moderate-income housing units, and develops commercial real estate. Perhaps its greatest triumph is the Jeffrey Plaza Shopping Center at Seventy-First Street and Jeffrey Boulevard. With one of Chicago's leading supermarkets as its anchor and twenty-one other stores to widen its appeal, this $9.4 million project has been Shorebank's most effective retail effort to date.

The Neighborhood Institute rehabilitates apartment buildings for cooperative ownership, manages small-business "incubators" in the neighborhood, and trains and places job applicants. It coordinates rehabilitation projects, such as a thirteen-story apartment building in which one-fifth of the units were reserved for very low income tenants, and an innovative artist's colony called One Artist Row. Its Career Education and Employment Center has placed more than twenty-seven hundred individuals in private-sector jobs.

The Neighborhood Fund, which makes equity investments in minority-owned companies, placed $625,000 in six businesses in 1990. Shorebank Advisory Services works with clients like Specialty

Mill Products of San Francisco, a nonprofit cabinet shop that trains low-income high school dropouts in cabinetmaking and millworking skills.

On the Road

This newest subsidiary has also helped Shorebank expand its concept into other geographic areas. In 1986, the corporation opened a variation in the far west side neighborhood of Austin, the largest in Chicago, with almost twice as many residents as South Shore. A year later, the Winthrop Rockefeller Foundation and the state of Arkansas asked management to help "accelerate the pace of economic activity" in a very rural thirty-two-county area. Grzywinski, Houghton, Fletcher, and Davis formed a second bank holding company, Southern Development Bancorporation, to do so.

Later, Shorebank officials also initiated a similar program on Michigan's Upper Peninsula; there they are in partnership with Northern Michigan University's Economic Initiatives Center in an effort to open a development institution that will provide a full range of financial and business support services. Even more recently, the corporation agreed to manage a recapitalized black-owned bank in Kansas City.

Perhaps the most challenging of all its newer undertakings have taken place overseas, where Shorebank has been developing credit programs in countries like Bangladesh and Finland since 1983. One of the most intricate began in Poland in 1989, where, in cooperation with the U.S. government–backed Polish-American Enterprise Fund, it is trying to introduce the same kinds of institutions Shorebank has been utilizing in its development efforts since 1973.

Back in South Shore the corporation has grown to some three hundred fifty employees. They generally fall into one of two categories: those who come to the corporation specifically because of its social mission and those who live in the area and simply need a place to work. Shorebank provides a good job for both as well as some excellent benefits—it is continually cited as one of America's top companies for mothers employed outside the home, for example—and long-range strategic planning is under way to move the company into the future.

Milton Davis says of the future: "Like anybody, I see changes and I'm willing to change my mind. If you asked me when we came here in 1973 how long it was going to take to get this neighborhood turned around, I would have told you two years. Well, I'll never say that again. Here we are more than eighteen years later and it's still going on. But if you stop and reflect, this neighborhood hadn't torn down in two years, so there was no reason to expect it could be rebuilt in two. Our time frame should have been much longer than it was, but after two years we didn't just say, 'let's turn around and go.' We stayed for the long haul."

Shorebank has indeed stayed and made a major impact. Its innovative development ideas have set the standard for community redevelopment, but other bankers have still not rushed out to copy its now-proven strategies. Of the more than eleven thousand banks in the United States, only Shorebank's South Shore Bank in Chicago and Elk Horn Bank in Arkadelphia, Arkansas—along with the unrelated Community Capital Bank of Brooklyn—operate under such a socially responsible mantle.

Nonetheless, the success of Shorebank's policies are apparent. To see them for yourself, go to Chicago's Stony Island Avenue. At a point about nine miles south of the Loop, where South Shore compares so favorably to Woodlawn, you'll understand exactly how effective they've been.

6

Selling What Comes Naturally

Name: Alfalfa's Inc.
Type of business: chain of natural-foods groceries
Locations: Denver, Littleton, Fort Collins, Vail, and
Boulder, Colorado
Number of Employees: 750
Year founded: 1983

It's a typical midweek morning at Alfalfa's Market in Denver. Several young mothers, their kids in tow, peruse the food store's narrow aisles for buffalo steaks, imported Italian pasta, and organic vegetables. Two business executives, taking an early break for lunch, wait at the deli counter for their order of black-bean cakes and tofu moussaka. A couple of college students, seated in the in-house Café, share an earnest conversation while sipping espresso. On the other side of the grocery, an elderly man picks up a few cans of nonfat soup and a jar of sodium-free tomato sauce and then stops to chat with a stock clerk in the bulk-grains department.

Alfalfa's Inc., a small chain of Colorado natural-food stores open six days a week from 8:00 A.M. to 10:00 P.M. (and till 9:00 P.M. on Sundays), appeals to a varied and devoted clientele. Local residents who want a wide array of high-quality foods have been frequenting its six dramatically different stores since the first in the chain opened in 1978. The company has since grown into one of the largest operations of its kind in the nation, with stores in Denver, Littleton, and Boulder, Colorado, and additional outlets in the planning stages.

In 1993, Alfalfa's had 750 employees and recorded gross sales of $142 million. It carries a well-deserved reputation for honesty, integrity, and knowledgeable service. Original employees remain committed to the company. The firm's extraordinarily generous donations policy has financially enhanced many community-based charities.

For example, during 1991, Alfalfa's contributed more than 24 percent of its net profits in cash and in-kind services to a wide assortment of local nonprofit organizations. That figure does not include any money realized through its regular company-sponsored fund-raisers or its daily contributions to local food shelters of a variety of fresh products that are perfectly edible but no longer salable.

Still, as befits a company with a conscience, many employees want to see Alfalfa's do more. They therefore take it upon themselves to initiate new charitable programs all the time. These include a solo trek along six hundred miles of the Continental Divide that raised $20,000 for the Food Bank of the Rockies; an all-you-can-eat spaghetti dinner—entirely stocked, prepared, and served by volunteers—whose total proceeds went to a group called Community Food Share; and an annual "Share the Spirit" program that, since its inception in 1988, has provided Christmas Eve dinners for thousands of needy local residents and Christmas presents for their children.

"Our approach to all of this, though, is pretty low-key," notes Marcus Christopher, Alfalfa's director of human resources. "If employees want to help out, that's great; if they don't, that's fine, too. We just try to educate them about what we do, and we end up getting pretty good participation. I think that speaks well of the type of employees we have—people who want to make a contribution."

Everyone agrees that this philanthropic spirit is symbolized by Sandy Stewart, manager of the company's store in suburban Littleton. Despite her extensive professional responsibilities—not to mention the personal duties that come with being the single mother of a toddler and the caregiver for three foster children—Stewart spearheads Share the Spirit in the southern portion of the metropolitan

area. She also consistently introduces new events, like a family bar-
becue, which benefits the Denver Emergency Housing Coalition's
"Adopt-A-Home" program. Her devotion and commitment to make
a difference instills a charitable attitude in her own employees and
others within the organization.

An active volunteer since age fifteen, when she spent the summer
working forty-hour weeks in the ghettos of Buffalo, New York, Stewart now embodies the people orientation that helps make Alfalfa's a
model of corporate generosity and community involvement. Her
impressive personal commitment, however, is just one of the many
things that sets the social agenda for this grocery chain. In the past
several years, for instance, her peers have organized additional benefits for the Make-A-Wish Foundation, the Humane Society, the
Denver Dumb Friends League, and the Arapahoe County Inter-Faith
Task Force for Community Service. Her co-workers have also initiated programs to inform customers about the plight of dolphins, the
use of pesticides, and the need for recycling.

"The owners and employees of Alfalfa's are as committed to the
ideals of customer and community service as they are to issues concerning health of individuals and the environment," proclaimed the
cover story in one issue of the company's monthly newsletter. "Our
philosophy of help encourages individuals—employees, customers,
citizens—to take an active part in programs of community service."

Stocking the Shelves

The shelves at Alfalfa's are filled with products, brand names, and
ingredients that are most likely quite alien to the average American
shopper. The likes of Knudsen's organic pear juice, fresh pâté forres-
tier, Health Valley nonfat chili, Siberian ginseng, and Coleman Natural Beef, after all, surely are foreign—and maybe just a little bit
frightening—to the unenlightened. To Alfalfa's customers, though,
these and thousands of other obscure items are everyday dietary staples. Their names, while hardly in the mainstream, roll off the tongue
of an Alfalfa's shopper with a trustworthy familiarity.

A sign in the window of Alfalfa's store in Denver, outlining the
company's purpose, explains it well. "We created Alfalfa's Markets
toward one aim only: to make people feel better by helping them eat

better," it says. "We believe that given the choice, people prefer honest, wholesome food that not only tastes delicious but sustains health. At Alfalfa's you don't have to wonder if the food you select is good food, free of harmful chemicals and insecticides, because good, natural food is the only kind we sell. So every choice you make is a healthy choice. That promise, and a commitment to integrity, quality, respect, and service, are the things we gladly offer our community."

Shahid M. Hassan—"Hass" to everyone who knows him—is Alfalfa's cofounder, president, and chief executive officer (CEO). Now in his mid-forties, the Kashmir-born, London-educated Hassan became involved with "health foods" almost immediately after moving to Colorado in 1974. By running a Denver food co-op and then a Boulder natural-foods store before opening the first Alfalfa's, he quickly learned that community service would amount to nothing without retailing integrity. And he also surmised that neither could exist until he developed an uncompromising consistency among his products.

"In order for a conscientious business to work, the number-one thing you have to have is the right product. You cannot be a business that sells something nobody needs and couch the whole thing in environmental consciousness and service to the community. You can do everything else right, but if your product's a worthless product, it isn't going to work," Hassan says.

"On the other hand, we'll never sell products that violate our standards just because they're in demand," he adds. "I know that a lot of our customers drink Pepsi and that they have to go elsewhere to buy it. Still, you'll never find Pepsi in our stores."

Hassan says he didn't expect his concept to catch on as quickly as it has, although he felt, right from the start, that he had the right products—and ones that nobody else was selling properly. He recognized it first at the Denver co-op, which grew out of a community-service requirement imposed by the "meditation community" to which he belonged at the time. He saw it again in his first Boulder store, the Pearl Street Market, which he opened in 1978 with meditational partner Mark Retzloff. He spotted it a third time in 1982, when he and Retzloff realized that they had already outgrown their original store.

Public acceptance and financial success appeared within their grasp, but the two understood that expansion would involve new challenges. With the help of Lyle Davis, the third original investor who was tapped to run the Pearl Street Market's produce department after his return from a ten-month sojourn to Italy, Greece, and North Africa, a $400,000 Small Business Administration (SBA) loan was secured for the relocation. Nonetheless, the partners were still about $200,000 short of the funds they needed.

"We had to raise money to do it on the scale that we wanted it done," Hassan recalls. "So we held a 'dog and pony' show. We rented the banquet room at a local hotel and invited friends and family, prominent people in town and good customers, and got several hundred people to show up. We took a lot of food down and threw a big party, showed our concept and our plans for the future, and said we were looking for investors. A lot of people liked the idea, knew they'd shop there, and said they would feel proud to be a partner in a good business that contributed to making Boulder good. Many pitched in five thousand or ten thousand dollars, and a few invested more. We got a big shareholder base, and enough money to open."

Alfalfa's eventually materialized a few blocks from the Pearl Street site, and it became deeply involved in community affairs. Free "tasting fairs" encouraged University of Colorado students and other local residents to check out the new store. The owners actively solicited customer feedback and paid strict attention to what they heard. A newsletter was distributed. Additional projects were soon initiated outside the confines of the grocery.

"We started staging events in which we were 'giving back' to the community, even if these events were not specifically geared to selling more products," remembers cofounder Davis. The first, which set the tone, was a downtown Denver picnic with free food and entertainment for low-income residents. "It felt good to see a lot of joy in people who would probably never be our customers," Davis adds.

The Community Expands

It's lunchtime on a late winter afternoon, and Alfalfa's store in Boulder is bustling with activity. College students—most of whom were just babies when Hassan opened his first store—are prowling the aisles, meeting friends, discussing coming events. The Café and take-out deli lines are so crowded that Hassan and Marcus Christopher take up places behind the counter to help out. Two middle-aged women sit at Al's Bar, a freestanding island that serves up juice and ice cream, and discuss a book on dream therapy. A young man listens in and then joins the conversation by adding a tidbit on Denver's C. G. Jung Institute.

Scenes like this one, say Alfalfa's employees and managers, take place every day in each of the chain's three locations. The image of Alfalfa's as a gathering spot, a place to meet friends or to find someone with whom to talk, never varies. And that, apparently, is entirely by design.

"Part of the initial concept," explains Hassan, "was that we wanted our store to be a community meeting place. It used to be that every community had its church, its post office, its village green—its center. But that doesn't exist anymore. We knew everybody goes grocery shopping and everybody needs food. So we wanted to make our store that community center, the place where people like to go because the environment is attractive, there's something going on, and you see your neighbors and friends. We thought there was a need for that, and we thought, businesswise, that it made sense." The cafés—unusual features in a grocery store—sprung from that belief.

One of Alfalfa's largest fund-raising events, the Pancake Breakfast, also is rooted in that idea of community. Every June, each store hosts its own version of this all-you-can-eat extravaganza at which whole-wheat pancakes, pure maple syrup, homemade, preservative-free sausage, and coffee, tea, and milk are served. All of the $4.00-per-adult fee ($2.50 for seniors and children) is donated to charity, but organizers believe the event really draws the masses it does because people enjoy the party and the chance to spend the day with others in the community.

Employees, too, seem to like to stick around, and the company tries hard to give them reason to stay. Tim Overlie, for example, initially moved to Colorado to become a solar engineer; a quirk of fate caused him to start working as a buyer for Alfalfa's a month before the first store opened. He stayed there because he liked the company and the people, and about seven years later he was named Boulder's manager. Marcus Christopher, the human resources director, came on board to stock shelves and build displays when Alfalfa's first opened. Another original employee, Paul Gingerich, was asked to run the meat departments of each new store before being named manager of the Denver location.

"Before I began working for Alfalfa's," Gingerich says, "the longest I was ever employed in one place was three years. It was not that those jobs were bad; it was just that I was bored or I had done everything there was to do and I saw no place to advance. But so far that hasn't happened here. There's always something coming up."

The future, apparently, offers even more opportunity for these and other employees. The company's most recent addition is a central commissary, run by cofounder Davis, that now prepares all of the chain's high-production items (including baked goods and salads). And Alfalfa's plans to open three more groceries in Colorado by 1994 (among the sites under consideration are Fort Collins, Colorado Springs, Vail, and another Denver neighborhood), followed by additional stores throughout the Rocky Mountain region.

This pending expansion presents an obvious challenge to a company that prides itself on its family-like atmosphere. Keeping employees informed of comings and goings at five, six, and seven sites is obviously much harder than it was when Alfalfa's was merely in one, two, or even three locales. Even more difficult, perhaps, will be the task of imparting the company's rather unique culture to new employees in far-flung towns.

To help it do so, in early 1992, Alfalfa's implemented its first-ever management training program. A dozen employees regularly meet with upper management to learn the ways of the company, and they then travel from store to store on their own time to see how things are currently done. When growth does take place, new management positions will be filled from this employee pool.

"We're finally getting smart and working on expansion in advance," explains Jon Payne, Alfalfa's vice-president of operations. "We've realized that more important than finding the perfect facility and negotiating the right rent and building at the right cost, is the need to have the staff to open these new stores and maintain the quality relationships we have between employees and customers." Payne joined the management team in 1990 after selling his own small grocery chain. He was, however, an early investor in Alfalfa's and has been a member of its board since 1986.

While programs like the training effort and a comprehensive employee assistance program are being added to help move the company into the nineties, Payne and other managers admit that Alfalfa's could do even more for its workers. Cutting-edge benefits are simply not yet a part of the package, for example, though additional perks are under consideration as the company grows more profitable. New ones, like a comprehensive employee assistance program, are being added all the time.

Nonetheless, the family atmosphere and people orientation appear to be the draw that keeps luring prospective workers, especially from among the ranks of existing shoppers.

"One of the biggest reasons people are with us is because of what we are and what we aspire to be," says Payne. "We're not perfect, and we make mistakes, but in general our philosophy, and our spirit, is to be all we can and to give back to the community. Yes, it's a job, and yes, it doesn't pay rocket-scientist wages. But here people can really affect their community and have a job where they can really have some say."

Such mistakes include the slow addition of improved employee benefits, the aborted attempt to place management in a central corporate office, and, until recently, the lack of adequate managerial training to provide for future expansion. Like Alfalfa's movement into increasingly innovative charitable areas, however, these problems are being rectified.

Easing the Growing Pains

Shahid Hassan's small, unpretentious office is located on the mezzanine level of the rambling Alfalfa's store in Boulder. Its walls are plastered with pictures of his family and posters of events that the grocery sponsors. A toy basketball hoop hangs over the door, and Hassan often challenges visitors to a shot. Classical music wafts into the room from the grocery below, while an interior window offers a good view of the activity on the market's main floor.

For Hassan, this vista is a constant reminder that the way Alfalfa's is today is not the way Alfalfa's has always been.

The biggest change came about in 1989, when management decided to decentralize its operations. Up until that time, Alfalfa's had a central corporate office, and major decisions were made there for all parts of the company. As the business grew, however, those in charge recognized that a new system was needed. There was some initial resistance, but a decision was made to move the power out to the stores themselves. And it seems to be working.

Now, for instance, store managers are referred to as "unit presidents." They have complete control of their domains, taking full responsibility for everything from hiring to merchandising to deciding how they will spend their individual contribution budgets each year. Within each store, managers of every department are given the same autonomy; individuals in charge of meat, produce, the deli, groceries, frozen foods, cheese, health and beauty care, and the front end are all allowed to run their areas as they see fit—within certain parameters, of course.

"We've all got roles and responsibilities that are very well defined, and there's a line of authority, and the clearer we can make that, the better," says Hassan. "But the idea is that everybody has a valuable role to play. If you're the person who runs the deli, that's your job. I'm not going to tell you what to do; you can do it any way you want within the context of what Alfalfa's is about."

The experiment has proved successful, and each store has developed a definable persona of its own. The 18,000-square-foot Boulder market, for example, is the youth-oriented store, designed and run for that town's young college-age population. The 23,000-square-foot Littleton store, opened in 1985 in a building that previously housed a standard supermarket, is a more traditional, open site with an upscale "suburban" feel. The 16,000-square-foot Denver store, opened in 1990 in the posh Cherry Creek part of town, offers a crowded urban ambience not unlike a small, old-fashioned grocery in an established ethnic neighborhood on the East Coast.

Significantly, decentralization has affected more than just the way the stores look. For one thing, it provides the company with a varying series of prototypes it can then use in its impending expansion. For another, says Boulder manager Overlie, it allows him and other store managers to "empower people from the top all the way down to the bottom," which has greatly cut turnover. "At one point, two people out of twenty here were on the job for more than six months," he explains. "Now there are two here less than six months."

The move also helped to shore up the chain's profitability picture, which solidified considerably about the same time the decentralization plan was implemented. Most groceries shoot for net profits of about 1 percent of gross sales; at Alfalfa's, the goal is 5 percent—and that is now being realized. While profits were lower than management originally hoped for, they jumped into the desired range even as annual gross sales doubled, from $15 million in 1988 to $30 million in 1991.

Still, the decision to decentralize was particularly difficult for those who brought Alfalfa's to the point where it was necessary.

"It has not been easy," Hassan readily admits. "It's worked, and that has greased its happening. But it's not always easy for me personally. I have a vision of how everything should be. When I go into a store, I look at every shelf and every can and every display and every interaction, and I have an idea of how every one of those things should be to be perfect. It's not easy for me to acknowledge that I wouldn't do it the way that it's been done, but now it's essentially someone else's store. And if I want them to take complete pride in it and to treat it like their own store, it isn't going to work if I constantly butt in."

In fact, Hassan and the other owners have allowed the company to become increasingly employee empowered. Spontaneous suggestions are taken seriously, companywide meetings are held monthly, and storewide gatherings are scheduled weekly to discuss such matters as pricing and marketing and customer service. Fiscal information is also shared regularly with all employees: Department-by-department sales and labor reports for all three stores are posted at all locations for everyone to see. "Basically, everybody in the company knows everything," says operations vice-president Payne. "We don't hide anything in the way of numbers."

One of Alfalfa's biggest changes was its search for venture capital to fund expansion plans. Everyone was informed of the lengthy step-by-step process that resulted in the New York investment company of Weiss Peck & Greer—which already managed about $6 billion in properties—buying out original partner Mark Retzloff for an undisclosed sum.

"They checked us out, obviously," Payne says. "And we checked them out. We wanted to know what other businesses they were in;

what kinds of things they were invested in. We did due diligence on our part to make sure we weren't aligning ourselves with someone who didn't have a culture or a belief system that meshed with ours. We want to make money, but we want to make it with a conscience."

The fit apparently was a good one. Alfalfa's managers, employees, and eighty shareholders were satisfied. And with the financial infusion, the company began plans for additional growth.

Alfalfa's Way

At the start of 1992, Alfalfa's Markets became the first major grocery chain in the United States to begin selling Coleman Natural Beef—exclusively—in its meat departments. The Colorado-based producer's cattle are given only organically grown feed raised on farmland certified free of herbicides, synthetic fertilizers, and pesticides. Its line, from ground beef to tenderloin, was subsequently the first in the world to be officially certified by the Organic Crop Improvement Association.

The move to stock it, Hassan told the local media, was part of Alfalfa's long-term and ongoing commitment to the organic-foods industry. "Organic farming has been the cornerstone of Alfalfa's philosophy of providing our shoppers with the best-tasting, purest, and healthiest food available," he explained.

Alfalfa's has also taken an active position in the drive to educate consumers about products that company personnel consider unhealthy. Its monthly newsletter, offered free to the public at all three stores, contains regular articles like "Pesticides: A Matter of Growing Concern" and "At Alfalfa's, We Believe in Organics" that pull no punches. "Pesticides are poisons," says the former. "They are designed to kill living organisms. Some are tailored to attack insects; others are used to destroy weeds, molds, and rodents. The same chemicals that are poisonous to agricultural pests can also be harmful to humans, causing cancer, birth defects, nerve damage, and genetic mutilation."

These and other articles go on to state that Alfalfa's supports over one hundred food producers that are dedicated to the principles of organic farming and "sustainable agriculture"—the process of preserving and revitalizing renewable resources by cooperating with nature rather than trying to control it. The company has had some of these relationships for eight years or longer. It buys such items from local sources whenever possible, but will go elsewhere to purchase appropriate products, if necessary. Additionally, it is an active member of the Colorado Organic Producers Association, which, among other things, has been responsible for the passage of relevant statewide legislation.

To further these causes, the company also suggests in its regular newsletters that customers work for the establishment of national organic standards, advise their favorite restaurants about the benefits of organic ingredients, and utilize organic growing methods in their own home gardens.

"Our products make us different from other supermarkets," says Jon Payne. "But the other thing that's different is our belief structure. We're committed to furnishing a product that is better for everyone. One of the slogans we use is 'We read the labels for you.' And that's quite legitimate. We won't carry things that don't meet our criteria of cleanliness and wholesomeness, sometimes to the sacrifice of sales."

The company also makes product choices—and takes sometimes-controversial political stands—on other food-related issues. One example is its campaign to raise awareness of the tuna industry's incidental killing of dolphins during the hunt for yellowfin. Beginning in 1988, Alfalfa's launched an extensive in-store and media campaign designed to bring the problem to the attention of its shoppers and the community at large. At the same time, it eliminated from its shelves all brands of canned tuna products that were produced by companies suspected of killing some of the tens of thousands of these air-breathing sea mammals slaughtered annually in the quest for tuna.

This and other related practices clearly define Alfalfa's position. But they also make running a profitable supermarket all the more difficult. "We don't do business with people we don't agree with," notes Payne. "Even if Dow Chemical had an organic field, we'd have trouble with that."

As a result, Alfalfa's managers are very critical when examining potential suppliers and their products. This is no small task. The average supermarket deals with sixty to eighty suppliers, one of whom usually provides it with 70–80 percent of its total selection. Alfalfa's, on the other hand, does business with fourteen hundred suppliers, none of whom provides more than 2 percent of the chain's products. "That's a drastically different picture, and it's very difficult to manage, to pay bills, to receive. It's very time consuming and inefficient," Payne admits, "but it works for us."

On the positive side, the complex makeup and ever-changing nature of Alfalfa's product line prevents newcomers from easily entering the local marketplace. But dealing with so many small vendors also stops the chain from developing profitable store-brand products and keeps prices higher than traditional competitors for the type of items that both carry. Payne says that regular markets make a 40 percent profit on house items and 20 percent on standard brands, for example, while Alfalfa's has to price its products from 15 percent to 20 percent higher across the board in order to make up the difference.

Fortunately for Alfalfa's, Denver was climbing out of its lengthy oil-collapse recession just as the rest of America was falling victim to a recession of its own. The growing economy in Colorado meshed perfectly with expansion plans at the grocery chain, and locals—hunkered down financially through most of the late 1980s—responded to the chance to buy quality products that complemented their healthy life-styles and dietary tastes. The markets filled a unique niche in each area they located and probably cut more into major-market competitors, like Safeway and King Soopers, than into any specialty shops in those neighborhoods.

"It's an investment for the consumer, but we think the benefits are high," Payne says, noting that Alfalfa's customers shop more for quality than they do for price. "Besides, this is a boutique, and there's not much that we have that's really comparable with other markets. It's like putting a K Mart up against Neiman-Marcus."

The chain has further tried to differentiate itself in recent months by opening an EcoShop in its Boulder locale. This "store within a store" features items like rechargeable batteries, energy-saving light bulbs, recycled paper goods, and water-filtration devices. The management team feels it is a good match with their other departments, and they now plan to add such sections to all new stores while retrofitting existing locations for these and similar goods.

Getting Its Just Desserts

It's a warm Saturday in early August, and a parking lot the size of two football fields at Alfalfa's in Littleton is filled with dogs. Doberman pinschers, Dalmatians, Labrador retrievers, Akitas, cocker spaniels, collies, German shepherds, mutts—the asphalt is crowded with canines of every imaginable shape, color, disposition, and size. Kids are being pulled to and fro by dogs. Adults are trying to hold civil conversations while their dogs wrap leashes around their legs. Barking, whining, growling, and yelping fill the air. Water and soap suds flow like rivers between the rows of parked cars.

The reason for this madness? An event that is admittedly unusual for a grocery store to sponsor: Alfalfa's annual dog wash. For a nominal charge—five dollars for dogs under twenty-five pounds, eight dollars for dogs over twenty-five pounds—residents of the area get a chance to socialize while their pets are hosed down, soaped up, and toweled off. Contests are held for biggest dog, smallest dog, fluffiest dog, shortest tail, longest tail, best master-dog look-alike, and best trick. All proceeds go to the Denver Dumb Friends League, which shelters thirty thousand lost and unwanted dogs each year before placing many of them in private homes.

While Alfalfa's does do a brisk business in dog food—organic, nontraditional brands, of course—the day's activities are planned for more than promoting its wares. Like the Denver store's participation in an event called Taste of Cherry Creek or the Boulder store's involvement in a yearly Thanksgiving food drive, the dog wash is a way in which company personnel can raise money for a worthy cause while getting involved with their respective communities.

The goal has not changed even as the employee base and the number of stores multiplied far more rapidly than anyone but the original founders ever had a right to suspect.

"I think our values are admirable, and they've always been so," says Denver store manager Gingerich, who grew up in a family that ran a traditional meat business. "In the past we were, many times, unable to really act on some of the things we really believed in. But since 1989, we have gotten our operations under control, and we are now making money. We have some capital to expand, and we are developing training programs. At last, we can afford to do what we need to do."

Gingerich, who also hosts a cooking segment on a local television show every Tuesday afternoon, pauses only momentarily when he is asked if Alfalfa's could ever get so large and formal that it forgets those values.

"We have too much pride in being on the cutting edge," he replies. "I go to industry conventions, and I'm proud to say I'm from Alfalfa's. People know we are leaders, and we aren't about to take a backseat to anyone."

7

Baking, Building, and Benefiting

Company name: Greyston Corporation
Type of business: umbrella organization for a bakery, a
construction company, and a nonprofit foundation
Location: Yonkers, New York
Number of employees: 65
Year founded: 1982

When you reach the Greyston Bakery in Yonkers, New York, you aren't quite sure you have the right place. The small, unassuming building with the rust-colored steel door blends in with other structures in this shoddy industrial section, just blocks from the Hudson River. If it weren't for the small, hand-carved wooden sign hanging above the doorway, you could easily walk right by.

Once inside the door, however, it is obvious you are in the right place. Invitingly rich aromas envelop the front doorway. A pumpkin cheesecake rests on a hallway table. Before you are asked who you are and why you are there, the receptionist invites you to sample a slice of the dessert. After two bites, you're encouraged to give your opin-

91

ion. Is it too sweet? Would this work well for the holidays? Would a chocolate glaze be overkill?

Before you've even been in the clean, efficient kitchens or up to the third-floor attic that houses the cubbyholelike offices, you are already part of the Greyston team. Everyone's thoughts count, and input is actively solicited. Later, it becomes apparent that this attitude—making everyone who in any way relates to the company an important ingredient—permeates the company.

Greyston Bakery is a supplier of elaborate pastries to gourmet shops, department stores, and some of New York's most celebrated restaurants, including Sardi's and Tavern on the Green. In addition, it makes the brownies that are used in Ben & Jerry's Chocolate Fudge Brownie ice cream.

The 8,000-square-foot bakery, named for the solid rock formation quarried in this lower Hudson Valley area, operates sixteen-to-twenty-four hours a day, six days a week, and employs forty-five people who work in two shifts. Sales have grown from $1.2 million in 1989 to a projected $3 million by 1992's year end. In addition to the excellence of the company's products (their cheesecake was rated New York City's best by the *Daily News*), Greyston Bakery, with its nonprofit affiliate, Greyston Family Inn, is acclaimed for its work to eliminate homelessness and poverty in one of New York's more depressed areas, the southern portion of Westchester County.

Besides providing delectable desserts, the organization has gutted and renovated a nearby abandoned apartment building, also in Yonkers, which now houses eighteen single-parent families that were, or currently are, on welfare. A street-level day-care center for infants and youths employs several of the residents. In addition, the Greyston Family Inn offers workers and tenants ongoing counseling services to meet such problems as financial troubles, drug and alcohol abuse, and job searches.

The organization is a shining example of how for-profit and not-for-profit companies work together under the same roof to achieve their goals: earning money and succeeding in a social mission.

Such an operation embodies Greyston's founder and president Bernie Glassman's holistic approach to business and social work. "We provide a circle of activities—a job, a home, counseling, and support—that are a complete method of healing a family," he says from his office, a small corner partitioned off by shelves filled with thick binders brimming with company information and books on philosophy and business.

Glassman, fifty-five years old, is a Zen Buddhist priest who speaks with a distinct Brooklyn accent. Zen Buddhism, a religious sect originating in Asia, is both meditation and community service oriented. Millions of Americans from a variety of religions follow Zen Buddhism under the guidance of people like Glassman. In 1982, as the recently appointed abbot, or leader, of New York's Zen community, he moved his religious group ten miles north of New York City to neighboring Yonkers.

In an effort by Glassman and his students to live self-sufficiently rather than on retreat donations, the group investigated a variety of business opportunities. From 1960 to 1980, Glassman lived in Los Angeles. First he was an aerospace engineer working for McDonnell Douglas Aircraft. When he left his position to devote himself to the Zen community, he became involved with a variety of enterprises, including a medical clinic, a publishing house, and a construction company.

"When I came to New York, I was interested in pursuing a business that would be a vehicle for growth and training, not just for us but for our community," he says. "Baking seemed ideal because it is labor-intensive. Plus, bread is wholesome, and it was something we could believe in."

Glassman sent six followers to the successful Tassahara Bakery in San Francisco, famous in the area for its multigrained, wholesome products. "They provided recipes, trained our people, and gave us great support," he says.

With $320,000 secured from grants and loans, Glassman founded the Greyston Bakery, but the product mix that worked in San Francisco was unsuccessful in New York. The bread-making business in the metro area is very competitive, and Greyston was overwhelmed by well-established bakeries.

"Breads are a nightmare to market," says Mitchell Zucker, resources development officer, who started working at Greyston in 1987. "There is a tremendous amount of competition in that field, and delivering the product fresh around the tristate area was impractical. It nearly bankrupted us from the beginning."

A New Direction

Luckily, the company was also producing gourmet desserts, thanks to the owner of a local Italian bakery who offered his help. Glassman and his students learned the fine art of dessert baking and the skill of decorating. With this, plus training from the Culinary Institute of America, delicacies like lemon tarts, chocolate mousse cakes, and pecan tarts appeared. "Ours are excellent because we bake from scratch," claims Glassman. "We never bake with premade mixes. We use the best real ingredients available."

Greyston's reputation as a serious confectioner soon flourished. The gourmet desserts were also a better business opportunity. "Cakes and pastries can be sold directly to restaurants and specialty shops, so this was the better way to go for us," says Glassman.

Though the bakery originated as a means by which New York's Zen community could support itself, it soon needed additional employees to help run the business. Because many of the students had volunteered their time and donated food to the local homeless shelters and soup kitchens, they were anxious to reach out to the many unemployed people they served. "First, we needed additional good employees," says Glassman. "Second, we felt we could help."

Their pool of potential employees consisted of totally inexperienced workers, so it was up to Greyston to teach them the craft of baking. "It was a challenge to think we could take people who had no skills, no job experience, and no affinity toward baking and train them to make excellent gourmet desserts," says Glassman. "I know there were some skeptics, but I never doubted our ability to make it work."

Along with the Yonkers school board, Glassman first developed a training program to teach their neighbors how to mix, spread, bake, cut, and decorate. Greyston employees then placed fliers around the neighborhood to recruit people for the training program. "We like to find people with both need and promise," says Tom, Greyston's rugged production manager, who looks more like a football player than a baker. "At first we ran the program in our place, but the school district had developed an excellent program of its own. We told them what we needed, and they followed through with a wonderful program."

Tom, a former counselor, interviews dozens of candidates for every job opening at Greyston. "There is a greater need for jobs than we have the capacity to hire," he says. "We get one hundred fifty applications for one single opening."

Tom considers a person's potential much more important than his or her past experience. Mark, for instance, was living in a men's shelter and had previously gone through drug therapy to kick a ten-year cocaine and crack addiction. When the youthful thirty-six-year-old interviewed for a position as a dough mixer, he met a few other applicants who were being interviewed. "One guy cooked for eight hundred people in the army and had all this experience," Mark says. "Another had already gone through the training program. After my interview, I went back to the shelter and said, 'no way did I get the job.' The next day, Tom called and said I was hired."

After a year of working on the night shift and making the brownies used in Ben & Jerry's ice cream, Mark was promoted to a supervisor's position. "I've been here fourteen months, and this is the longest period I've ever held a job," he says. "I'm paying my own rent for the first time in my life, and I now have greater responsibility. I got it through a lot of hard work."

It's up to Mark's boss, Tom, to identify good workers and help them evolve within the company. "I look at my job as developing people," he says. "My personal philosophy is to give those who show promise plenty of space to advance as much as they possibly can."

Greyston Bakery is filled with success stories. The production crew consists of six foremen and three dozen production workers. Carmello, head foreman of the day shift and responsible for the intricate pastries, began as a dishwasher. Millie, a single mother of two daughters, was formerly on welfare. She was in the company's training program in 1987 and now is considered a top "finisher," or cake decorator.

"It's great to see people getting somewhere," says Tom. "We have ex–drug addicts and dealers who were in jail. We have people who were homeless and lots of people who never held a job for more than a couple of months. Often this is their first paycheck. Here," he says, "I see people taking responsibility for what's going on in the business and in their own lives."

It's up to Tom to encourage the workers to take charge. "What I try to instill in everyone is that this is 'their own' bakery. I want to give the bakery away to these people. Sometimes they're not sure they can do this. But it's their ideas, energy, and input that make it all happen. We are working to empower people," says Tom.

The bakery is now developing a program of self-directed work teams. Ideally, each team, consisting of the cakes and tart crew, the ice cream brownies shift, and the cookie group, would manage itself. Groups would maintain communication with the company "buyer," who would inform them as to what they needed to produce to fulfill the quota. The team would do its own scheduling. Each group would also order needed ingredients and be in charge of hiring and firing within its team. Finally, the team would be paid a lump sum, and it would be up to the members to determine the proper allocation and distribution of money.

"We're working on this gradual transfer of authority. A natural leader will evolve from the group, and it would be up to each team to ensure it is productive," says Jef Hoeberichts, a management consultant who was retained in 1989 to help the company become more efficient. It's a system Greyston Bakery hopes to have in place within the next year.

The Right Fit

Though just about every white-capped employee at Greyston is a success story, many employees don't work out.

"I'd say one in five workers end up being successful," says Tom. Family, money, and drug problems all contribute to a hired employee's failure. "These people are facing extraordinary conditions. Unfortunately for many, holding down a forty-hour-a-week job is sometimes too much."

According to Tom, Greyston used to be almost too lenient regarding employee relations, but recently the company has toughened up. "Employees must come to work on time and always be responsible. Obviously, alcohol and drugs are out of the question," says Tom. "It's hard to be strict sometimes, but I do have to remember that we are running a business."

It's disappointing to Tom when an employee does not work out. "What's hardest is when a person shows great promise. They have the aptitude, but because of the way they operate or the way their lives are, they can't hold jobs."

Mark, the newly promoted supervisor, recalls his own attitude toward work before joining Greyston. "When I was on drugs and on the street, I used to look down on people with jobs like this," he says. "I used to think it was much cooler to hang out all day and the only jobs worth having were high paying. Soon I realized how wrong I was. I was strung out on drugs and hadn't worked in years. I got $22.50 every two weeks from welfare. Now I make twenty times that, and I'm proud to say I mix the brownie dough for Ben & Jerry's ice cream."

Wages for employees on the brownie production line start at $6.50 per hour, and the average now is $7.75. For skilled pastry makers, the average salary is more than ten dollars per hour. "Part of helping these people is getting them off of welfare and helping them be self-sufficient. You can't do that while working a minimum-wage job," says Tom.

New Challenges

For its first five years, the Greyston Bakery enjoyed steady growth, baking the fancy tarts the company sold primarily in the New York area but also as far away as Florida, Washington, D.C., Chicago, and Boston. When Glassman met Ben Cohen of Ben & Jerry's ice cream at a business conference, the two men discussed their personal and professional lives. Soon a friendship blossomed. "Ours is an interesting relationship," says Glassman. "Ben is a businessman reaching toward spirituality. And me, I am a spiritual person who is reaching toward business. We meet at the intersection."

The connection eventually resulted in a business deal. Ben & Jerry's asked the bakery to duplicate the recipe for the chewy brownie used in its brownie ice cream so that the ice cream maker wouldn't have to rely solely on their then current supplier. If successful, they could win a contract for more than $1 million worth of business a year.

For weeks, the bakers worked and experimented with all sorts of chocolate variations; finally, in August 1989, they were awarded the contract. "It was great getting the business, but it almost did us in," says Glassman with a smile.

Greyston's production manager, Tom, agrees. "What was unique was that we had to bring in a whole new production team at once. I hired a lot of unskilled people who all started at the same time."

For the first several months, employee turnover was high, and production was slow and limited. "At first it took twenty workers to bake seven hundred pounds per week," says Tom. "Now ten people produce two thousand pounds per week."

In 1991 the company contracted with Community Products, Inc. to bake Rain Forest Cookies made with nuts harvested from Brazil's rain forest. Sixty percent of the profits from the cookies go to environmental and peace groups. Ben & Jerry's subsequently projected a 100 percent increase in brownies, and Greyston reacted. "I held off automating the brownie production kitchen because I didn't want to lay off workers," says management consultant Jef. "Now, with the increased orders, we can get the dough depositor, the second oven, and the cutting machine that will make us more productive, and we will be able to maintain our number of employees."

From Baking to Building

In 1988, with a small profit and an endless supply of energy and ideas, the Greyston Family Inn, the nonprofit arm of the bakery, turned its focus to the greatest problem facing the neighborhood: homelessness. Westchester County, north of New York City and home to some of the wealthiest areas in the state, also has the highest per capita rate of homelessness in the country: 18 out of 200 residents. More than half of the estimated forty-three hundred homeless are in southwest Yonkers, where Greyston Bakery is located. Most are single mothers with children.

"None of the $50 million our government spends to house the homeless goes into permanent shelters," says Glassman as he briskly walks the several blocks from the bakery to the newly renovated apartment complex. "We learned from our work at the shelters that most of the homeless families from this area were being placed in motels all over the county. When we saw the conditions they were living in, we were amazed. The rooms were roach infested. Then, on weekends, the families would often be kicked out if the motel thought the rooms could be rented to someone else for a higher rate. Children would have to take the bus for hours to get to school. Often the mothers would keep them at the hotels, fearing they might be kicked out during the day. In our own small way," he says, "we wanted to tackle this issue."

After buying the apartment complex for $250,000 from grants and bakery profits, the Greyston Family Inn secured a $2.8 million state grant. The nonprofit organization then created yet another for-profit company, Greyston Builders, which totally reconstructed the building.

Once again, Greyston hired those who needed jobs and a chance. "I had run a construction company in Los Angeles, so I knew what was needed," says Glassman. "We had some good people running the business, and they were in charge of hiring the right contractors and employees." The Greyston builders finished the building in the summer of 1991, both on budget and on time.

Greyston Family Inn estimates it saved hundreds of thousands of dollars by training and employing its own workers versus contracting the work out to others. After two years, the revised building houses eighteen single-parent families as well as a youth and infant day-care center.

As Glassman and a visitor reach the front of the freshly painted building with a brand-new awning, they are greeted by Joan, who warmly grasps their hands. "How are you today, Bernie?" she asks. "Why, you shouldn't be out today without your coat on!"

Joan, a middle-aged former homeless woman who for the past decade was moved from shelter to shelter in New York City, had learned about the Greyston permanent housing project when it appeared on a television program. She wrote a letter directly to Glassman and asked if there might be room for her as well. The complex did include a studio apartment, and Joan is now anxious to show off her new home. The clean, though sparsely furnished studio is filled with her favorite mementos, including a statue of the Virgin Mary and a small vase of cloth flowers. On her counter rests a portable typewriter next to a stack of neatly typed pages. Joan is a writer and dreams of having her life story published.

"This place is my heaven," the native of Ireland says with a thick brogue. "I never thought I would be a person who would live on the streets, but circumstances came up that I just couldn't handle. I think

Bernie is a saint. I don't say that to him in so many words, but I hope he knows it."

Next door to the studio apartment, the youth and infant-day-care center bustles with activity. Toys and furniture, donated by a local Junior League chapter, are scattered throughout the brightly lit rooms. "This is the only infant-care center in all of Westchester County," says Glassman.

The two-bedroom apartments upstairs are also bright and clean. The official rent for the apartments is $780 per month, though no tenants pay more than 30 percent of their gross income.

They include Mary, a grandmother living with her ten-year-old grandson, who is now completing a high school equivalency program; Monica, a woman in her early twenties with a four-year-old son, who had been homeless for more than three years; and George, a single father to two young children. He had lost his job as a building superintendent two years before and soon found himself unemployed and homeless. He is now the building superintendent for the Greyston apartment complex.

More than sixty families applied for the permanent housing at Greyston. Those accepted were chosen carefully after inviting candidates into a training program. Greyston employees conducted classes on a variety of subjects, ranging from personal finances to hygiene and self-esteem.

"From there we were able to see what families had the determination to change their lives, who would be good to live in the building," says Glassman. All residents signed contracts with Greyston before moving in. Each document states that the resident wants to get off welfare and is dedicated to self-improvement.

Once chosen, the training workshops continue, and weekly meetings take place in the downstairs child-care center. "We are all interested in living in a safe, clean home," says Joan. "We meet and discuss everything from how to prevent robberies and how to clean up any graffiti on the building to what to do if a neighbor has the radio on too loud," she says. "We've all become one big family with our own separate opinions. We also realize how lucky we are to be here."

Mitchell Zucker, who was responsible for attracting most of the grant money needed to renovate the building, says a special bond has developed between the families. "All of the families have gotten to know each other, and an open-door policy exists in the building," he says.

Most importantly, Zucker and the child-care-center employees have noticed the children's improved behavior. "Living here has transformed the children," he says. "Many of them were emotionally troubled, coming from overcrowded environments with drugs and alcohol. The most common characteristic was inactivity and boredom. Their emotions ranged from being hyperactive to despondent. Now they are best described as normal children."

There are benefits for the adults as well. All tenants receive job training in conjunction with the bakery, the child-care center, and the builders. A job counselor is available to help with these and other employment opportunities.

"None of the adults were employed when they moved in here," says Zucker. "Within a year, ten were employed either at the bakery, the child-care centers, or at other neighboring businesses; eight were in job training; five were working toward getting their high school degrees, and one went to college."

Now that the first permanent housing project is complete, the company is negotiating to buy three more abandoned buildings on the block.

Trends in Community Development

Greyston is committed to creating jobs for the unemployed and housing for the homeless. According to the company's brochure, "Greyston Family Inn's long-term goal is to end homelessness in Westchester County by the year 2000 and in the process establish a working model of community development for the entire nation."

Part of the objective is creating a network of for-profit and not-for-profit companies that interrelate and support each other. Greyston Corporation is a holding company for the for-profit Greyston Bakery and Greyston Builders as well as for the not-for-profit Greyston Family Inn, a social-service organization that handles the housing, jobs, child-care services, counseling, and youth programs.

"For tax reasons, it's beneficial for us to have both the for-profits and not-for-profits working together," says Glassman. The Greyston

Family Inn grew out of the social activities of the bakery. It is, according to Glassman, "a nonprofit organization with entrepreneurial consciousness."

Originally, Glassman determined that the for-profit companies would provide money and resources to enable the not-for-profits to function. Now he believes the for-profits act as a vehicle for social change, and their role is also to create jobs, and therefore improvement, in the community. If excess profits exist, they are used to fuel other companies in the community.

"At this point I'm looking at the for-profits to help develop more for-profits, too," he says. "I believe that our building and baking companies must have a not-for-profit bottom line. Further, our not-for-profit must have a for-profit mentality."

Accordingly, the Greyston Family Inn, originally funded by New York's Zen community, receives money from foundations and grants. The bakery and builders have become self-sufficient, and their profits are used to spur additional businesses.

New businesses on the horizon include forming their own distribution company so that Greyston could sell not only their cakes and tarts but additional related products, such as small breads and additional gourmet foods from other contractors. Second, Greyston plans to develop more retail products, such as smaller-sized cakes and tarts, that will be sold to gourmet stores and upscale delicatessens.

As the bakery and the building businesses flourish, the Greyston Corporation continues to focus on its first and foremost concern: to improve the lives of many who live in their neighborhood. "We want to help those most in need, and our business here is the best way of achieving this goal," says Glassman.

8

Rolling Along

Company name: Sunrise Medical/Quickie Designs, Inc.
Type of business: wheelchair manufacturer
Locations: Torrance, and Fresno, California, Avon
Lake, Ohio, and Kent, Washington
Number of employees: 525
Year founded: 1980

It's a summer afternoon in Birmingham, Alabama, and the three-day Randy Snow Tennis Camp buzzes with activity. About two dozen eager participants—beginning and advanced players alike—are working intently on the sport's fundamentals. They repeat drills in forehand, backhand, and directional delivery. They rehearse strategies on power, placement, and groundstrokes as weapons. They practice exercises for relaxation, concentration, and confidence building. This, however, and other sessions held around the country each year in the Quickie Sport Series, is no ordinary sports camp.

"This camp has something for everyone," Snow tells representatives of the camp's primary sponsoring organization, Quickie Designs, shortly after the lessons come to an end. "We not only try to improve the players while they're here, but we give them the materials they can take with them so they can continue to develop their skills."

Snow, who was a nationally ranked junior tennis player before a

103

ranching accident left him a paraplegic, offers his instructions and advice from a wheelchair. His students, all physically challenged individuals who range in age as much as they do in tennis experience, are as interested in chair-mobility tactics as in serve-and-volley techniques.

The thirty-two-year-old Snow—nine-time U.S. Open Wheelchair Tennis singles champion, five-time doubles champion, former national track record holder in the 200-, 400-, 1,500- and 5,000-meter races, two-time Gold Cup winner in World Wheelchair Basketball, and Olympic silver medalist in the 1,500-meter wheelchair exhibition—is one of forty-three disabled athletes associated with Quickie, the number-one manufacturer of lightweight wheelchairs. In addition, the company runs annual basketball camps featuring David Kiley, considered the world's top wheelchair athlete, and regularly sponsors a variety of competitive events, such as the Junior National Wheelchair Games.

These numerous alliances, like the company itself, are the brainchild of Marilyn Hamilton. Hamilton, an accomplished athlete and high school teacher, was paralyzed in a 1978 hang-gliding accident. Remarkably, she completed her rehabilitative therapy in record time and experienced great frustration with the cumbersome wheelchairs then available. She wanted to resume the active life-style she enjoyed prior to her accident, and that included a return to the ski slopes and tennis courts. But she immediately recognized that the heavy steel wheelchairs of the day would not allow for that; in fact, they actually hindered her rehabilitation.

"I realized I needed more performance in a wheelchair, and one that would make me feel better," recalls the forty-four-year-old Hamilton, back in her office in Fresno, California. "I felt okay, but people didn't allow me to feel okay in that steel dinosaur. They would pat me on the back and say, 'Can I help?' Or they looked the other way."

So Hamilton—whose office walls are adorned with pictures of her meetings with famous admirers, like Barbara Bush and Tommy Lasorda, as well as a photo of her soaring through the air on a hang glider—asked two friends to build her a customized, ultralight wheelchair. What they came up with was a chair that weighed just twenty-six pounds—about one-half the weight of existing models. She took that first version to the 1980 Handicapped Ski Championships in

Winter Park, Colorado, and was overwhelmed by the positive reaction from other disabled athletes. Hamilton felt this new wheelchair would fill an important product niche. She and the designers then formed a company to manufacture the model, and within two years this formerly nonexistent product category of high-tech, lightweight wheelchairs blossomed into one that now represents more than one-quarter of all wheelchairs sold.

Company sales grew by about 200 percent in one year as word about the new and improved chair spread among athletes from all over the world. Hamilton herself tirelessly promoted it by competing in, and winning, various sporting tournaments. A folding version was introduced in 1983, and later, others that also appealed to non-athletes, who appreciated their convenience and style. Models in a palette of fourteen striking colors, for example, purple and neon pink, told observers that people in these sleek and sporty chairs were feeling good about themselves and their lives.

While its customer base has expanded greatly over the years—Quickie Designs now generates about $75 million in annual sales and employs 525 people at its Fresno headquarters as well as its satellite plants in Ohio and Washington—the company's focus on sports has never wavered. Convinced that disabled athletes are virtually indistinguishable from their nondisabled counterparts, Quickie continually pioneers equipment that takes wheelchair athletics to an increasingly competitive level. In the process, it enables individuals like Randy Snow and those who attend his annual tennis camps to achieve a degree of personal accomplishment that eluded Hamilton immediately after she crashed on Tollhouse Mountain in California's Sierra range.

"I found myself lying on the side of that mountain, at the age of twenty-nine, and wondering, Why me?" she says today. But a little luck and something Hamilton now calls her ABCs gave her the impetus to go on. "The 'A' is adjusting your attitude, like when someone comes to me with a problem and I just flip it to the solution. The 'B' is believing in yourself. And there are actually two 'Cs': challenging yourself to do things that you never imagined and having the commitment to do what it takes," Hamilton explains.

"But there is also a 'D,'" she adds quickly. "You have to dream. And you have to continue to dream."

Reinventing the Wheel(chair)

Marilyn Hamilton was well acquainted with wheelchairs. Her uncle, Bill Hamilton, was thrown from a Model T while in high school and had been a quadriplegic since the 1920s. Gregarious and likable, he easily proved to those around him that people in wheelchairs could do anything that they set their minds to. Bill Hamilton, in fact, defied the odds from the start by making the most of the crude rehabilitative therapy and equipment available prior to World War II. His first wood-and-wicker wheelchair weighed ninety pounds and required attendants to push around, but he still went to college and law school before turning the family fruit orchard into a successful brokerage business.

Like her uncle, Marilyn Hamilton is strong-willed and has an insatiable zest for life. She graduated from college with a degree in home economics, an art minor, and a secondary teaching credential, taught high school in Australia for two years, and traveled extensively throughout the Far East before returning to her native California for another teaching assignment. She was in her fourth year at a West Coast high school, while enjoying the sport of hang gliding, when the accident occurred that forever altered the course of her life.

Bill was at Marilyn's side immediately after the incident to offer both reassurance and advice. When her employer proved reluctant to take her back, Bill also offered her a job in the family fruit brokerage. It was a seasonal business and provided Marilyn with enough free time to travel around the country and participate in various sporting competitions.

She refused, however, to accept the limitations of the chrome-steel wheelchair she was given after her release from the hospital. It was too heavy for the tennis courts, too clumsy to get her near the ski slopes. So Hamilton contacted two inventive friends, glider pilots Don Helman and Jim Okamoto, and asked them to build her an ultralight wheelchair out of the same aluminum tubing they were using to construct hang gliders.

In a 600-square-foot shed behind Helman's house, the two combined their knowledge of thermodynamics and engineering with seamless drawn aluminum developed by the aerospace industry. They conceived of a revolutionary wheelchair that would be more

mobile, more adjustable, and ultimately, more competitive than anything that came before it. Their creation—which they dubbed the
Quickie—looked more like a racing bicycle than a rolling hospital
bed. It was sleek, sky blue, had comfortable nylon upholstery (instead
of the standard vinyl or Naugahyde), and it offered a variety of adjust-
ments that enhanced safety as well as performance.

Hamilton paid $700 for that first chair and immediately took it on
the road. After the 1979 Colorado ski championships, she moved on
to other events. With the help of her new equipment, she won the
National Wheelchair Tennis Championships in singles and doubles
both in 1982 and 1983. She also captured the National Disabled Ski
Championships six times, from 1981 to 1988, in addition to other ski
and tennis honors. As she met with athletic success, other members
of the disabled athlete community—who had been modifying standard wheelchairs in order to compete—began clamoring for Quickies. Hamilton teamed up with Helman and Okamoto to form a
company they initially called Motion Designs in 1980 and used the
proceeds from each sale to fund construction of additional models
that would change the industry.

"Everything was shoestring, garage mentality," says Hamilton
today. "We weren't taking salaries. We had no overhead. There was
no cost."

The three did, however, sell Quickies as fast as they could produce
them. Hamilton believes fifty chairs were sold the first year, maybe
two hundred the second, but exact figures are unavailable because all
of those early records were subsequently lost. Rapidly expanding sales
required the partners to move to larger facilities twice in the first four
years. And she did, however, convince an initially reluctant medical
community of the potential for their unique new product.

"We filled a niche," Hamilton recalls. "When I look back, the success of the company came from finding a need and filling it, doing it
better than anyone else, hiring great people, and having fun."

The need for wheelchairs was expanding year by year. Many of
those who now utilized them were attracted to Quickie's stunningly
original design. In addition, the number of people who used wheelchairs rose from 500,000 in 1960 to nearly 1.25 million in 1980. During this time medical advances allowed accident victims to survive
catastrophic injuries. More and more paraplegics and quadriplegics

were released from rehabilitation centers and hospitals. Growing numbers wanted to pursue active life-styles like Hamilton's, and the bright colors and performance orientation of Quickies appealed to them.

Quickie Designs promoted its product in a new way as well. Existing manufacturers had long aimed their ad materials solely at medical personnel, and they usually pictured empty chairs in a hospital setting. Hamilton's promotions, on the other hand, used real people competing in wheelchair athletics. She also bombarded the industry with provocative slogans like "Nothing beats a Quickie" while appearing at the usually staid medical trade shows in a splashy black, silver, and red booth.

In addition, she and her partners developed a second model, the folding Quickie 2, which was aimed at the nonathletic wheelchair market. Within six weeks of its release, three hundred of these easily maneuverable lightweights were sold.

Quality remained the main emphasis at Quickie, and the company's blend of revolutionary ideas and advanced materials produced farsighted concepts. The resultant pediatric Zippie line and low-cost Breezy line eventually captured the attention of even more new customers, while Quickie's innovative business practices drew overtures from an equally resourceful young public company named Sunrise Medical. In 1986, after three years of courting by Sunrise, Quickie became a part of its fast-growing empire.

A New Dawn

Richard H. Chandler believes in teamwork. Most executives say such things these days, of course, but Chandler, who has a background in competitive sports as well as in corporate America, definitely practices what he preaches. At forty-nine he is chairman and president of a $320 million New York Stock Exchange company that he built, piece by piece, beginning in 1983. The firm, Sunrise Medical, now employs thirty-two hundred in eight manufacturing divisions, including Quickie Designs. Located throughout the world, each operates independently under Chandler's hands-off philosophy.

"I believe that a committed team of individuals will always win out over a disconnected group of individuals, no matter how talented, who are not working together," he explains. "It's like raising children: Any time you say, 'Do this because I'm your father and I say so,' you've really lost. There's no way your child will ever do what you want willingly. But if you can say, 'Do this because it's the right thing to do, and let me explain why,' you're going to end up with someone committed to doing something on its own merits."

His style has always been to rely on gentle persuasion rather than power, adds the father of three. "I'm not comfortable with authority as a leadership tool," he notes. "True power comes from authenticity, which means demonstrating ethical values and a concern for people, not giving orders."

Chandler has proven that tight corporate control is unnecessary when it is supplanted by progressive management concepts and people-based philosophies. His ideas developed at Princeton, evolved at the University of Chicago where he got his MBA, and finally coalesced at the University of Louvain, in Belgium, where he earned a master's degree in international economics with distinction in 1967. Three years later, in Chicago, at the age of twenty-seven, he put these principles into practice outside of his job. The result was Chicago Community Ventures, Inc., the nation's then largest investment company devoted to funding minority-owned enterprises—an organization that still exists today—by organizing a volunteer group of young professionals to raise funds from the city's major corporations. Meanwhile, he further honed his leadership style in executive positions at several Fortune 500 firms.

Chandler's rise through the corporate ranks culminated in 1979 as a group vice president at the Sara Lee Corporation, when that company sold off its Abbey Medical Division to an investment group. He served as president of this nationwide chain of home health care stores until he sold it to American Hospital Supply in 1981. He took a year off to write a novel and travel with his family and then, at age thirty-nine, formed Sunrise Medical. "I was too young to retire and still had a number of unfulfilled career goals," he says from Sunrise's Torrance, California, headquarters.

With a $25 million credit line, $4.6 million from venture capitalists, and some cash of his own, Chandler set up Sunrise Medical in early 1983 and acquired five medical businesses and went public in November of that year.

"We emerged fully grown as a $50 million public company with no operating history," he says. With plans to build a worldwide company that designed, manufactured, and marketed high-quality medical products, he eventually acquired twenty-five more companies. Four were later sold off so that Sunrise could concentrate on those committed to the rehabilitation and recovery phases of patient care. The rest were consolidated into eight manufacturing divisions. Their products—manual and electric wheelchairs, ambulatory and bath safety aids, patient-room beds and furnishings, and specialty mattresses—are made in the United States, the United Kingdom, Germany, and Spain and distributed in eighty-five other countries.

Sunrise's financial and design successes are striking. Sales and net income increased 31 percent and 50 percent, respectively, in the poor economic climate of 1992, and seventy-six new products were introduced. These statistics are also representative of Chandler's progressive management techniques. Despite the crash-and-burn fate suffered by other acquisition-based organizations initiated during the same period, for example, Sunrise's various divisions continue to operate happily and successfully under its corporate umbrella. And, Chandler notes proudly, not one of his many deals has ever sparked a single lawsuit.

"We're very idealistic," he explains. "We really believe that our mission in life is to improve people's lives by creating innovative, high-quality products. So if there's somebody who believes that their mission in life is to acquire as much money as possible, they're not going to fit. We're bottom-line managers, but we find that the best way to increase sales and profits is to do the right thing. Profits are a by-product of doing other things well."

Such thinking is manifested across the board. All employees are referred to as "associates," to show they are partners in a common enterprise. Liberal bonus plans and incentives are extended to workers at every level along with companywide profit sharing and stock options. Everyone is on a first-name basis. There are no executive perks, such as reserved parking spaces. And in its decentralized atmosphere each Sunrise company is run autonomously. In fact, just twenty people work at corporate headquarters.

In addition, valuable prizes for cost-saving ideas and large cash awards for divisional improvements are regularly distributed to workers in departments from sales and production to accounting and administration. The various efforts that Chandler has devised to elicit such responses—including his "Pursuit of Excellence" program, "Sunrise Olympics," and "Project EXCEED"—have increased productivity and cut turnover. "I've always believed the strongest motivation for most people is peer recognition," he says. "We're big on plaques and awards."

Most importantly, perhaps, the existing management teams of all acquired companies are kept intact while their operations and goals are smoothly integrated with those of Sunrise. Companywide conferences are held annually devoted to growth, manufacturing and administration so that managers in all divisions can share ideas. This procedure stimulates teamwork and cooperation but allow the organizations to flourish their own way and supports them by tying bonuses to performance within a division, not to companywide activity.

While he looks carefully at prospective new acquisitions, they also look carefully at him. "Dick Chandler impresses you not only with his intelligence but with his value system. There are very few people who you run into in a lifetime who have such strong values—and that's important to us," says Hamilton. After three years of "low-key courting," the two developed a friendship and a mutual trust.

In 1986, Hamilton and her partners sold Quickie to Sunrise for $21.3 million in cash, subordinated notes, and stock. In return, the new owner helped bolster Quickie's financial management, customer service, manufacturing efficiency, and overall growth. Hamilton was promoted to senior vice president of marketing, reflecting her special position as company founder.

Two years later, Sunrise shifted its executive vice president of operations, Thomas H. O'Donnell, to the post of Quickie president. Placing the former IBM executive at the head of the wheelchair division has allowed the company to continue its impressive growth record. "We felt that Sunrise would continue the company in a way that we would be proud of," Hamilton says of the acquisition and subsequent changes. "And it's worked out well."

Commitment to Quality

Quickie's Fresno headquarters, with a 135,000-square-foot manufacturing area, stands at the edge of town bordering central California's vast farmlands. Extraordinarily clean, strikingly colorful, and exceedingly bright, the plant is obviously a cheerful and efficient place. Sky-lights open the ceiling to the California sky; bold pictures and pithy slogans adorn the freshly painted white walls. Although more than one thousand custom wheelchairs are now turned out weekly, the atmosphere is more reminiscent of a high-tech firm or a sporting-goods manufacturing facility than a medical-products company. This is, however, no illusion.

"For research we go to consumer electronic shows and bike shows," says Wayne, the head of engineering, who has been with Quickie since 1983 and a paraplegic since age fifteen. "We're all techno-nuts."

Wheelchairs are incredibly important to those who use them, Wayne points out, and that is why so much time is spent at Quickie on technical advancements geared to fit, comfort, and adjustability. Each of the company's chairs is totally customized for the needs and size of its new owner. Exacting attention to minute details as well as to both praise and complaints is required. Not surprisingly, these characteristics are high on Quickie's corporate mandate.

"I put a lot of emphasis on recognizing that all of us have a customer. Whether to a dealer or to someone who only works internally, every piece of work we do is going to someone," says O'Donnell, who has fit in well with the division since becoming its president in 1988. This attention to overall quality has led to numerous industry firsts, such as Quickie's pioneering use of com-puter-milled or machined components for tightly controlled and bet-ter-functioning parts. It also resulted in the company's Opportunity for Improvement program, which solicits and acts upon ideas put forth by all associates on everything from safety issues to process improvement.

"We all get involved," confirms Dan, who has been with the com-pany for five years and is now in quality assurance. "We are given freedom to try things, and our supervisors listen to us. This company has the best open-door policy I've ever seen."

Others at Quickie enthusiastically share his positive view and readily tout additional benefits that make the firm special. There are no time clocks, for example, and workers choose their own flex-time schedules. Internal training is always available—classes in topics like remedial English and sign language are just two of those offered—and

75 percent of the cost of outside educational programs are reimbursed. No one has ever been laid off. Associates even receive birthday cards at their homes.

The company's generous benefit package and excellent working conditions helped stabilize Quickie's employment force to the point where turnover dropped from 27 percent when Sunrise took over to 9 percent in 1992. Moreover, it definitely helps the company attract a diverse associate mix—40 percent are female, 40 percent are minorities, and 11 percent have disabilities. They are all deeply committed to Sunrise Medical's mission and values and work hard to make Quickie the world leader in its field. Many in the 380,000-person Fresno area, in fact, aspire to positions in the company.

"This factory is like a breath of fresh air, and the people are special," agrees Ramona, a grandmotherly type who sews upholstery for the chairs. "I was fifty-nine when my previous employer moved to Arizona. I'm not a young person, but Quickie hired me. And they made me feel at home."

Albert, a thirty-four-year-old welder who has been with the company for five years, says, "The greatest thing about this company is the respect we get."

Indeed, many of Quickie's underlying operations and systems have been changed since Chandler and Hamilton and her partners made their deal in 1986, but all of the alterations have occurred without obliterating the company's soul. The introduction of state-of-the-art production methods, for example, just-in-time manufacturing, freed floor space while improving quality and efficiency. New products, such as pediatric, geriatric, and power wheelchairs, beefed up its product line. The implementation of sophisticated financial controls and modern management information systems upgraded engineering, quality control, and personnel functions. And in the process Quickie's sales have grown nearly five-fold in the six years following the acquisition.

All of this will be more important in the decade ahead as the division further expands a distribution network now reaching more than two thousand dealers and hundreds of rehabilitation hospitals in the United States, along with emerging outlets in twenty other countries. The market in which it has successfully carved its niche, too, is expected to grow far larger in the coming years as medical advances continue to lead to increased survival rates of those suffering spinal cord injuries.

Thousands will benefit from Quickie designs. Former White House press secretary James Brady, who was paralyzed in 1981 during the assassination attempt on former president Ronald Reagan, uses a Quickie. A decade after the shooting, Brady arrived in Fresno to be fitted for yet another neon-yellow Quickie, which he says he favors because of his heavy traveling schedule. "One of the better things in my struggle has been my Quickie," he told a reporter for the *Fresno Bee.* "It never complains, it doesn't eat too much, it's always up in time for the ironsides van to take me to the hospital, and it's there for me to sink into when I'm done with the pain and the suffering."

Giving Something Back

The large gymnasium at northern California's San Jose State University is filled with dozens of strapping male athletes in colorful T-shirts. The young men, who are all in wheelchairs, represent ten teams from throughout the United States in the national Quad Rugby Finals. With four players from each team on the court at a time, their object is to carry the ball—a volleyball—over the goal line. They work toward this with a series of forward passes, while teammates defend them with picks and screens. Quickie Designs is a national sponsor of the sport. A Quickie booth in the corner offers assistance, for example, pumping tires and replacing spokes.

The game was originally called "murder ball" because it tends to get physical. Players often crash into each other when passing or blocking. During the fast-paced game, it's not unusual for a player to be thrown to the floor.

Thirty-one-year-old Brian Hanson is captain of the Berkeley Quad-zillas. With muscular arms and lean body, he pushes the slanted wheels with concentration. While some players rely on their considerable strength to overpower weaker opponents, Hanson—who is also a member of Team Quickie, the promotional group sponsored by its namesake—uses finesse. He eyes his teammates carefully and then passes the ball for a victorious goal.

"We're athletes here, and our chair is our tool for achieving our goal," says Hanson, a physical education instructor at a public school in nearby Hayward. "It's amazing what a good chair does for your ability to get around. My Quickie allows me to lead the life I would have if I wasn't disabled."

The company has literally changed the lives of all those who use its products. Ranging in price from $800 for a Breezy to $8,000 for a top-of-the-line power chair—with ultralight manual sports models selling for under $2,000—customers get a wheelchair made to their personal seat dimensions and back height, choice of wheels and front casters, and preferred color. They also get it in two to ten days, as opposed to the eight to ten weeks it took for delivery of a custom chair before Quickie came along.

In the process, they become involved with a company that has dramatically altered the direction of the entire wheelchair industry. The lightweight portion of the market was nonexistent when Quickie was formed in 1980, and Sunrise estimates that it now constitutes more than 25 percent of the total, with growth trends indicating it could someday represent 60 or 70 percent of all wheelchairs sold.

Still, Hamilton and the others were not completely satisfied. They recognized that even with improved products like Quickie wheelchairs, disabled adults generally end up with less education, lower income, fewer job opportunities, and less social contact than their nondisabled peers. They also realized that the root of the problem stemmed from their experiences as disabled children. So they set about developing a program that would help these youngsters grow into adults who would be able to share in the American dream.

The result was Winners on Wheels, or WOW, a not-for-profit organization designed to "empower youth in wheelchairs to be all that they can be." Conceived by Hamilton in 1991 and initially funded by Sunrise and Quickie with a $200,000 grant, the program is designed to create Boy Scout/Girl Scout–type chapters across the country that meet every other Saturday at sites provided by local sponsors. Along with Hamilton—who is spending much of her time these days on organizational duties and the search for additional corporate partners—board members include Quickie president O'Donnell, Sunrise chairman Chandler, and several Fresno business and education leaders.

"When you think about it," Chandler says, "the time after school and on Saturdays, when kids are out doing sports, is the time that has to be the loneliest when you're ten years old and in a wheelchair. You can sit in class and do everything everyone else is doing, but when they go outside for sports, you can't."

WOW strives to build self-esteem and problem-solving skills—while offering a regular opportunity for fun activities—through "Circles," comprised of twelve to fifteen youngsters, ages seven to fifteen. The program is structured so that members, who participate at no cost, can earn "Wheel" awards (like Scout merit badges) in areas like Family, Community, Games, and Crafts. Adult leaders include parents, community and business representatives, and health-care professionals. After a year of pilot operations in Fresno, Circles have been extended to more than twenty other locations nationwide.

Quickie continues spending a lot of company time and energy on other efforts, too, donating gifts-in-kind and services to appropriate organizations and individuals. It remains directly involved in the sponsorship of four wheelchair sports teams and eight wheelchair sporting events, and company personnel devote several weekends each month at tennis, track, basketball, rugby, and skiing competitions. The division also presents ongoing hands-on professional workshops throughout the United States on the latest advances in rehabilitation concepts and wheelchair technology. Topics include "Understanding the End User," "Seating and Positioning," and "Fitting—The Team Approach."

Additionally, Quickie still sponsors its annual basketball and tennis camps, in conjunction with The Med Group, an organization of independent rehab equipment dealers, at locations around the country—Kansas City, Las Vegas, San Diego, and Newark, Delaware. Participants tout their personalized approach, inspirational atmosphere, and top-notch staff and rave about the improvements they see in themselves after the programs have come to an end. The benefits, however, run both ways—as tennis-camp leader Randy Snow eagerly points out in an interview that appeared in Quickie's own *Q* quarterly magazine. Associated with the wheelchair company since 1982, he says his sponsorship has evolved into much more than a standard business deal between athlete and corporation.

"It's a relationship with one of the most dynamic and personal companies in the country," says Snow, who also enjoys track and field, kayaking, scuba diving, basketball, and road racing. "They provide the opportunity for me to pursue my wheelchair sports with every type of support. They allow me to concentrate on my sports by taking care of things that other athletes might have to worry about."

Since she saw the reaction to that first lightweight wheelchair in 1980, Marilyn Hamilton dreamed that she might someday have a similar impact on the world of sports.

It was about the same time that Dick Chandler was dreaming about the public company he wanted to create that would embody the ideas and values he'd developed in his earlier business career with Fortune 500 America. It was the intersection of these two paths—and the sharing of their dreams—that has led to Sunrise Medical/Quickie Designs achieving their joint success today. It's a classic case of business meeting a consumer need with the result that both the company and the customers are the winners.

9

Less Is More

Company name: Patagonia Inc.
Type of business: clothing designer and distributor
Location: Ventura, California, and Bozeman, Montana;
retail stores in Santa Barbara, San Francisco, Seattle,
Boston, Salt Lake City, Freeport, Maine, and Dillon,
Montana, Haleiwa, Hawaii, Washington, D.C.,
Munich, Chamonix, Tokyo, Dublin, and Buenos Aires
Number of employees: 525
Year founded: 1974

Employees at Patagonia Inc. knew that 1991 was not destined to go down as one of their finest years. Despite record sales and increasing worldwide recognition, the Ventura, California-based designer and distributor of functional outdoor clothing had trouble obtaining an increase in its credit line. It was unable to adequately absorb, train, and devise internal systems for the hundreds of new workers demanded by rapid growth. On-time product delivery was threatened. The company was forced to withdraw from all consumer and trade shows. Moreover, in July it laid off one hundred twenty employees—some 20 percent of its work force.

So how did Patagonia, one of America's most conscientious and successful young companies, respond? By reorganizing its management team, restructuring its product line, and downsizing its sales goals to account for more realistic growth projections. Although it involved some very painful decisions, this combined action immediately put the company back on the path that brought it unbridled success in the seventies and eighties. Consequently, it mollified employees who thought the company was moving in a direction that was increasingly beyond their control.

Simultaneously, Patagonia redesigned its "corporate tithing" program, which already had given away millions of dollars to hundreds of environmental organizations. While other companies facing similar corporate conditions might have vastly reduced or even eliminated such efforts, Patagonia chose instead to bolster its charitable agenda. Previously structured to donate 10 percent of pretax profits to a wide variety of carefully selected donors, the company's so-called Earth Tax would now give away 1 percent of total sales if there were no pretax profits to pass along. For employees and officials, that decision came much more easily than the reorganization, the downsizing, and the restructuring.

"Just because we don't make a profit doesn't mean we don't have a responsibility to give money away," says Yvon Chouinard, Patagonia's intense yet unpretentious founder, owner, and driving force.

Chouinard was an accomplished outdoorsman long before he was a successful businessman, and his love of the land still takes precedence over everything he does. Argentina, Belize, Colorado, Hawaii, Kenya, Nepal, Wyoming—he's likely to see more than a few of these destinations as he mountain climbs, surfs, fly-fishes, kayaks, and skis his way around the world during the eight months each year that he spends away from Patagonia's home base. But it is there, among the rocks and water and sun and snow, that Yvon Chouinard put together everything that makes his company what it is today. And it is there, outside the door to the Ventura offices, that Patagonia has chosen to make its stand in good times and in bad.

"We will continue to donate one percent of our total sales (or ten percent of our profits, whichever is greater) to saving and restoring the environment. We will also continue to work with dealers on shared environmental projects," the company concluded in a letter to retailers that explained its 1991 changes. Even in a follow-up announcement on the layoffs, Chouinard emphasized that donations would be continued. With sales expected to hit $117 million, they would donate more than $1 million for the year. "That's something we'll do regardless of the economy," Chouinard reiterated. "It gets to the heart of why we're in business."

Patagonia has donated its time and expertise to such groups as the Southern Utah Wilderness Society, Trout Unlimited, the Wyoming Outdoor Council, and Friends of the Payette for the past two decades. This is not surprising considering the fifty-five-year-old Chouinard's commitment to preserving the great outdoors and his company's stake in its future. Every one of Patagonia's products, after all, is designed to function under the type of demanding active use that its president and employees engage in regularly. A diminishing outdoor experience, either through active encroachment by anticonservation forces or passive neglect by uninterested conservators, would have a devastating impact on Patagonia's work force as well as on company sales.

But there also is far more to the way this company operates. A perfect example is Chouinard's decision to put the brakes on his corporation's previously unchecked expansion after a 16 percent sales increase from 1990 to 1991 threatened to undermine his future plans.

"We don't want to exceed our resources," he says, explaining recent changes, including management shuffling, newly downsized product line, and self-imposed limit on growth. "That is the one thing that rock climbing, whitewater kayaking, and some of the other risk sports tell you: Don't exceed your limits. If you do, you are dead."

It was, in fact, this potential transcendence of Patagonia's veritable economic and personnel assets—owing much to its garments' increasing acceptance as a fashion statement by self-styled outdoors enthusiasts who rarely traveled farther afield than their own backyards—that led the company to put its corporate foot down. Growth had been rapid but manageable almost from the beginning; starting around 1988, however, the demands on employees and finances started to spiral out of control.

Chouinard had yet another good reason to slow down. He absolutely abhors conspicuous consumption and has continuously worked to convince Americans that their throwaway mentality is destroying much of what he and his friends hold dear.

"We're not trying to get people to stop consuming; we're trying to get them to cut back and consume better," Chouinard explains. "But if I say we must confront these problems and also have a business that grows and grows, then I'm a hypocrite. If I don't put the halt to this company and stop the growth, then I can't expect anyone else to do so, either."

The Accidental Businessman

Yvon Chouinard never planned on being a businessman. He envisioned himself instead as a craftsman. His goal was improved products that helped their owners perform chosen tasks more effectively and lasted forever while they did so. Although he most certainly has become a businessman since starting his first company in the mid-sixties, Chouinard succeeded on these other fronts, too. His products have played an integral role in countless expeditions and even made it onto at least three space shuttles. And longtime customers can point to at least one piece of gear that looks and functions as well as it did when it was purchased a dozen years ago.

The company sells its products through fourteen-hundred outdoor specialty stores in the United States and distributes to Europe, Asia, and South America. Patagonia has sixteen retail stores and factory outlets in such locations as Seattle, Boston, San Francisco, Ventura, and Chamonix, France. Worldwide sales for the fiscal year ending April 30, 1993, were $112 million.

"My mandate is to produce the most functional products in the world, with the greatest technological improvements," says Richard, who works closely with Chouinard as the company's head designer of alpine, mountaineer, and marine and water-sports products. "My father worked for a company that manufactured steel parts in the Midwest. It was a very classic company, very hierarchical, and the hourly wage earners were treated like dirt. But it taught me how special it is here."

Special, though, is not a word that many observers would use on an initial visit to the Patagonia complex. In fact, except for the absence of traditional business clothing on employees and a totally open floor plan with no private offices, the company, on the surface, looks and functions much like many other small or midsized corporations. Beneath the surface, however, Patagonia's true strengths are apparent. And like everything else in the company, the lens through which the viewer can see the company and its purpose is brought into focus with Yvon Chouinard.

Born to French-Canadian parents in the French-speaking town of Lisbon, Maine, Chouinard started life as an outdoors type. He stayed that way when his father, a plumber and handyman, moved him and his mother, two sisters, and brother to Burbank, California, when Yvon was eight. But the California sunshine and nearby Hollywood hills soon helped him discover his first true love—the mountains— and by the time he reached high school, Chouinard was banding eagles and hawks for the U.S. Fish & Wildlife Service. Before graduation, he summered in Jackson Hole, Wyoming, where he further honed his climbing talents in the spectacular Teton range.

By the time he finished high school, Chouinard had become an accomplished climber. He tried taking a few geography courses at a California community college after graduation but left before earning a degree in order to better concentrate on his sport.

Chouinard's affinity to climbing quickly opened his eyes to the inadequate equipment then available. He grew frustrated by the primitive quality of essential tools like pitons (steel spikes driven into cracks in the mountains) and carabiners (metal rings that serve as links between the pitons and climbing ropes). Chouinard decided to try and improve his equipment, and in 1957 he bought a book on blacksmithing, gathered $100 to buy an anvil and coal-fired forge, and began making his own pitons in his parents' Burbank backyard. About a year later he borrowed a little more than $800 from his parents to buy an aluminum forging dye to make his own carabiners. He decided to make a large quantity of them and became a climbing-products salesperson. As he traveled from climbing site to climbing site, he sold this gear to his many friends right from the trunk of his car.

Within five years Chouinard Equipment Ltd. had become well known among climbers because of its design innovations and high-quality products. Chouinard himself was on his way toward developing his now-legendary nontraditional approach to business. For example, he made his pitons of tough steel alloy rather than the malleable iron used by his European competition. Serious climbers recognized high-quality merchandise and were willing to pay four times the price of existing gear. The market, however, was small, and he had to support himself by working part-time for his brother, Jeff, who was Howard Hughes's chief of security.

In 1966, after two years in the army, Chouinard moved to Ventura with fellow climber and longtime friend Thomas Frost. The two rented a tin shack behind an abandoned slaughterhouse and proceeded to redesign all of Chouinard's hardware. They put together a one-page mimeographed "catalog" of their offerings and mailed it to all of their friends. By 1970 they had captured some 80 percent of the domestic climbing market and were grossing close to $300,000 a year. In 1972, Chouinard and Frost incorporated as Great Pacific Iron Works.

It was during this period that Chouinard also decided to manufacture clothing in addition to climbing gear. On a climbing trip in Scotland, he found a regulation team rugby shirt. Chouinard believed it was the best shirt available for rock climbing. He brought it back to duplicate and made matching shorts, called Stand Up Shorts, on a machine used for sewing leather patches onto climbing packs and quickly sold both items to eager friends through his catalog.

Within a year sales had more than doubled to $1 million, and in 1976 a new company—dubbed Patagonia for the South American region that Chouinard liked so much—was spun off.

Frost, who always favored climbing over business, left the company soon thereafter. Chouinard and his wife, Malinda, were left as sole owners of the company, which now fell under the banner of the Lost Arrow Corporation—named for that first piton, called the Lost Arrow, that Yvon designed in his Burbank backyard.

The climbing division continued to lead all domestic-gear manufacturers in sales through the 1980s, but the nation's liability mania—in the form of accident-related lawsuits—finally caught up to Chouinard. His insurance premiums rose 1,000 percent, and while he never lost a lawsuit resulting from faulty climbing gear, both he and others feared that their very threat clouded the future of what was then the $67 million Patagonia line. Chouinard Equipment filed for bankruptcy protection in 1989 and was sold the following year to a group of employees who renamed it Black Diamond Equipment Ltd. and moved its operations to Utah. The company continues, but without Chouinard.

Clothes Make the Company

Today Yvon Chouinard's desk, which sits next to his wife's, is clustered in an open area that serves as Patagonia's main office. In this atmosphere he seems a bit reserved, even somewhat shy. Wearing unironed Patagonia clothing that has seen more than a few seasons of rugged use, he appears very much the regular guy who can focus equally on a weighty global issue, a product-development question, or the pounding surf he is about to attack with people thirty years his junior.

"I'm the outside man," he offers. "My job is to be away from the office, getting ideas—on future life-style changes, where the world is going, how all this effects the company—and bringing them back." It is in this "outside," where Chouinard spends the better part of each year, that he feels most at home and does his best "thinking" about the company's direction.

While he is still very much revered by his peers for his knowledge of the outdoors—his 1978 book, *Climbing Ice,* remains the Bible on this subject—Chouinard doesn't get an opportunity to pursue many real "adventures" anymore. Or so he has said. But consider a story from the man who told *Forbes* that his "number-one priority is to have free time."

The incident in question took place in the late eighties and also involved three of Chouinard's close friends (including Doug Tompkins, cofounder of Esprit de Corp). The four were dropped off in Chile by a fishing boat, where they proceeded to climb an as-yet-unclimbed peak in very bad weather. The wind was so strong during their after-dark descent that the men had to crawl for four miles on their hands and knees to reach level ground.

They embarked on a seventy-mile kayak journey in rough seas to return to their starting point, only to be blown over by strong winds not long after they began. Chouinard was forced to bail out, abandon his camera gear, and swim through cold water to the shore. There he and the others built a fire for warmth before forging ahead in wind and water so rough that the four had to hold tightly on to each other until the strongest waves passed. "It turned out to be more than we bargained for," Chouinard once told a magazine editor. "It turned out to be an adventure."

Some would call Patagonia's adventures in the clothing industry an equally unnerving experience, and for Chouinard and his wife, Malinda—who quietly and effectively handles the human relations side of the company, while Yvon remains immersed in product development and long-term planning—the ride has been equally fast and intense.

It started with those rugby shirts and Stand Up Shorts, but Patagonia's line quickly expanded to include other products that Chouinard deemed to be as technically sound. His first major innovation came in 1976, when Patagonia began offering lightweight jackets made of a warm, fast-drying, synthetic fleecelike material called pile. Within three years, pile garments accounted for at least half of Patagonia's total sales. They also became de rigueur in mountain getaway towns like Chouinard's old haunt Jackson Hole, where he coincidentally had bought a cabin and was beginning to spend large chunks of time.

In addition, pile's popularity spawned immediate competition from other companies whose designs included appreciably fewer features and carried significantly lower price tags. So Chouinard moved on to bunting, a similar product with a tighter weave that offered superior performance. The competition again followed suit, and by the mid-eighties, Patagonia had advanced to Synchilla—an exceedingly soft polyester version developed along with Malden Mills. This, too, was also picked up on quickly by other companies, which began to churn out their own, less costly copies.

But Patagonia will never compete on price, Chouinard emphatically declares. Patagonia is constantly creating even better products once the rest of the industry finds a way to muscle into the markets it develops. It has done it with climbing hardware and long johns—Patagonia's second-largest product line, polypropylene underwear, was eliminated from this line when other companies, for example, L. L. Bean to K Mart, started selling cheaper versions; its successor, Capilene, has been worn by crews on at least three space-shuttle missions—and it will do it again. Chouinard's customers know this and follow his company's lead. Unlike other companies, Patagonia has never had to pay athletes to wear and thus endorse its gear. The true sportsman knows superior gear.

"To this day," reads the Patagonia design philosophy, "we make clothes that are long-lasting and of the highest quality, using as a benchmark a rule Chouinard followed when making the Lost Arrow piton: 'Any number of shapes will work, but there must be one shape that will ultimately work best; by best I mean it is the most functional, with the least material, with the smoothest lines, with strength and lasting qualities.'"

Chouinard himself still agrees with that sentiment wholeheartedly. "We never invented anything here," he says respectfully. "When we made climbing equipment, we took existing products and made them better. Same with clothing. We have a commitment to make a better product." And if you can't get the best-quality product available, he advises, "save your money until you can buy the one that will last the rest of your life."

Power to the People

By midmorning, the day is fully under way at Patagonia's on-site child-care facility. Toys are everywhere, and the walls are decorated with brightly colored drawings. A healthy lunch is being prepared. As many as eighty-five kids, from eight weeks to ten years old, are playing. The high ratio of staff to children is noticeable throughout the age-specific groupings: infants/toddlers, two-year-olds, three-to-five-year-olds, and the children in the school-age Kids Club. One employee is taking a break from office duties to breast-feed her baby. Another is here because his child didn't want to stop crying. A few Patagonia employees without youngsters of their own have stopped in to play with the children of others.

This, in short, is exactly the kind of center for young children that working parents everywhere long to find. "It's good for the company because it protects Patagonia from losing employees of child-bearing age," says Anita, the facility's director. "And it's part of Patagonia's social responsibility."

The seven-year-old in-house department—which accepts nonemployee children whenever there is space—is also good for employee morale. Because it is right next to the offices, the close proximity reduces stress on both parents and children. Between the subsidized charge to employees, the higher but still competitive rate for nonemployees, and the federal and state tax benefits, it's operation is less cost-prohibitive than one would expect, Anita notes.

"Benefits are here to make our employees more productive," says Chouinard, who has two teenagers of his own. "Child care is here so that someone with a kid doesn't have to worry about what is going on in some child-care center. No one will have to quit work just because they have a young child."

Other extraordinary benefits include a cafeteria serving the type of healthy foods that Patagonia employees tend to prefer and a liberal flex-time work schedule. If someone like Rosie, a five-year employee in the personnel department, wants to go out for a bike ride on a nice afternoon, she feels free to do so—but may come back to the office to work until as late as ten o'clock that night. Rosie's tan shows that she regularly takes Patagonia up on the opportunity.

And Rosie's circumstances are as unique, yet as common, as those of many of her co-workers. She met Chouinard while she was a climbing guide for the Outward Bound program in upstate New York and followed him back to Patagonia when he offered her a job. "Patagonia was willing to take a chance with me," she says. "Since I was a guide and had never committed to any company, a lot of other employers would have wondered what was wrong with me. Patagonia took the risk."

Now Rosie helps her co-workers reach for their own peak performances. She enjoys her work developing internal training programs for the company and planning employee classes on topics ranging from personal finance to drawing. She also feels comfortable as part of an organization in which women and men are on equal footing. "Sixty percent of the company is female, and that includes the CEO, CFO, design head, retail operations head, personnel head, and data processing head," she says. "Gender is not an issue here."

All jobs at Patagonia, in fact, appear to be good stepping-stones for any employee committed to the company and its ideals. Not surprisingly, it consistently attracts people like Paul, who—at age twenty-eight and with a master's degree in environmental biology—accepted a $4.75-an-hour part-time job with Great Pacific Iron Works just to get his foot in the door. Later, for two years, he managed a company-owned retail outlet in Ventura. And now, some ten years later, he has gone from being Patagonia's environmental affairs director—where he organized in-house environmental awareness programs and offered business advice to non-profit groups throughout the country—to heading up the company's internal environmental assessment program. In this position, he organizes in-house environmental awareness programs and offers business advice to nonprofit groups throughout the country.

Chouinard thinks he could do even more to motivate and retain employees like Paul but concedes it has become harder than ever since the work force reached 525. He rectifies this as best he can by pulling out groups of twenty-five or thirty and offering them week-long classes and single lectures on different aspects of his unique business philosophy—he doesn't want Patagonia to become an impersonal corporate vacuum. An employee newsletter also relates similar information, and Chouinard estimates that the messages, for example, "Quality is foremost" and "People have a say," get across to at least half of those at the company.

"But we're not all clones. We disagree with Yvon on certain issues, and he certainly listens," says Libby, Patagonia's "environmental grants" coordinator, who helps determine where the company's donated funds should go. "For instance, after the liability problem led us to sell off the equipment division, he wanted to take climbing gear out of our stores. I felt very strongly that it should stay in. He finally agreed."

The best example of Patagonia's overall attitude toward its employees, of course, is illustrated by Kris McDivitt. She was nineteen and a student at the College of Idaho in 1969 when she was hired part-time to pack climbing equipment into shipping boxes. In 1978, six years after she completed school with a double major in psychology and sociology, she was the company's chief executive officer (CEO). She retained that position until 1988, when she asked to step aside to become director of image and design. In the recent management shuffling, she returned to Patagonia's top position. She left full-time employment there at the end of 1993 for personal reasons, and now is a member of its board of directors.

Eyes of the Beholder

The Patagonia catalog reads: "Everything we make pollutes; the production of every piece of clothing we make has a negative impact on the environment. Period."

Strange words in an era when businesses everywhere strive for the green seal of approval. Stranger still—at least at first blush—coming from the corporate pen of Patagonia, a firm consistently in the forefront of environmental responsibility. Honesty, though, is a virtue this company never lacked. It's not surprising, then, that such an unflattering admission appeared in the opening spread of Patagonia's semiannual catalog, which was mailed to more than four-hundred thousand households. After all, this highly regarded sales piece—successor to Chouinard's original one-page product sheet and cornerstone of an astonishingly successful marketing program that includes only minimal print advertising—has never been shy about promoting issues close to Patagonia's heart.

The company regularly spices up its thick book, with poignant articles like "Save the Salmon" and "The Mountains Are Dying." The back cover is devoted to causes Patagonia helps develop. Two examples are a move to save stands of the world's oldest tree in the Cani mountains of southern Chile and a "Coat of Many Colors" program to supply needy children with free Synchilla jackets made of discontinued fabric, trim, and zippers. The former led to the creation of a new rain-forest preserve; the latter put more than six thousand jackets on cold children in just one year. Patagonia invited its customers to send in the names of youth groups that could use the donated coats. Thousands have been given away since the program's inception three years ago.

The catalog also informs customers of its industrial expenditures. It lists exactly how many trees, gallons of water, and kilowatt hours of energy (enough to heat 130 homes, incidentally) that it saves each year by utilizing recycled paper. Figures also include how much solid waste and airborne pollutants it doesn't create for the same reason. To further underline its commitment, Patagonia recently trimmed the size of its premier selling tool from an oversized 10 1/4 by 12 3/4 inches to a more traditional 8 1/2 by 11.

This follows a move to eliminate waste and inequities in all Patagonia products, starting from the raw materials themselves and moving through the complete manufacturing and distribution processes. The company is undergoing an environmental assessment. "We are evaluating every piece of the trail that a product goes through," Kris McDivitt told a radio reporter. "The way it is dyed, the way it is spun, the way it's cut, the way it's transported." The subsequent effort, now headed by salesman-turned-environmental assessment leader, Paul, is ongoing.

Patagonia additionally offers employees, customers, and residents of its communities a vast array of information on the environment, and now, on human rights issues as well. It sometimes takes the form of an employee class on landfills and water treatment or a traveling exhibit to show Californians the benefits of conserving old-growth forests. It might include appearances at public hearings, massive letter-writing campaigns, and impassioned newspaper Op-Ed pieces. There have even been singular consumer-directed ads, such as the controversial 1991 full-color magazine piece on beach pollution that featured a large photo of a littered waterfront and the word "SHIT" as a prominent magenta headline.

"We debated whether or not to use that word," says Paul, the environmental assessment director, "but we wanted to wake people up." Unfortunately, he adds, more was made of the word than the message. But it is always the responsibility of employees and others to first comprehend, and act, on any of the messages that Patagonia puts out.

Chouinard used the company to promote such ideas from the beginning. His catalogs supported the move to so-called clean climbing well before it became popular, for example, even though it spelled doom for his signature pitons and other products that climbers physically wedged into rocks.

In the mid-eighties, he came to the realization that Patagonia could be more than a sporting-goods company; it could be used as a tool to change things he could not change on his own. The result was a more environmentally focused company. Patagonia cut its own trash by 50 percent; it developed a special recycling program for plastic bags that cover its garments as they travel to the United States from overseas. Patagonia dealers send back the used plastic bags and packaging, which are then reused or recycled. It also helped form an active corporate conservancy group—the Outdoor Industry Conservation Alliance—which counts Patagonia's chief competitors among its members.

Yet the company does face difficult business decisions when Chouinard and his senior managers must step in to find a way to match their environmental conscience with their quest for product perfection. One example was the company's recent attempt to use buttons made from Ecuadorian palm tree nuts in an effort to discourage destruction of the rain forest in which they are found. The resultant tagua-nut buttons eventually proved too fragile for Patagonia's quality demands, however, and the project has been temporarily shelved until a workable solution can be reached. Furthermore, the company has invited its customers to send back any shirts with the buttons for a replacement.

One direct and highly successful outgrowth of Chouinard's mideighties' activist push was his creation of the Patagonia grants program, which still stands as the company's single most significant ongoing effort. Quietly planned and administered—only small notices in the catalog and on clothing "hang tags" mention its existence—this Earth Tax nonetheless sparks some ten grant requests each week. Millions of dollars are subsequently given away, generally in smaller amounts to lesser-known grass-root organizations. Additional assistance, like brochure creation and letters of recommendation, also may be offered to the nonprofit groups.

Not everyone, employee or customer, supports every one of the company's activities, though. Some of its more controversial beneficiaries, for example, have been Planned Parenthood and Earth First! (the most radical of today's environmental organizations). Patagonia's association with both has caused some hard feelings with employees and customers. Yet for Chouinard it is more important that their company serve a greater good. "Maybe some of our employees don't agree with all of the groups we give money to," he said. "But most likely they back ninety percent of them. And that's more than most companies would do."

The company does communicate with upset customers. "We write letters that say we are sorry we lost them, but this is the way it is," Chouinard says. "As for our employees, I tell them that they should work for another company if something we do really bothers them.

I don't want them to compromise, and I want them to get behind what we are doing."

The Patagonia Shuffle

The 1991 announcement that Patagonia was about to undergo a significant upheaval shocked the tight-knit outdoors community. Yvon Chouinard's company, after all, had been phenomenally successful throughout its existence, with annual sales growing from $300,000 when it incorporated in 1972 to $117 million some two decades later. Sure, profit margins tended to fall a percent or two below the industry average, but that stemmed predominantly from the cost of innovation and quality and the money given out rather freely to nonprofits.

Yet the company has a new goal for the 1990s. "I'm sick and tired of being under the thumb of the banks," says Chouinard. "I've always controlled my own life, and now we're too heavily dependent on banks. We've lost control. We want to make profits, retain profits, and be out of debt in four years."

The first salvo in this effort was fired on May 22, 1991, when a letter signed by the company's vice-president/wholesale and sales manager went out to all dealers. Its main point was that Patagonia was "curtailing domestic growth" for economic and moral reasons. "We've taken a public stand in favor of more rational consumption in order to benefit the environment," it read. "We have practical reasons as well. We simply can't control this vehicle at a high rate of speed, no matter what the condition of the road."

The letter cited personnel, production, and financing problems associated with rapid growth. It announced that the company would keep sales level for the following twelve months and then raise them modestly. Planned job additions were scaled back, trade- and consumer-show participation was eliminated, "some marginal products" were dropped from the imminent line, and certain new styles were trimmed from future catalogs.

The company's next move was to cut its overall product line back from 360 items to 280. The objective was to eliminate duplication and increase production capacity.

In addition, in 1991, Chouinard removed the outside management team that he placed in five key positions in 1988—CEO, Chief Financial Officer, Chief Operations Officer, head of mail order, and director of personnel—and he asked former CEO McDivitt to return to that position. It was not that the newcomers were not qualified—the CEO had been vice-president of operations at a major ski resort and head of a large environmental program, for example; it was just that they were, well, outsiders.

"The only type of management that works is self-management," Chouinard says now. "When we realized that we were about to become a midsized company and our thinking was still small sized, we brought in so-called experts to take us to the next step. But it was a disaster. I don't think there is anyone you could bring into this company who would fit in and know what to do. This is a unique company."

The reorganization, however, was not quite over. On July 2, 1991, Patagonia announced the layoff of 120 employees, one-fifth of its total work force. The dismissals covered all levels of the company, including management; most were concentrated at the Ventura headquarters, but others hit the mail-order center in Bozeman, Montana, and the overseas offices in Europe and Japan. Each employee let go received ten days' notice as well as a severance package, including at least four weeks' pay plus one week's pay for every year of service to the company.

Chouinard attributed the problem once again to rapid growth and the company's inability to reach what proved to be unrealistic sales projections, especially during recessionary times. "To hit the sales goals we set, we would have had to move well beyond our core customers, beyond the specialty outdoor business," Chouinard noted in the layoff announcement. While many companies leave their laid-off employees feeling as if they had not done a good job, Patagonia took the blame. "It was a case of mismanagement, and it was painful to effect so many people's lives," says Chouinard. "I never want to be in that situation again.

"If we didn't recognize the need to scale back and retain a focus on our core customers, we might have considered other options," he added. "But it's clear to us that we've hit the ceiling in this industry.

To try and grow beyond the industry would change the nature of the company. And in the long run it would probably hurt us."

Patagonia's iconoclastic founder is certainly not ready to change the well-regarded business he created by moving his products into department stores like some of his competitors. Instead, he's content to service the seven hundred or so outdoor accounts that treat his garments—and his customers—with the same respect that he displays toward them. Chouinard has gotten as far as he has by knowing his limits, in business and in the out-of-doors. Now happily ensconced in middle age, with a solid business and an enviable personal life, he's not about to go back to the drawing board.

Chouinard often says that he has a hundred-year plan for Patagonia and that he wants the company to become a sort of nonprofit foundation when he leaves it. He also says that his greatest desire is to use it while he can to set an example for other businesses around the world.

"If we can take the radical end of it and show it's working for us," Chouinard notes, "the more conservative companies will take that first step. And one day they'll become good businesses, too."

10

Grateful—and Generous

Company name: The Grateful Dead
Type of Business: rock-and-roll band
Location: San Rafael, California
Number of employees: 60
Year founded: 1965

It was the rain forest that did it. The Grateful Dead always played benefits of one sort or another, starting with those regular Saturday night gigs for Ken Kesey and the Merry Pranksters. But this was different. This was a full house at New York's Madison Square Garden. Opening performances by Hall & Oats, Bruce Hornsby, and Suzanne Vega. Commemorative posters by Robert Rauschenberg. And a cause—preserving the world's rain forests—that almost no one could oppose. The mainstream press, which had blatantly ignored or patronizingly dismissed the band for years, suddenly grew interested.

Publications everywhere began pulling old photos and files on the band to update their readers on the state of The Grateful Dead in 1988. The timing was ideal. The Dead was coming off its best-selling record of all time and its most successful touring year ever. The performing unit was stable, the creative juices were flowing, and the group was flexing its considerable public relations muscle for a cause that made good copy.

135

Not surprisingly, though, most newspapers and magazines that went digging came up empty. The majority found the same old psychedelic sixties rockers that they always saw and agonized anew over the cultural and societal declines that they attribute to The Dead and its ilk. Some discovered what they thought was an entirely new angle: a group of middle-aged musical relics who somehow managed to transcend the acid-rock mantle and then move on to become the top live draw in the music industry and one of the highest-grossing acts in all of show business.

Precious few, though, really came close to understanding The Grateful Dead. That's partly because mainstream America never has understood the band that rose from cult favorite in the sixties to wildly successful road show in the nineties. And partly because the individuals who make up this legendary ensemble really wouldn't have it any other way.

Musicians in The Grateful Dead prefer, instead, to communicate through their music. Band members are hardly press-shy, but they are not particularly forthcoming, either. They don't talk to local papers just to sell tickets. They don't hold press conferences to announce their charitable contributions. They don't encourage articles about their positive treatment of employees and fans. And they don't discuss The Dead as a successful business, even though in 1993 it accounted for $45.6 million in concert ticket sales alone while also overseeing the production and sale of an entire catalog of recorded music and an eclectic mix of licensed products.

Moreover, The Grateful Dead seems to relish its long-standing image as a somewhat mysterious collection of tie-dyed musician-philosophers who have provided a distinctive soundtrack to American life from the sixties' Summer of Love to the nineties' Era of Safe Sex.

Band members rarely sit down for serious interviews. They never converse with their audiences while on stage. And they keep their private lives mostly private. But they play extraordinarily long concerts on seventy or eighty occasions every year—shows lasting four hours are still standard—and their repertoire, which is never the same from night to night, connects with the audience in an uncannily direct way that absolutely baffles outsiders.

There they were, working with Greenpeace and Cultural Survival and the Rainforest Action Network on a celebrity-studded event designed for an audience far broader than their usual crowd of appreciative fans. After a while, even the musicians felt a little estranged from the situation they had helped to create. "We've put a lot of time into this because it's important," Jerry Garcia, a founding member of the group and one of its two singer-guitarists, told *Rolling Stone* magazine. "Somebody needs to do something—it's just incredibly pathetic that it has to be us." But The Dead's participation continued to be supported by the entire band, he noted, despite being an organization whose six members usually had six different opinions on every subject.

"Nothing is quick and easy with The Grateful Dead, but that particular one was quick and easy," Bob Weir, another cofounder and the other singer-guitarist, agrees today. "A couple of us were invited to a dinner in San Francisco, which was held to save this grand benefit that was falling apart. We realized it was going to fall apart, and there was no way of stopping it. But the people who were involved were great, and the cause that stood to benefit was important, so we decided to help them start fresh."

The result was the sold-out Madison Square Garden concert on September 24, 1988. The band ensured that all proceeds from the evening—about a quarter of a million dollars—went to rain-forest preservation. It put together an extensive press package to spread the message. And it gave its time freely for months beforehand to help keep the event on track.

But by the time they mounted the Garden stage, the musicians—Garcia, Weir, bassist Phil Lesh, drummers Bill Kreutzmann and Mickey Hart, and keyboardist Brent Mydland, ages forty-two to fifty-one—were once again ready to let their music do the talking. The enthusiastic crowd experienced an unpredictable and exhilarating evening. The rain forest received widespread media attention and considerable financial aid. The Dead got to play on something of a national stage for one of the rare times in its long history.

Immediately afterward, though, The Grateful Dead slipped easily back into its more accustomed role: that of an extremely popular but still unpretentious rock-and-roll band committed to those around it and willing to help needy people and worthy causes without a lot of fanfare.

Uncle John's Band

It would be nice to say that The Grateful Dead simply ambled onto a Bay Area stage one moonlit evening long ago and without a word cranked out a pair of killer sets highlighted by a version of "Dark Star" that fans everywhere still talk about with reverence. Unfortunately, the band's beginnings were far more mundane. Jerry Garcia—the folk-musician son of a jazz clarinetist—was making the club rounds in northern California when he met up with sixteen-year-old guitarist Bobby Weir. After a spontaneous New Year's Eve, 1965, jam in a music shop where Garcia taught banjo and guitar, the two joined together with a few friends to form a jug band.

The new group played pure folk music from the start, but influenced by the emergence of the Beatles—and Garcia's side jobs as a guitar and bass player in rock bands—it soon shifted toward Chicago-style blues. In came Ron "Pigpen" McKernan on organ, Kreutzmann on drums, and classically trained trumpet player Lesh on bass. With the addition of second-drummer Hart a few years later, the lineup was essentially set for good.

That first band was called the Warlocks, and in many ways it remains the group that exists today. In fact, except for a succession of five keyboardists—three of whom died tragically—the band's personnel line-up has remained stable since its beginning. No mean feat in any industry, to be sure, but a particularly impressive accomplishment in this one.

Other changes have taken place, of course. The most obvious was the new name, which came about in December 1965 because band members believed the "Warlocks" label had already been claimed. The new name was chosen from a definition someone happened upon in Funk & Wagnall's *New Practical Standard Dictionary of English*. Essentially, it described a cycle of "Grateful Dead" folk tales in which a kindhearted person receives his just rewards from an appreciative corpse.

By the start of 1966, it seemed as if the band really did have such a grateful cadaver on its side. The group landed as many as eight jobs a month, putting it constantly on the road and kicking off the habit of regular touring that continues to this day. These early performances showcased The Dead in well-known San Francisco halls—the Fillmore, Winterland, and the Avalon Ballroom—and also included long free-form concerts at that infamous series of multimedia happenings produced by novelist Ken *One Flew Over the Cuckoo's Nest* Kesey known as the Acid Tests. (These Saturday night events from Portland to Los Angeles were promoted with cards reading: "Can *you* pass the acid test?")

Of this constant cycle of early shows, those held weekly in association with Kesey—an association that lasted about a year—probably had the most impact on the band. For one thing, they introduced members to cultural icons like Neal Cassady and Timothy Leary, future literary stars like Larry McMurtry and Robert Stone, and kindred souls like Mountain Girl and Ram Rod. (The former became Garcia's wife, though they're now divorced; the latter was hired to handle the group's drums, a job he still holds in addition to serving as president of The Dead's corporation.)

More importantly, perhaps, the weekly no-holds-barred shows gave the band a chance to play exactly the way it wanted—and the way it increasingly wanted to play was definitely more jazz-inspired jam than top-forty pop. The Acid Tests thus gave the still-jelling musical group a chance to stretch out on songs that sometimes ran a half hour in length, or more, as well as an opportunity to learn a little more about itself and its sound.

Playing so many live shows also forced the musicians to keep up with the technical side of their performance, and a deep-seated commitment to deliver the highest-quality sound possible led them to constantly update their always state of the art concert systems. They began their long-running, mutually beneficial relationship with the late Bill Graham in 1966—performing for the legendary promoter at his first annual New Year's Eve concert, among other shows that year—and by 1967 they were poised for big things. They released their first album, debuted in New York (at the Cafe Au Go Go), and added second-drummer Hart to further bolster their sound.

Touring remained their major emphasis, though, and they saw the world while the world saw them: Portland, San Diego, Athens (Ohio), San Francisco, Boston, New York, Denver, Philadelphia, Cleveland, St. Louis, Brooklyn, Eugene, Los Angeles, Nashville, Woodstock, Europe. A slew of songs—written mostly by Garcia and Weir in collaboration with Robert Hunter and John Barlow—were introduced and ironed out before live crowds. Albums were released regularly, too, but few caught the excitement and spontaneity of the marathon concerts. These records generally sank quickly from view, and most radio stations never played them. But hard-core fans, called Dead-heads, swore allegiance to the group in astounding numbers all the same.

By the early seventies the band was playing in as many as fifty-six different venues a year, in sites as large as RFK Stadium in Washing-ton, D.C. Its music was better than ever, but the pace and the life took their toll as McKernon—who often served as front man in this early lineup—developed the liver disease that would kill him in 1973.

The band took a yearlong sabbatical from touring shortly there-after and worked with two other keyboardists before hiring Brent Mydland a few months after its series of seminal 1978 shows at the Pyramids in Cairo, Egypt. (The second of these replacement musi-cians, Keith Godchaux, was killed in an auto accident two years after leaving the group.)

The Dead had the lineup and the sound that it would build on through the eighties as well as the technical crew and office staff that would carry its music to their followers, who were, almost inexplica-bly, growing in both number and intensity as the years wore on.

The band attained the all-time height of its popularity about the time of the rain-forest benefit and continued to ride that crest unchanged into the nineties. At least, that is, until July 26, 1990, when Mydland died of a drug overdose.

The band was devastated, but like any organization with a lot of people depending on it for paychecks, business went on. Old friend Bruce Hornsby sat in until band members hired Vince Welnick, who once played keyboard in a popular San Francisco band called The Tubes. The Dead then set out on tour once again.

Eyes of the World

In the summer of 1990, Bob Weir helped organize a mountain bike tour through the northern Rockies of Montana. The group—which included John Oates, from the Hall & Oates musical duo, and Howie Wolke, cofounder of the radical EarthFirst! eco group—covered 150 miles of grizzly bear territory, from Glacier National Park to Missoula, in three days. The tour was planned to dramatize the wanton destruction of wildlife habitat and backcountry wilderness by the timber industry. Media throughout the country picked up on the issue, which Weir continued to support long after the pedaling ended.

Such hands-on commitment is not uncommon in members of The Grateful Dead, which, individually and collectively, aims to "make the world the place it should be," as Weir explains. These mostly unsung projects also include drummer Hart's various environmental efforts, bassist Lesh's continuing support of avant-garde musicians, and cofounder Garcia's regular donation of his royalties from the sale of Ben & Jerry's Cherry Garcia ice cream to the nonprofit foundation associated with the band—which gives away these funds and much more to some of the numerous causes constantly clamoring for The Dead's attention.

"Back in the early eighties, we realized that there were just too many ideas for benefits—that we felt aligned with—being presented to us," Weir says. Following the suggestion of the band's attorneys, the musicians helped create the Rex Foundation to suggest appropriate charitable recipients and award them with as much as $10,000 apiece from funds primarily generated by the group. Many, but not all, of the band members sit on its board; most, but not all, of its funding is derived from a three-day series of concerts held at Sacramento's Cal Expo fairgrounds each spring.

The Rex, as the foundation is called, is named in honor of longtime crew member Rex Jackson, who died in a 1976 car crash. It has made "dispersals on the order of about $3 million to this point," says band spokesman Dennis McNally. Beneficiaries, which are all organizations that promote "social healing," he adds, include many inner-city, AIDS, Native American, and ecological causes. Examples range from the San Francisco Mayor's Fund for the Homeless to the United Anglers of California and the San Francisco school system. "We gave the schools $10,000 to buy instruments, which has been my single favorite Grateful Dead donation," McNally says. In addition, the foundation recently funded a recording of the men's choir at San Quentin prison and produced four thousand cassettes. The money generated from the sales of the tapes will promote the prison's music program. The Dead also contributed $5,000—plus a set of tie-dyed warmup suits—to the 1992 Lithuanian Olympic basketball team.

The foundation is run quietly by a board that meets twice a year, he continues. On it sits band members, staffers, famous friends, like former NBA star Bill Walton, and not-so-famous friends, like Alabama dentist and certified Deadhead Bernie Bildman. The board's operation, in fact, mirrors that of the band itself: Members from every level of the organization consider ideas suggested by everyone involved with the group and find a way to make the best of them work.

"In a way," Weir muses, "I think our attitude basically boils down to enlightened self-interest. We are the kind of people who want to live in the everyday world rather than cloistering ourselves off from it. So in order to make the world we live in a more livable place, we have to work on it a bit. And the better it gets out there, the better a time we are going to have. It's pretty much that pure and simple."

Weir, who also has organized a nonprofit foundation of his own, seems to have taken these words to heart as much as anyone in the band. Immediately after the rain-forest benefit, for example, he and his sister, Wendy, began working on a way to increase interest in this endangered area among those who will play the most vital role in its future: today's children. The resultant book, *Panther Dream,* and accompanying audio cassette was released by Hyperion in the fall of 1991. Intelligently written and beautifully illustrated, it spins an engaging tale of the rain forest and a young boy's discovery of its secrets.

"The impetus was supplied by my sister," Weir says. "She knew that I would get involved with a project that had an environmental bent. And she was right. She got me hooked."

Wendy Weir, a financial consultant and self-taught painter, says the pair decided on a children's book as a logical extension of The Dead's rain-forest concert. They began by enlisting Simon Muchiru, a native of Kenya and director of the African Non-Governmental Organizations Environmental Network, to ensure the accuracy of their story line and all peripheral details. They agreed Wendy would make her drawings—of which almost three dozen were used—as zoologically and botanically precise as they were visually arresting. And they decided Bob would produce a cassette featuring his narration over a complex and original musical score.

Not surprisingly, this last idea took on a life of its own as the project moved along. Bob Weir not only ended up writing the music and playing guitar and synthesizer on the soundtrack; he also developed a new technology especially for it called Virtual Sound. Effectively surrounding the listener with a carpet of music and junglelike noises, the tape has appealed to fans of The Dead as well as to six-year-olds who enjoy its realistic sound and the way it enhances an already enticing story.

"We did the whole thing with children in mind and felt that if we did the best we could do—if it came from our hearts—the children would appreciate it," says Wendy. A portion of the proceeds is being donated to the Rainforest Action Network and Cultural Survival, she adds, while the publisher is replanting trees for those used in the book's production. In addition, the brother-sister team is working with the Walt Disney Company's Epcot Center in Orlando, Florida, on related educational projects, and it prepared a free teacher's guide to *Panther Dream* and the rain-forest issue.

Such commitment—which on one level or another has been a part of the band's culture for almost three decades–also impresses its peers in the music industry. Recently, some have recorded *Deadicated,* a tribute compact disk featuring a diverse assortment of musicians—Midnight Oil, Dwight Yokam, Elvis Costello, and Lyle Lovett—covering a variety of Grateful Dead songs. The CD's recycled cardboard longbox featured a cutout postcard to be mailed to Sen. Robert Kasten, Jr. (R-Wisc.), of the Committee on Appropriations, noting that the sender is "upset to learn that my tax money is being used for World Bank and IMF schemes that destroy the rain forests, flood farmlands, and dislocate native peoples and others." The fourteen performers, along with The Dead, also donated all royalties from the project to Cultural Survival and the Rainforest Action Network—nearly $1 million in its first year of release alone.

One More Saturday Night

In its twenty-second year, The Grateful Dead finally hit the big time. Its 1987 *In The Dark* album—the first released by the band in seven years—sold a million copies in just a few weeks when most of their previous albums never cracked the half-million mark. The single, "Touch of Grey," became the Dead's first top-ten hit and even spawned a popular video. Previously, the group sold out nine of ten shows; now it sold out 96 percent over the course of a year that took it to the nation's biggest arenas and stadiums. Within two years, in fact, 3 million concert tickets were sold.

Other than finally releasing the album that longtime fans always knew these musicians had in them, The Dead really wasn't doing anything differently than it had done for the previous two decades. The band developed a steady traveling pattern that took it and some two dozen support people around the country in three relatively short bursts, offering about twenty shows during each trip before returning home or going off somewhere on a break. (The musicians also play a number of West Coast dates, such as the Rex Foundation benefit concerts, during these "respites" from touring.) But since *In The Dark,* more and more people were waiting for them in every city that they played.

The Dead always attracted a phenomenally faithful audience, which enthusiastically attended shows night after night in an ongoing display of adoration never seen before or since in the world of popular music. Elvis and Sinatra saw larger individual crowds. Bruce Springsteen and the Rolling Stones tallied larger touring grosses. The Beatles drew more enthusiastic fans. But none of them ever had thousands of followers travel around the country (or the world) with them for a while—a couple of days, several weeks, a few months, even longer— just for the chance to be there on a memorable night that everyone would talk about for years to come.

"Our audience is like people who like licorice," Jerry Garcia told Geraldo Rivera on ABC's *20/20* back in 1981. "Not everybody likes licorice, but the people who like licorice really like licorice."

This faithful multigenerational audience—which includes graying baby boomers as well as youthful fans born well after the band—has long been rewarded with relatively low priced tickets, mail-order ticket lotteries that provide equal access to the usually sold out shows, marathon concerts that are totally different every night, special areas at every venue where "tapers" are free to set up their personal audio recording gear (to make cassettes that are freely traded with the blessing of The Dead), and even campgrounds at certain multishow locales.

Most seats at the shows were still being filled by dedicated Deadheads, but publicity surrounding the band's resurgence drew others to the scene. Because the band attracts fans who may travel thousands of miles for a specific show or follow the group throughout all or part of one of these twenty-show minitours, the concert halls along the way become temporary stopovers for the traveling caravan of Deadheads. A lot of newcomers gravitated to these campground/marketplace/gathering spots, and some never set foot inside a concert hall. The development was bound to cause some friction, and eventually it did.

One by one, some of The Dead's longtime second homes—like Stanford University and the University of California at Berkeley—announced that they could no longer handle the crush of fans. Other communities, from California to Maryland, tried to block future visits. A few cities that did host shows were the scene of clashes between crowds and officials. Ironically, The Dead's newfound popularity looked to be the biggest threat it ever faced, even though it was now responsible for pumping more than $1 million into local economies on every night it played. So it stopped performing in places where it was not wanted.

But when the community of Deadheads started to mushroom beyond the logistical capacities of the arenas willing to host it, the band intervened. It distributed fliers and produced public-service radio spots asking fans not to ruin a good thing by giving authorities a reason to step in. The Dead's road manager, Cameron Sears, began working with local officials on crowd management a year in advance of the band's appearance. It sought to ban alcohol sales at shows, booked fewer multinight dates, halted camping at some sites, and played more concerts that were announced only a few days in advance. It took about three years, but these relatively soft interventions succeeded, and the band was able to continue its regular touring pattern into the nineties.

One of the major reasons the group could pull this off, of course, was its staff. From the beginning, The Grateful Dead has treated its employees with respect and appreciation—like members of the family, in a very literal way—and it has in turn been rewarded with one of the most loyal and talented crews in the industry. In a business like this, that is important: Misjudge an arena's acoustics and fans in the back of the hall may be so disappointed they'll never return; place the drums one inch too close and one of the drummers could break a finger. Additionally, the technical expertise that's been associated with this band has been responsible for pioneering sound and lighting systems that remain the envy of other musicians to this day.

The Dead know this, obviously, but it is still significant that in all its many relationships with employees, fans, and neighbors the band continues to epitomize the counterculture tenets it has always espoused. It still operates out of the same clean but cluttered Victorian house in Marin County it has rented since 1972, where as many as three people share cozy upstairs offices that once were bedrooms. Modern computers clash with the old-fashioned wallpaper, and the friendly atmosphere is enhanced by such homey—if unexpected— touches as a kitchen filled with Easter candy each spring. In the past, staffers have even sent Christmas greetings to everyone on their 100,000-name mailing list.

While they don't like to admit it, the musicians also follow most of the tenets of a socially responsible business. The band (which incorporated in 1971) works hard, consistently offers a high-quality product, and demonstrates fierce dedication to its work force, its customers, and its community. It is entirely self-managed and tries to meet monthly to discuss new projects and interesting offers. Outside help is used only when necessary. And even though these traits have on occasion had a short-term downside—some decisions wind up needlessly costing the band money, for example—in the long run they've proved successful.

The album sales racked up by its successful 1987 recording may never be repeated, but the band was happy with its position before that release, and it is certainly happy that the frenzy surrounding it has died down somewhat. "We became more of a household word because we hit the top forty," says Bob Weir. "But right before *In The Dark* we were still one of the top-grossing acts. *In The Dark* didn't make that big a difference."

Interestingly, the band is not often recognized for its business prowess. Though a few other musicians, including U2 and Metallica, have come to The Grateful Dead for advice, the band appears to the outside to be in a world of its own. "There's a stigma of who we are," explains Sears. "They think we are in another galaxy, so what we know is not applicable. We would love to see other musicians take more control. But the artists themselves have to want to be involved."

The Grateful Dead often makes decisions that follow their consciences instead of the music-industry norm. Recently, for example, the Grateful Dead's record company overproduced its most recent album, called *Built to Last*. The tendency in the business is to either price the CDs and tapes at a reduced price and sell them through discount stores or to destroy them. The band had never discounted any of their albums and was not about to start now. It could not abide with the waste of destroying thousands of CDs and cassettes. So, working with the record company, The Grateful Dead sent a mailer out offering the CD for five dollars plus a handling fee; all money generated from the sale was donated to promote forestry issues. The mailer included a piece that encouraged the public to write to Congress about the current state of our forests. In addition, thousands of cassettes were sent free to fans in the former Soviet Union.

Built to Last

In 1986, Cameron Sears was a river-rafting guide with two passions: organizing float trips to benefit a group called Friends of the River and listening to The Grateful Dead. He wrote a letter to The Grateful Dead inviting both the band members and office staff on a river trip. When he followed up his letter with a phone call, he was told, "Don't call us, we'll call you."

Two months later, Sears received a call from Danny Rifkin, who had been The Dead's manager since its inception and said that he had twenty-five people who wanted to take a raft trip down the American River. Soon Bill Graham also signed on for an excursion down the Tuolomne River. The promoter was so impressed that he wanted to work with Sears on a long-term series of excursions for his own employees; that didn't pan out, but Sears soon found himself performing odd jobs at some of Graham's rock-and-roll shows.

What came next is the stuff of which Grateful Dead legends are made. John McIntyre, who had been with the band off and on since its formation, took over the job of road manager from Rifkin and wanted an assistant. He knew Sears from the prior river trip and offered him the position for a four-month probationary period. The band liked Sears and asked him to stay on permanently. After three years, McIntyre left, and the job was given to his protégé.

"I'm in a one-in-a-million situation," Sears, thirty-four, says over a cup of cappuccino at a Bay Area coffee shop. "When I first started working for these guys, I didn't have a clue in the world what the music business was about. Now I have the equivalent of a Ph.D. in it."

Sears is not the first Dead employee to literally fall into a position of responsibility with the band. Many have been with the group since the beginning, and several have been rewarded with additional positions of trust, for example, the naming of Ram Rod as president of The Grateful Dead corporation and the choice of Bill "Kidd" Candelario (who handles bass and keyboards) to head Grateful Dead Merchandising. On occasion, selected employees also have been known to receive hefty bonuses.

"The band has faith in the people who work for it, and it gives us autonomy," Sears notes. "We are empowered to go out and do our jobs in the best way we know how without feeling encumbered. At the end of the day, we are accountable for what we do."

This symbiosis between musicians, crew, office staff, and fans sets The Dead radically apart from other bands. Real Deadheads, for instance—who are doctors and lawyers, carpenters and plumbers, waiters and saleswomen, kids and grandparents—rarely cause any commotion at concerts because they see eye to eye with the band and wholeheartedly support the atmosphere it is trying to create. Instead, most of the trouble that developed in recent years stemmed directly from the infusion of newcomers. Many of them physically joined The Deadhead caravan without understanding it or believing in what it represents. They felt no compunction to abide by its unspoken rules.

Nonetheless, The Dead's support team has become quite adept at handling any concert problems that do arise as well as the concerns and requests relayed to them by tens of thousands of regular followers who consider themselves an integral part of the band's extended family. In addition, the no-nonsense "roadies" who set up and break down as many as eighty shows a year ensure that this demanding task is performed consistently and professionally. To this end the band maintains a very close relationship with Bill Graham Presents, the

San Francisco firm that has worked with it virtually from the beginning.

Over the years, this association has certainly proved to be satisfying and mutually beneficial. And on January 1, 1992, the two organizations were hooked up once again at the Oakland Coliseum for what was supposed to be the twenty-sixth consecutive New Year's Eve Dead concert sponsored by Graham. Tragically, however, Graham had been killed in a helicopter crash several months earlier. For the first time since January 1, 1967, the popular promoter and his most popular act were not ushering in the New Year as one.

In its own inimitable way, however, The Dead offered a quiet tribute that wasn't missed by anyone in the full house. The break prior to midnight was used to show videotaped highlights of the special events Graham had scheduled at these New Year's shows for years—like bungee jumpers bouncing down from the ceiling or African fire dancers captivating everyone from the stage. After the countdown to the New Year, the band returned with its usual series of postmidnight songs, altered slightly to pay tribute to their friend: Graham's favorite Grateful Dead song, a twenty-year-old tune called "Sugar Magnolia," highlighted a special set that Deadheads were still buzzing about weeks later.

This gesture provided a necessary release, but the deaths of several close friends—an artist long associated with the band died around the same time as Graham and Mydland—only served to compound the stress generated by constant traveling, growing crowds, and increasing demands on their time. Jerry Garcia, for instance, fell ill in August 1992 with what his doctor called a "chronic" reaction to "lung disease related to years of smoking"; fall concerts were cancelled but physician Dr. Randy Baker reported that Garcia "should regain good health and continue performing for many years." He and the others recognize that their responsibilities spread much further these days than the six band members and their families. There are some sixty other employees dependent on them now, as well as the vast array of Deadheads who consider each of their appearances an event worthy of more than a little celebration.

So they will undoubtedly head out on tour again and again: to the East Coast, the Southwest, the Midwest, or the Northwest. Then there are the local California shows, the performances by various offshoot bands, the recording sessions, the books, the benefit concerts. Band members may now be able to take refuge during breaks in places like Hawaii, but they've managed to remain pretty much the same band of unpretentious sixties products that they've always been. Bob Weir, for one, heartily endorses The Grateful Dead's approach for other musicians who also want to be true to themselves, their employees, their fans, and their art.

"Get a good lawyer, one who shares an open-ended view of how things can be arranged, and have him set up a corporation that takes into account everybody's contributions," Weir advises. "Not just the musicians' or the management's but the people who do the grunt work as well. Everybody. Everybody has to contribute as a team, and however you set up your business mechanisms, they should reflect everybody's efforts and contributions. If they do, chances are the organization is not going to fold on itself and be diseased from within."

Weir, after all, should know. He and The Dead have watched as scores of other musical acts self-destructed after mistreating each other and those around them. The Grateful Dead, on the other hand, has been relatively stable, personnelwise, for nearly three decades. Its music, most say, is as good as ever. And sales of concert tickets, recordings, and licensed merchandise remain at an all-time high.

"All I can suggest is that people give it a try," Weir says of the band's conscientious approach. "It's worked real well for us."

11

Back to the Land

Company name: Yakima Products
Type of business: manufacturer of car-roof racks
Location: Arcata, California
Number of employees: 145
Year acquired: 1979

The 145 employees of Yakima Products are seated in neat rows in their vast shipping department. Standing before them is Bruce Hamilton, the company's general manager and chief executive officer (CEO). He holds up a newspaper clipping.

"This article in today's *Wall Street Journal* reports that General Motors lost $4.5 billion last year," he says into a small microphone, emphasizing the word "billion." "Let's assume the company runs 365 days a year, twenty-four hours per day," says the forty-six-year-old manager. "That means GM lost $12.3 million dollars per day, a half a million dollars per hour, $8,500 per minute, and more than $140 per second.

"Now, you have to ask," he continues, "how did our company do in comparison? Well, we made in one year what GM lost in one hour."

So started the Yakima Products biannual companywide meeting. At this formal gathering, management reports on the state of its company, and employees have the opportunity to ask any questions they want answered. The gathering includes shop room employees, customer-service representatives, sales managers, and engineers. It's a chance for everyone to speak out.

After a report on a recent trip to Japan, a discussion of new packaging products, and an update on new products, Hamilton invites the audience to ask questions. Yakima employees are not shy and are eager to voice their concerns.

One worker complains that managers use the lunchroom to discuss company business. "Isn't the lunch area a place where employees should get a break from company talk?" he asked.

Another employee says she thinks workers should be able to evaluate their supervisors, just as supervisors evaluate them.

A production worker asks Hamilton, who has been with the company for two years, how much money he earns. Without flinching, he tells them the high five-figure amount. A few eyes roll, and some of the hourly wage earners could not contain a gasp. Hamilton, without hesitation, goes on to discuss his background. His premed degree from Vanderbilt University, his years as president of a large manufacturing company, the amount of budget he is responsible for, and the fact he took a pay cut to come and run this company two years before.

Open. Honest. Vocal. Three attributes that have been consistent themes at Yakima Products since Don Banducci and Steve Cole, two renegades from the sixties, bought the company from a native of Germany in 1979. Yakima Products designs, manufactures, and distributes state-of-the-art automobile roof racks. The carriers hold sports equipment, including bicycles, skis, snowboards, kayaks, sailboards, and canoes.

Yakima Products is based in Arcata, a small coastal city near the Oregon border. It's the sort of area where many lifelong residents have never been on an airplane or made the five-hour drive to San Francisco.

Yet Arcata is an outdoor enthusiast's mecca and a haven for artists, entrepreneurs, and environmentalists. The city is surrounded by the Six Rivers National Forest and the rugged Pacific Coast. Nearby rivers attract whitewater kayakers, canoeists, and fishermen. The forests provide miles of trails for hiking and mountain biking. Thousands of students, professors, and support staff are associated with the local university, Humboldt State. With a total population of fifteen thousand, it is considered one of the country's most progressive small cities.

Indeed, more than one thousand acres of protected forest are within the city limits. Mining-era buildings, now housing cafés and retail stores, are preserved in the downtown area. There are laws that ban the use of herbicides within city limits, a sewage systems treats wastewater without chemicals, and Arcata has had a recycling program for two decades.

Yet this seemingly well balanced community is rife with controversy. Living side by side with the environmentalists, including artists, those associated with the university, and a handful of entrepreneurs at progressive companies like Yakima, is the quickly deteriorating timber industry. Timberworkers are desperate to hold on to their jobs, and environmentalists are fighting to halt old-growth destruction. The two groups have been battling for more than two decades. Yakima, behind its vocal leader and president, Banducci, is one of a few businesses in the area that doesn't rely on the area's fragile natural resources. In fact, the company has always embraced a progressive business philosophy—it cares.

"The chasm dividing Arcata," reported Jennifer Warren in the *Los Angeles Times,* "is rooted in its evolution from a town of timber families, fishermen, and small-business owners to its modern status—as a bastion of environmentalism and small-is-beautiful beliefs, where unorthodox approaches to life and business are welcome, even encouraged."

In the Beginning

Sitting around a picnic table in Redwood Regional Park, Banducci and Cole relish telling the story of how they bought Yakima. It's a tale that has been repeated many times. But it's not a polished version company presidents often tell to journalists, bankers, or customers. Rather, it's a story that seems to have been shared while enjoying a beer with friends.

Though Banducci and Cole are close friends as well as business partners, they are opposites in both temperament and interests. The forty-six-year-old Banducci, ruggedly handsome with salt-and-pepper hair, is outspoken, enthusiastic, and filled with ideas. Some of his employees consider him an eccentric. He handles company communications, advertising, and keeps a strong hand in product development. He has the title of president. Cole, forty-six, who is quiet, intense, and mechanically oriented, is the company's vice-president of engineering. Employees at Yakima privately compare the partners to a longtime married couple, bickering with each other one moment, flattering each other the next.

Don Banducci met Steve Cole when they were both in their early twenties and living in Arcata. Banducci, whose father and mother were born and raised in the area before moving south to the Bay Area, spent countless summers on the Eel River. Cole, a former McDonnell Douglas engineer, moved to the area from Los Angeles. He was a student teacher at the university and worked in the local bike shop.

Banducci and Cole shared a passion for whitewater kayaking; a host of rivers in this northern Californian area offered invigorating challenges for kayakers. In the late 1970s, to help pay for their own activities, the duo launched Six River Float Trips, a rafting company based in Arcata.

Cole and Banducci received a letter in 1978 from Otto Bagervall, the head of Yakima Industries, which was then based in the Washington State town for which it was named. The company manufactured handmade foot braces that were used in canoes and kayaks to help users keep their bodies stable. "We were at the point where we were trying to figure out what direction our lives would take, and this letter from Otto arrived," says Banducci. "He wrote that they were going out of business, that the government wanted them to pay too many taxes, and they had had enough. We called and asked if the company was for sale, and he invited us to come up and be apprentices for one month and he would see."

Banducci and his wife, Maggie, and Steve and his wife, Jan, drove up to Yakima and checked into a transient hotel within walking distance of the company. "We learned right away that this man was quickly losing his memory. He had no memory and worked in a chaotic, nonsensical manner. The operation was like a Santa's workshop," says Banducci. Besides the foot braces used to secure feet within a canoe or kayak, Yakima Products—which was founded after

World War II—built snow shovels, music stands, canoe racks, even crossing flags for the local schools. "If anyone had a need, Otto would try to help out," says Banducci.

For the next month, the two couples worked tirelessly in the shop, following Otto around. "It was a totally bizarre, dangerous operation," remembers Cole. "There were no guards on the saws, and everything was made by hand."

Though more than a dozen groups or individuals had already negotiated to buy Yakima, the staunch Otto said no to everyone. "After we were there a month, Otto said he would sell it to us," says Banducci. "I guess we passed his test."

With money saved from various entrepreneurial pursuits, Banducci and Cole bought the company in the fall of 1979 for $80,000. Their first decision was to move the company to Arcata. They set up shop in a small shed where the foursome built the foot braces and continued selling them to the more than eighty dealers Yakima Industries had established throughout the country.

"Our first thought was that this could be a nice little cottage industry for the four of us," says Banducci. "If we could pay ourselves $12,000 a year, keep the foot braces on the market, and be gainfully employed while involved with the sports we loved, then we were happy."

Focus on Racks

Within a year after they purchased Yakima, the two couples realized they could not sustain themselves by making only foot braces. Banducci and Cole soon discovered that Otto's books were not accurate. In fact, they learned he had actually been selling his products for less than it cost to make them. "We should have known there was trouble when Otto told us that if you don't make a profit, you don't have to pay taxes," says Banducci with a laugh.

Banducci and Cole realized they had to both improve their existing products and design some new ones as well. Cole, who enjoyed working with tools, pulled out the automobile roof rack Otto made to transport canoes. "It was very, very complicated," says Cole. The first thing he did was use better materials and simplify the method of attaching the canoe to the rack with straps. Cole soon developed attachments so that bikes could be placed on the same rack. That winter, he made another set of brackets that would hold skis. "Though I had a college education, my best training to do all this came from all of my years working on cars and bikes," says Cole.

In the summer of 1980, Banducci received a call from one of their dealers in Kansas City. He had bought the rack for canoes but wanted to know if it would hold a sailboard. Though Banducci had never seen one before—the sport was just becoming popular in the United States—he said he was sure it would. They quickly found a sailboard and developed the brackets, pads, and straps needed to secure the board, its boom, and its mast all on their rooftop rack. "It was with that phone call that I understood that we were in the multisport roof-rack business," says Banducci. Banducci and Cole created a new product category in the United States, all-in-one roof racks, a sports enthusiast's dream come true. Though a number of companies sold racks—for skis, for bicycles, or to hold lumber—no company built one rack that would hold a variety of equipment.

Excited with the new concept, the partners were ready to sell the system. Banducci and his wife set out in a used van to cross the country and show the rack to their established dealers and anyone else who might be interested. Their first sales call was at Recreational Equipment Incorporated (REI), an outdoors specialty chain store, with a home office in Seattle.

Banducci gleefully tells the story of how he and Maggie arrived the night before their meeting with a buyer and scoped out the office. They then found the local high school. After spending the night in the back of their van, they drove to the high school and sneaked into the showers with a group of students in gym class. Arriving fresh and clean at REI, the buyers liked what they saw, and the duo secured its first order. Similar successes followed. As they traveled throughout the country, they received both orders and interest.

Back at Arcata, however, it was obvious they would need more capital to produce the racks. "We had been hand-tooling everything ourselves, cutting, angling, and finishing each piece of the rack," says Cole. In order to produce the larger quantities, Yakima needed to invest in additional tools, including molds to form plastics and large dyes to stamp out steel parts. The partners needed capital in order to buy the industrial tools required to fulfill their increasing number of orders. The foursome put on their business best and tried to get a bank loan, but after a half-dozen rejects, Banducci remembered hearing about a man who was originally interested in buying the company from Otto. As it turned out, he had told Otto to call if the new owners ever wanted to sell the company. After a few calls, Banducci contacted the investor at his downtown San Francisco law firm. The lawyer, an avid kayaker, and a dozen of his friends who worked in the shipping industry formed an investment group that frequently helped burgeoning businesses get off the ground.

"We wrote a business plan," Banducci recalls, "and, dressed in a suit coat, tie, and blue jeans, Steve and I presented it to this group in a San Francisco skyscraper. We were asking for less than $100,000. Considering Yakima's annual sales were less than $150,000 for the year before, it was a significant investment relative to what they were purchasing."

The investors agreed. Though Banducci and Cole planned on buying back the percentage of the company they sold, the company flourished so quickly that the value of that percentage grew. They never did buy it back. The relationship between the investors and the company has been positive, though. Three of the investors sit on the company board, along with Banducci, Cole, and Hamilton. For ten years they have been supportive advisers, sharing their business and financial expertise. "Our partners steered us away from the cliff any number of times throughout the years," says Banducci.

With capital, a growing staff, and marked consumer demand, Yakima was a young company positioned for rapid growth in the early eighties. Two major factors directly contributed to its success: nationwide recovery from the ongoing recession and baby boomers reaching their income-producing years. As a result, many people were seeking outlets for their disposable income. Health, fitness, and outdoor recreation became the surest investment. Simultaneously, cars were becoming smaller and more fuel-efficient, and their owners still wanted to be able to transport their bicycles and skis.

From 1981 through 1986 the company doubled its sales volume each year. When sales reached $8 million, the annual growth slowed to 40 percent in 1987, then held at 30 percent. The company predicts 1992 sales will exceed $20 million.

Much of this is due to Yakima's continued focus on making the highest quality products available. "Steve's focus on technical function has made our products the best they could possibly be," says Banducci. In order to be the best, the company must employ highly skilled workers to design and develop the hundreds of intricate pieces that are used in the racks. Indeed, in the eighties, Yakima had trouble attracting top engineers to work in Arcata because it was too far from a major city. "Now," says Banducci, "if we run an ad in a Los Angeles or Sacramento newspaper, we get hundreds of responses."

Industrial designers and engineers, culled from both the computer and aerospace industries, work on technical, state-of-the-art computers, optical scanners, and CAD machines to contrive the rack's many parts. "These racks go on hundreds of different cars, and it's imperative that the fit is perfect," explains Cole. "Attention to detail is a must."

At the same time, through the years Yakima Products held true to the beliefs of its founder, Otto, and so enthusiastically embraced by his young protégés. The company catalog pays tribute to the now-deceased German, and its letterhead includes the words he often expressed: "Let us serve with honesty, wisdom, and skill."

The Company Today

Yakima's new office building and manufacturing facilities are within a few blocks of Arcata's celebrated square. Local residents can shop at a food co-op, visit a herbal therapist, and enjoy gourmet coffees and zucchini muffins at a downtown bistro.

The city of Arcata, much like Yakima Products, thrives in a county whose economy has withered. For the past century, the area's economy was extraction based. The timber, agricultural, and fishing industries accounted for the greatest source of income for generations of residents.

As resources have declined over the past thirty years, the unemployment rate has risen. Unemployment figures in 1991 rose to 12 percent in Humboldt County. The state of California, on the other hand, has as of the sumer of 1992 an unemployment rate of 10.5 percent.

"We take 'Think Globally, Act Locally' to heart here," says Banducci as he gives a visitor a tour around the large two-story building that now houses the administrative offices and the engineering and research and development teams. "The greatest impact we have is the fact we are located right here in Arcata and that we don't rely on local natural resources for our business."

Indeed, Arcata is not the most practical place to run a business. There is no interstate highway, and it is far from the suppliers who provide components used to make the racks, increasing freight in/ freight out costs. Traveling employees must often add an extra day to their plans in order to make connections at large-city airports. The company estimates it costs more than $300,000 per year to be located in Arcata.

Nevertheless, the company is committed to remaining in the community and adding to the area's economic prosperity. With its current 145 workers, many of whom were born in the area, Yakima's payroll exceeds $3 million per year.

But Yakima provides more than a source of income. It's a company that believes in worker empowerment. Yakima trains and educates its workers and believes in promoting them to higher levels. It helps employees work out personal and family problems, and management actively listens to its employees' concerns about the company.

Yakima built its new offices four years ago, after the company had outgrown the building across the street that now houses the manufacturing shop. Gray movable walls delineate the work area in a mazelike structure. "At first we thought we wanted a large, open work space, much like a newspaper office," explains Banducci. "But people learned they wanted a defined space and a sense of privacy."

Huge murals adorn several of the walls throughout the company. Images of families enjoying the outdoors enliven the entry hall and lunchroom. Another similar mural is in progress in the main office. They are the work of artist Duane Flatmo, a lifelong Humboldt County resident famous in the area for his cubist-style drawings. His work is found on numerous walls—the outside of a barn along the highway, in the middle of town on a pharmacy exterior—throughout Arcata and neighboring Eureka. "We believe in supporting local artists, and there is no one more fitting than Duane," says Banducci.

Yakima will pay the artist a total of $22,000 over a two-year period to paint the murals and use the images in the company catalog, in its ads, and on promotional materials.

Yakima is a company that embraces the needs of its community and its employees. Martha, the company's personnel manager for the past six years, is the self-described Yakima "den mother." In addition, she feels her role is to keep supervisors "supertrained" on how to effectively manage employees.

"We have paid for drug and alcohol recovery programs for our employees and have provided loans to buy home computers," she says. "We also pay for half of any educational program, whether it's a college degree or a special training situation."

The company offers full health and dental benefits to its employees as well. "Yes, Yakima is good to its employees, and I'm sorry to say it's not the norm in this county," says Martha.

With such a high unemployment rate in the surrounding area and a well-trained applicant pool of college graduates who want to stay in the area, many local companies skimp on benefits. "But not here," says Martha. And the word around town is that Yakima is a great place to work.

In fact, more than three hundred people apply for each entry-level position on the shop-room floor. Wages start at $4.50 per hour, and the average hourly salary in production is $6.50.

In the company's voluminous shop floor, workers wear protective eyewear as they bolt, drill, and assemble the heavy-duty zinc pieces used to make Yakima racks. Nineteen laborers and two expediters are responsible for turning out more than 100,000 roof racks per year. The workers smile and acknowledge a tour of visitors who watch them operate their machinery. "These particular mounts are for sports cars," says Michelle, who has worked on the shop floor for more than three years. The crew of four creates a mini–production line. Workers are cross-trained so that they can assemble any number of the 150 products Yakima offers. The various models are specific to the year, make, and model of car that the buyer owns.

Besides the machine-shop workers, Yakima employs several developmentally challenged workers from the Redwood United Organization. One of them, Sherry, puts accessory pieces in a plastic bag and seals them. She smiles as she works.

"These employees don't work on the machines, but in every other way they are totally integrated with the rest of the company," says Tracey, manager of the production facility. "It's amazing to see the progress they make after a while."

Others agree that working at Yakima is a positive experience. "We have a good familylike atmosphere here, and that helps us all enjoy our days," says Duke, a three-year employee. The production workers also feel a sense of pride. "We may not get out of town too much," says Michelle. "But it's great to know that our work is all around the country. It's nice that these racks are made in Arcata."

Many workers here are excited about their prospects for advancement. The company actively promotes from within. Indeed, more than a dozen former manufacturing workers have been promoted to supervisor and manager levels in the warranty and shipping departments and customer service.

Different Views

Yakima is environmentally sensitive. Like many conscientious businesses in America today, the company observes Earth Day each year by organizing employees in a one-day cleanup activity. In 1990, the company further celebrated the day by running one-page ads in *Outside* and *Bicycling* magazines that effectively communicated their company philosophy:

> We made our stand in Humboldt County because of our love for the people, the ocean, the rivers, and the redwoods. As ne'er-do-wells of the sixties we had an appropriate contempt for malignant capitalism. So we went into business to make honest, durable products that would help people have fun outside. We hoped to one day be a model for our country's economic future: an energetic, non-polluting, light manufacturing business, and a strong alternative voice on economic and social issues not often or popularly embraced by local business.

In Arcata, California, that alternative voice has expressed an anti–corporate timber message: They don't want big business ruining the forests. Much of this came to a head in the most recent timber crisis during the summer of 1990, known in the area as the Redwood Summer.

In the late 1980s, Houston-based Maxxam Corporation acquired Pacific Lumber, one of Humboldt County's most respected and responsible lumber companies, through a leveraged buy-out (LBO). Up until that time, the family-owned business had a long-term timber harvest policy that focused on maintaining a sustained production yield. Because of this long-term practice, Pacific Lumber owned some of the only old-growth redwood trees remaining in the country.

Under the direction of the new owners, however, Pacific Lumber doubled and some say tripled its cut rate within a year. It downed not only the second-growth trees but old-growth ones as well. Many of the trees were more than six thousand years old. The reaction around Humboldt County, whose residents saw their landscape quickly deteriorating before their eyes, was profound.

Timberworkers, many of whom were following in the steps of their fathers and grandfathers, saw the action as a necessary step to feed their families. Environmentalists, on the other hand, saw a precious and irreplaceable resource being recklessly destroyed. Pacific Lumber's blatant action ignited a fury that had been simmering for a decade.

"The last remnant of old growth was going down, and only because Maxxam needed more money fast to pay off their loan," says Banducci.

The Arcata community, as well as Yakima Products, reacted to the controversy. The local environmental newspaper, the *EcoNews,* ran editorials blasting the most recent pilfering of the timber industry and Pacific Lumber. "We weren't against the timber workers," Banducci goes on to explain. "We were against the action that was the result of corporate raidership." The timber industry and its supporters took the editorials as a direct attack. The timber workers called a boycott of any business that advertised in the monthly publication. Given the numbers of people and the economic power they wielded, advertisers quickly felt the effect of the boycott. They had lost half of their potential customers.

Although many of the advertisers cut their ad schedules, Yakima Products reacted in an opposite vein. The company actually increased its support of *EcoNews.* Yakima bought a half-page space on the editorial page and wrote pointed ad copy that renounced the timber industry's most recent activities.

Banducci wrote the opinionated pieces. One such statement described how the high cost of timber had forced him to downscale plans on his new home:

> Lumber prices are going through the roof! . . . All because of Spotted Owls, canceled timber sales, and the shrinking log supply. . . . As for our own house, we'll down-scale, simplify, and pay the higher price for the lumber we do use with no hard feeling. On balance, we choose spotted owls over vaulted ceiling, wild steel head over an expanse of deck. And while the old-growth clear-heart Redwood siding would look perfect in our wooded setting and last for a long, long time, I'd rather see it upright on the slopes of Salmon Creek than on the side of my house.

The ads were signed "Don Banducci, president, Yakima Products" and included the company logo. The pieces provoked controversy within both the community and the company. Employees were harassed by family and friends who worked in the timber industry. People wearing Yakima T-shirts in town were cursed and spat on. Some employees felt their president had gone too far and brought this up at a companywide meeting.

"I shot from the hip," explains the ever-enthusiastic Banducci. "People very quickly knew that I was anti–timber policy. That's not to say I'm antilogger or anti–mill worker. But this place had been ransacked and raped over the last century, and yes, I did and do feel upset about it.

"What I forgot was that it wasn't just me, Maggie, Steve, and Jan at the company. In writing the ads, I was speaking for more than a hundred people, many of whom don't share or can't share my somewhat harsh views," says Banducci.

Banducci responded to his upset employees by writing a heartfelt letter explaining why he feels so passionate about saving the wilds of Humboldt County. He also apologized.

"It is not my intention to alienate people within the company, nor to turn a segment of the community against the people of Yakima," he wrote. "In the future, if I feel the need to personally editorialize, I will do it as a private citizen in the Letters to the Editor column."

Yakima employees appreciated this gesture. "His ability to see both sides of the situation was insightful and appreciated. It was a great thing," says Charlie, manager of the company's product-development department. "He had to separate his private feelings and his company rhetoric."

Other employees agree. "Our entire area is divided on this issue, so it's no surprise that we are polarized within this company as well," says Martha, the personnel manager. "It was tough for many employees who felt threatened by the outside forces and couldn't admit that they work at Yakima. And most of us have husbands, brothers, fathers, and uncles who have or who do work in timber. The employees let Don know that they don't want him speaking for the entire company."

Though Yakima continues to run monthly advertorials in the *EcoNews,* the tone of the articles is less blasting, less accusatory. Like many people involved in the controversy, the company wants to get its message across, but in a more positive, constructive manner. And it is opening its doors to timberworkers looking for new work: The company has hired several ex–lumber workers. "It may seem that we have softened on some of the issues," says Banducci today. "But, in fact, we've replaced words and emotion with money and time to help make our little piece of the planet healthier. Business isn't an end in itself to us. It's a means to another end."

Looking Ahead

Since its origin, Yakima Products has always been a company that practiced what it preached. While its competitors package its racks in glossy boxes with four-color photos, Yakima ships its products in recycled cardboard. The company catalog as well is printed on recycled paper.

Yakima's careful attention to reducing the amount of waste it produces is exemplified in a current packaging decision. Yakima recently introduced a new lock system that can be placed on both the racks and the components that hold skis and bicycles. Since the locks are far more expensive to produce than they appear to be, the company knew it would have to produce attractive packaging to enhance the product's appeal.

"To stick four locks in a plastic bag with a cardboard header wouldn't have worked," says Banducci. However, the idea of creating extra waste to sell a product went totally against the company's philosophy. So Yakima responded by developing a cardboard box and internal components, such as foam, that can be returned to Yakima after the locks are installed by the end-use customer. Yakima pays for the postage, and anyone who does return the package is enlisted in the company's "Key Club." Members are entitled to free replacement keys. Yakima reuses the returned components in future packaging.

Throughout Yakima's decade-long growth spurt, company leaders also have learned the importance of bringing in additional employees who, as Banducci says, "know much more about something than we do." As the company looked to increase its distribution base within the United States as well as in Europe and Japan, it knew it needed a person with good business experience. After a nationwide search, Yakima brought in its new CEO, Bruce Hamilton, in April 1990.

"We want to be a world-class company," says Hamilton. "That means we want to sell our products around the world and produce them in a fashion that is true to the beliefs of our founders, that Yakima shall 'serve with honesty, wisdom, and skill.'"

As the company looks to broaden its scope both within the United States and abroad, Yakima Products plans to further influence those closest to its hearts—and its home.

The company's president, Banducci, expresses his sentiment similarly. "You know what it's like when nature speaks to you. Once you've seen how it all fits together, and that you're a part of it, and how miraculous it all is, you can't go back. You can start a business, raise a family, mow the lawn, watch TV. But you can't turn your back on the knowledge that there is something out there far more powerful than oneself. And everything you do should reflect that sense of wonder, respect and humility. That's what Yakima is about for me. It is our instrument."

12

The Spirit of Esprit

Company name: Esprit de Corp
Type of business: clothing manufacturer
Location: San Francisco headquarters, with company-owned stores in Los Angeles, Costa Mesa, Santa Clara, and Sherman Oaks, California and Aspen, Colorado
Number of employees: 1,200
Year founded: 1968

It's a mid-April morning at northern California's Briones State Park. Two dozen workers clad in matching T-shirts pick up shovels, spades, and trowels. While some members of the group clear away weeds and rocks from an overgrown hiking trail, others are rebuilding a deteriorating fence high up on a ridge. It's Earth Day, 1992, and the workers, employees of San Francisco–based Esprit de Corp, have abandoned their desk jobs for the day to help preserve the environment. Other Esprit employees are performing similar duties throughout the Bay Area: trail restoration at Muir Woods and on Angel Island, tree planting at a state penitentiary, and at Golden Gate Park employees are clearing a grove.

"This is a companywide event," says Quincey Tompkins, twenty-six, director of the company's Environmental Department, known as the EcoDesk, and daughter of Esprit founders Doug and Susie Tompkins. In fact, 80 percent of the 550 San Francisco–based employees devote the day to maintaining the pristine beauty that is so important in both their professional and personal lives.

Esprit is one of the country's most renowned manufacturers of women's, junior, and children's clothing as well as shoes, accessories, and bed linens. In addition to twenty-five of its own outlets, the company sells its products to hundreds of department stores throughout the United States. With domestic sales reaching an estimated $350 million per year and a longtime commitment to addressing social causes, the company is one of the largest and most famous of all socially conscious businesses. Currently, Esprit also does business in thirty-five countries through partnerships and licensing agreements.

Besides the annual Earth Day excursions, the company is involved in a variety of social and environmental programs: An in-house speaker series provides information on business, environment, and social issues; employees are encouraged to embrace volunteer activities, including group cleanup and renovation projects, caring for crack-addicted babies, and feeding the homeless; a multi-million-dollar ad campaign addresses the issues most important to its youthful customers; and, most recently, the company introduced a clothing line that was designed and manufactured to have less detrimental environmental impact than other contemporary garments. Finally, the nonprofit Esprit Foundation provides grants to educationally oriented causes. Company employees who are involved in such projects can submit proposals for grant funds.

From its origin in the late sixties, Esprit was known as one of the most refreshing companies in the competitive fashion industry, primarily due to the innovative approaches to business its founders adopted. Esprit's social and environmental dedication attracts much media attention and greatly influences millions of devoted customers. For this reason, it has become a big player within the fashion world.

Entering a New Era

Susie Russell met Doug Tompkins in 1963, when she picked him up hitchhiking in California's Lake Tahoe area. She worked as a card

dealer at a Nevada casino; he was a tree topper. After a brief court-
ship, the couple married and moved to the Bay Area, where Doug
opened a ski and outdoors shop in San Francisco's North Beach. In
1969, Susie started a dress company with her friend Jane Tise. The
company, which primarily manufactured simple all-cotton dresses,
was initially called Plain Jane. In 1971, however, the name was
changed to Esprit de Corp. After selling his retail store, Doug managed Susie's thriving business, and in 1976 the couple bought out Tise
and another partner.

Esprit's fresh designs of dressy sportswear quietly caught on. Esprit
styles were fashionable, not trendy, and its exciting colors and style
became a favorite of the booming junior sportswear market.

In 1979, Esprit launched its line of clothing with a colorful, oversized catalog featuring the "Esprit Girl." The company asked
employees to model the clothing. The poses were accompanied by
quotes like "One of my favorite things to do is just stay in my night-
gown all day." The promotional campaign generated mail-order sales
and sales within the growing number of major department stores that
sold the line. Retailers, such as Bloomingdales and Marshall Fields,
opened specially designed Esprit boutiques. Esprit was flourishing; its
products were soon selling throughout the world.

As a result, Esprit became one of the most successful husband-and-
wife entrepreneurial efforts in the country. In the first half of the
1980s, sales for the company increased 500 percent, to $800 million
worldwide.

Many believe Esprit's success was due to its ability to sell life-style.
The image of young, healthy, and active women was evident not only
in its ads but in all levels of the company. Employees were treated to
foreign-language lessons and lavish overseas adventure trips and had
use of the company-owned ski cabin in the Sierras. In fact, Esprit
soon became known as "little Utopia," for all of its employee perks.

In 1984, Esprit aggressively entered retailing, opening fifteen stores
in eight cities, reportedly costing the company $50 million. Within a
few years, however, the strain of company-owned stores would prove
to be too great; many were sold to franchisers. Today the company
owns six Esprit stores, nine outlets, and it franchises twelve stores
throughout the United States.

In 1987, Esprit's rise to success abruptly faltered. Though sales had reached $412 million in the United States, profits fell to only $5 million. At the same time, the couple's marriage was unraveling as they disagreed over the company's direction. Susie preferred to focus on the maturing working woman; Doug wanted to continue designing for the junior market. In 1988, Susie physically left the company, and Doug became chief executive officer (CEO). In December 1989, the couple put their company up for sale. The time for its employees was tense.

"Doug did his best to keep our morale up, but it was tough," says Una, a designer with Esprit since 1985. Not knowing the company's fate was a growing concern for everyone involved. Finally, one June morning in 1990, the company's employees were invited to meet outside in the park. "Doug and Susie both stood up there and said that it was important to them that the company not be sold to strangers, that they had agreed that Susie would take over the company," says Una. "There was such a feeling of relief, there were tears in everyone's eyes."

Susie Tompkins, with three shareholders, completed the buy-out in June 1990. Doug reportedly received $125 million, far less than if the company had been sold on the block. Since then, Doug has started a foundation that is acquiring threatened land in southern Chile's rain forest.

"The experience of having left and having all that time to myself was very important to me," Susie said to a magazine reporter at the time of the sale. "I learned so much being away. But this company is my life. I have spent my whole adult life here, and it was strange not being here."

In the end, the couple knew they had a lot more in common than the differences that were so widely publicized in the industry and business press. They were both committed to reducing the amount of environmental damage needed to produce their products, for instance. Both Susie and Doug believed in contributing to the environment and to the communities in which they do business. Both stressed the importance of worker empowerment and the capacity for goodwill their employees can share with the community.

Doug knew he wanted to keep the company in the family rather than risk its going to someone who would destroy the culture he so carefully cultivated over the years.

In spite of the turmoil within the company during this time, Esprit never lost its passion for being a conscientious business. Many of the programs in place today, including the company's EcoDesk, its speaker series, and its corporate giving program, were developed during the late 1980s. These programs have since flourished.

Committed in the 1990s

Following the successful company sale, Esprit experienced a rebirth. "The eighties were about style and life-style," Susie Tompkins, a petite blonde, says today from her sunny corner office in the company's design area. Books, shoes, magazines, photos, and a large bowl of apples lend a homey, inviting ambience to her office. "The nineties are about soul searching . . . about encouraging volunteerism. Before, we gave our employees French lessons, sent them on river trips—all of those personal things. Now we're giving them character-building opportunities," the fifty-year-old Tompkins says.

At the end of 1991, for example, the company did not hold a holiday celebration. Rather, each department was given a small budget to host a Christmas party for a needy group—a senior-citizen center, a shelter for homeless families, a halfway house for teenagers. The Esprit groups brought trees, decorations, food, and refreshments and put on a Christmas party for people who needed it more than they did. In addition, the company gave presents, ranging from canvas bags for senior citizens to blue jeans for the teenagers.

A few months earlier, more than three hundred employees participated in the company-sponsored Labor Day workday. Event organizers received "wish lists" from a San Francisco community center and a rehab center for the homeless. The employees devoted a Saturday to stripping, painting, and cleaning. The company donated more than $16,000 worth of materials.

To many associated with Esprit, such actions have long-term advantages. "These programs give me something that is not quantifiable," says Tompkins. "Helping our employees contribute and feel good about what they do and who they are buys us a loyalty that money cannot."

The employees agree. "This is my third Earth Day event," says Simon, who works in the company's production department. "It's great to get out here, to achieve a goal for the day, and to collectively make a difference."

While Esprit continues to lead the way for socially conscientious corporations, its leader realizes the need to focus on its product. "We're not a foundation doing handouts," says Tompkins. "In order to do good, we have to put out a good-looking product at the right price." Creating a balance between social causes and commerce is Esprit's challenge for the upcoming decade. With retail businesses floundering, Esprit knows it must also adapt. "It's important to focus. Things are changing, and we must be fast and strong and flexible and create a product that will make sense to buy. It has to be a good value.

"We've never been a company that makes clothes," continues Tompkins. "Rather, we're a company that makes clothes, and a profit, and has good social values. And because we make a profit, we can contribute to the community and learn from that and grow. Though we're not a bottom-line-driven company, we clearly have to make money so we can do good things."

With annual sales remaining level for the past several years, many industry observers believe the company must expand its scope to create the demand Esprit experienced throughout the eighties. Therefore, the company has developed new products, such as Susie Tompkins's own line of serious go-to-work clothing targeted for the twenty-five-and-over crowd. Launched in New York City in February 1992, the line's foremost message wasn't about styles and colors but about social justice. Though the crowd of savvy store buyers and press assembled in the company's showroom was accustomed to slick presentations by professional runway models, the new line of mid-priced clothing was introduced by the Reverend Cecil Williams, minister of San Francisco's Glide Memorial Church. After leading a chorus of "Amen," he launched into a sermon about social justice.

"We were attempting to inject some reality into the fashion world," says Tompkins, who believes her industry is sometimes too shallow. "I'm an activist in my personal world, and I want to share that with the buyers and journalists."

Infusing her personal convictions into her business life has remained important to Tompkins. "Esprit has always been an extension of our life-style. Going to the office is like going to another part of my home. I don't wear different clothes, and I keep the same hat on. I talk to people the same way, and I think with my heart," she says. Tompkins's mission with Esprit is easily stated: "My aim is to have Esprit inspire good values," she says.

In fact, one of her first duties when she returned to Esprit was to rewrite the company mission statement. "We hired meeting facilitators, and we went over and over what we wanted to say," Tompkins remembers. Finally, the collective group of Esprit employees came up with a simple three-line statement: "Be informed. Be involved. Make a difference."

Tompkins feels if you follow this, everything else falls in place.

Fashion and Flair

It's immediately obvious when entering Esprit's wood-beamed offices in a quiet San Francisco neighborhood that this is a company with a unique knack for good taste. Various departments are sectioned off by tinted glass, so that the executives work in full view of their employees. Tasteful floral arrangements from the nearby flower mart adorn desks and tables throughout. The company's Amish quilt collection, once shown at a nearby museum, graces the walls. Recycling baskets are stored at every work station. Across the street, a full fitness center holds noontime aerobics classes, and sporting-goods equipment, such as tents, windsurfers, and kayaks, are available for employees to borrow.

The company's in-house café, selling healthy lunches, a slew of teas, and fresh-squeezed juices, bristles with activity at all hours of the day. No paper products are used here; employees eat off china and stir their gourmet coffees with stainless-steel spoons. At the San Francisco headquarters, this in-house café served gourmet California-style meals, as it does today. Esprit bought and built a nearby park so employees could enjoy their lunches outdoors. The bulletin boards list company-sponsored events, including a fund-raiser for U.S. senatorial candidate Barbara Boxer and an upcoming rafting trip. Voter-registration cards are available below a sign reminding employees that the deadline to register is quickly approaching.

"All of our offices are central, and we don't have a conference room, so this is where we often hold meetings," explains Una, the designer, as she sips her carrot juice. Next to the café is an outdoor terrace. Esprit, she says, has adopted a European attitude toward work. Employees are encouraged to take an hour lunch break and not just eat a quick sandwich at their desks. In fact, the company forbids its employees to eat at their desks, and all drinks must be placed in insulated cups with tops. "The thought is that if you are hungry or thirsty," Una explains, "then your body is telling you you need to get away from your desk and your phone and take a break. Then you will return refreshed."

For Una, working at Esprit has been an invigorating change from her days as a designer with Seventh Avenue–based fashion firms. Working at Esprit, with its emphasis on human values, opened her eyes. "I had never realized how caught up the New York fashion world is in material things. Here they know there is something to the bigger picture," she says.

Dan, who works in the company's international communications department, agrees. "Esprit is a conduit for what is going on in society," he says. "We are young in attitude, aware, encouraged to be fit, to read, and to basically get more out of life." Indeed, one of the company's main goals is to educate, inform, and therefore inspire its employees.

Education as Success

The company's large showroom has been cleared of racks of product samples and is now filled with more than four hundred Esprit employees. Petite women from the sewing room sit on the carpeted floor beside burly shipping-room workers as everyone nibbles on their lunch. They have all gathered to listen to feminist and best-selling author Gloria Steinem encourage them to contribute to society.

Esprit employees have anticipated this gathering for weeks. Standing before them on a stage set with dramatic flower arrangements, the author and activist tells her audience to do something "outrageous" in the days ahead of them, to act on a belief they feel, and to make a difference. The audience reacts with booming enthusiasm and applauds the speaker. A professional film crew tapes both the speech and the reactions of the crowd. The resulting videotape will be distributed to Esprit offices and retail outlets throughout the world.

Though Steinem's visit is undoubtedly considered a special event, it is by no means unprecedented. Since 1986, the company has regularly invited people with messages to speak at its corporate offices.

"Although we take what we do very seriously, we don't believe the world revolves around the fashion industry," reads a brochure explaining the company's social and environmental programs. "Education and understanding current affairs are an essential part of our jobs and our lives."

To company cofounder Susie Tompkins, the speaker series provides a chance for her to share her contacts and inspirations with her employees. "I've had the pleasure of knowing Gloria for many years and have had lunch with her several times," says Tompkins after the speech. "She's such a guiding light to me, and I wanted to share her with everyone here."

Every two months, speakers ranging from The Body Shop's Anita Roddick to Ben Cohen of Ben & Jerry's Homemade and author Jeremy Rifkin come to educate, inform, and inspire Esprit employees at companywide gatherings. In addition, Esprit invites representatives from a variety of Bay Area environmental programs to speak during lunch hour. "In the past few weeks we've had a representative of the Marine Mammal Center talk about the facility," says Quincy. "Plus, we've had a representative of an electric car company and another speaker who talked about arms proliferation." When an employee recently got lost in a Sierra Mountain snowstorm during a backcountry ski trip, he told his fellow employees about his two-night ordeal on his first day back at work. A week later, the company brought in an expert on mountain safety.

Most employees relish the brown-bag programs. "I'm very much into marine life and have learned so much through our programs here," says Alfonso, the company's twenty-eight-year-old shipping and receiving manager. "I did not go to college, and in many ways I feel like I'm getting a good education here, with so many interesting programs all the time. It's an opportunity to learn."

It's also an opportunity to act. At the company's EcoDesk, or social and environmental affairs department, three full-time workers act as the "conscience of the company," says Quincey. They book the speakers, organize group volunteer activities, control the company sponsorship program, run the company's Eco Audit, and arrange for employees to organize tennis and yoga classes. A company Culture

Club reimburses employees up to 50 percent for two tickets to plays throughout the year. But the trips, once fully company subsidized, have been toned down. Esprit does organize rafting, canoe, and kayak excursions for its employees, but participants pay a percentage of their own way. Employees are encouraged to join the Esprit Corps. According to its employee manual,

> Esprit is dedicated to making the Earth a better, healthier place for all its inhabitants. Each one of us has a role to play, for example, by teaching someone to read, running errands for an elderly person or someone with AIDS, cradling a baby born addicted to drugs, working on environmental issues, or organizing a letter writing campaign. . . . To provide support for such volunteer work, the Esprit Corps . . . allows up to ten hours per month paid leave—to be matched by a similar amount of the employee's time—for an approved volunteer activity.

Esprit is committed to providing employees with endless opportunities to grow and develop both as professionals and as people.

The result, many Esprit employees believe, is that they are far more interesting—as well as interested—people. "The effort to educate makes this a much more fascinating place to work," Una says. "There is a great encouragement to read, be informed, and be interested in the important issues around us. Most of us thoroughly read the paper every day, and we stay on top of what's going on around us. We don't just talk shop around here."

Indeed, a job at Esprit is well coveted. The company receives close to one thousand unsolicited résumés each month from applicants throughout the country. The company looks for employees who are energetic and flexible. "No two days are alike around here, so employees have to be able to shift priorities very quickly," says Esprit's human resources manager, Daryle, who has been with the company four years. The work force is 70 percent female. Daryle feels the high number of résumés is due to Susie Tompkins. "Women read about her or see her on the news and believe in what she says and who she is," he says.

The company also is attractive to people who will mesh with the corporate culture. "We want people who will be influenced by what we have here," says Tompkins. "It is a benefit to hear speakers, to go on rafting trips, to contribute to the community." The company's EcoDesk includes a library with videotapes of the speakers and a wide variety of books on environmental and social issues. They are available to all employees.

Putting Words Into Action

As of 1990, the company was fully entrenched in becoming a committed, conscientious company. It had written about environmental concerns in its catalogs, changed its paper and stationery to recycled stocks with soybean-based inks, and initiated the companywide social and environmental programs.

As early as 1986, in fact, Esprit hosted an AIDS-awareness day. Seven speakers, including doctors, hospice workers, and AIDS victims, spoke before the hundreds of employees. "I had the misfortune and the fortune of losing my best friend to AIDs," Susie remembers. "The misfortune was losing and missing someone I love. The fortune was it motivated me to do something about it, and helping those closest to me understand AIDS was a first step."

In 1987, the company followed up by devoting a full page in its catalog to a piece designed to increase AIDS awareness. The catalog, which was sent to 1.4 million customers, included the National AIDS Hotline number.

At the same time, Esprit looked at its own industry a little differently: Besides examining the look and feel of the fabrics and raw materials used in Esprit clothing, the company examined how the materials were designed and produced.

"Food can provide an excellent example," explains the company literature. "A piece of fruit can look impeccable on the outside. But there may be another story underneath, something you can't see or feel. There could have been heavy applications of pesticides and herbicides on the trees, which contaminate the soil and groundwater. On the other hand, it could have been grown with no synthetic substances at all."

In the fall of 1990, Dan, who works in the company's communications department, read an article in *Utne Reader* magazine about the amount of pesticides, herbicides, and fertilizers used in cotton fabric production. Disturbed by what he read, he passed the article on to Doug Tompkins, then the company's president. Within days the article was posted on the design-room bulletin board. Soon another article about the effects of stonewashing denim appeared alongside it. Considering the hundreds of thousands of yards Esprit uses to make its clothing, the company knew it was in a position to act on this situation.

The articles prompted Lynda, then a four-year Esprit designer, to look into possible alternatives. The energetic woman researched unexplored areas of manufacturing like processes that minimize resources and wastes and simultaneously value hand labor. "She was looking at design and manufacturing from an ecological point of view," says Dan.

Dan and Linda first took a trip to North Carolina, where they met with mill representatives who produce natural fabrics. "Being at Esprit, we were in a nice position," says Dan. "We were interested, and we came from a large, influential corporation, and the mills had to act on our requests to develop the fabrics in less harmful ways.

"Esprit gave Linda the space to do the research, and that in itself is quite special. There was a lot of time and company resources directed toward the effort. No other major clothing manufacturer had ever done anything like this," says Dan.

"How you make something is just as important as the finished product, and Esprit has started a journey of self-examination," says Linda.

The dozen-plus pieces in the resultant Ecollection introduced in March 1992 include skirts, pants, jackets, and blouses in natural, unbleached, undyed linens and cottons, poplins, denims, and knits. The colors are earth-friendly—greens, warm browns, and natural. The charter for Ecollection incorporated many environmental ideas, such as reduced packaging. Esprit also eliminated or modified various manufacturing processes, such as chemical washing and finishing garments, stopping electroplating treatments on metal zippers, snaps, or other hardware, choosing dying methods with low impact, and supporting organic and sustainable agriculture whenever possible.

The Ecollection design charter also included a nondesign objective: to support endangered areas and cultures and work with artisans. For instance, the company buys hand-painted buttons from a rural North Carolina artisan group, and it uses cotton that grows naturally colored; it therefore does not need dyes. Finally, the line eliminates harmful hardware processes: Colored alloys replace the usual electro-plating process for zipper finishes.

That the company launched such a line is remarkable, particularly since doing so further emphasizes how damaging the rest of its clothing production can be. As Esprit discovers further ways to reduce this negative impact, it plans to incorporate several of the methods used in Ecollection in its other clothing lines as well.

Sending the Right Message

A huge blowup of a recent Esprit advertisement hangs in the front entrance of its corporate headquarters. A headline asks: "What Would You Do?" The ad responds: "End racism and the killing of people in the streets." In the café, another ad on the bulletin board reads, "Pay the police to serve and protect. Not maim and beat."

It is two days after a Southern California jury rendered its astonishing verdict in the Rodney King case, and like the rest of the nation, employees of Esprit are stunned by both the verdict and the violence that resulted in Los Angeles. These ads, produced just months prior to the chaos permeating the nation, were two of dozens used in Esprit's $10 million campaign on television, in fashion magazines, and in stores.

Replies to its question were chosen from the more than three thousand responses offered by Esprit customers who replied to an invitation in the spring 1991 catalog. "If you could change the world," it asked, "what would you do?" The answers ranged from clever and witty to serious and thought provoking:

- "Keep a woman's right to choose unless George Bush is free to baby-sit," Rachel Hirsch, Massachusetts.
- "I'd teach everybody that nobody is a nobody," Shannon Going, California.
- "I'd ban high heels and teach the world to groove," Angelle Brooks, California.

Not surprisingly, the ads provoked a nationwide response. While thousands of customers heartily embraced the campaign, others objected. Letters poured into Esprit's offices and pro-life groups threatened a boycott of Esprit products. The company decided to suspend the campaign. "If we had all of our own stores, it would be one thing," says Tompkins. "But we are in department stores where business is less than great right now. In terms of advertising, we have to be softer." The company's newest ad campaign features the product more than a message.

While some employees felt the company was buckling under pressure, Tompkins feels its decision to curb the campaign was right. "Today I think we are all proud with our $10 million campaign of last year. We addressed important issues. But I know the importance of balancing commerce and social goodwill. Now it's time to focus on making money."

This goal included stabilizing management and finding a business leader. A yearlong executive search resulted in the April 1993 appointment of David Folkman as president and CEO. "We needed someone with a heart and soul and also someone with good business acumen," says Tompkins. "We knew right away that David was right. His values matched our own, and he has a clear perspective of what business should be doing."

Indeed, in the emotionally charged hours following the King verdict, Tompkins's conviction that businesses need to address social issues grows even stronger. "The government is just not doing it— they can't do it," she says. "It's up to businesses, and it's up to us."

And though finding the balance between producing a profit and promoting change is integral to the company's success, the maturing company, like its founder, is altering its focus. "Ten years ago I would have been thrilled to get a fashion-design award," says Tompkins. "Now our inner-city work is what makes me most proud, and knowing that we are working to change things. That's what it's all about to me now. I want to make a difference."

With a focused line of clothing, a committed work force, and a founder embracing the issues close to her heart, Esprit is likely to do just that.

13

The Additional Enlightened

There are many other companies that are excellent examples of corporate and social responsibility. The following case studies are therefore presented to recognize these businesses and to illustrate the vast array of activities that companies with a conscience are currently implementing to advance their social goals.

Newman's Own Inc.

These days, movie stars are often as well known for their offscreen antics as their on-screen performances. One of today's most famous, Paul Newman, is unique because his private-life notoriety comes partially from his establishment of a multi-million-dollar food company. And partially because Newman's Own foods—founded in 1982 by the actor and his friend, author and playwright A. E. Hotchner—gives away 100 percent of its after tax profits. To date, the private company, based in Westport, Connecticut, has donated more than $50 million to hundreds of charities while selling more than $60 million in salad dressings, popcorn, lemonade, pasta sauces, and salsa in 1991 alone.

"What I particularly like about this company," Newman says from his office, "is that we furnish people with wholesome food that they enjoy. And this enables us to take the profits we make and give them to the unfortunate people of the country who, because of poverty, sickness, old age, or illiteracy, need help. That's what makes this business such a kick—this mutually beneficial recycling from the 'haves' to the 'have-nots.'"

The company was created after Newman spent many December evenings packaging homemade salad dressings in old wine bottles for Christmas gifts to friends. He and Hotchner eventually decided to market the dressing, believing what was good enough for their friends was good enough for the general public. They contracted with a small bottling company in Boston and sold the product locally under the label of Newman's Own olive oil and vinegar dressing. Within months, stores across the country were requesting it.

The two friends invested $40,000 to set up Newman's Own, Inc., with Newman as the president, Hotchner as executive vice-president and treasurer, and the author's wife, Ursula Hotchner, as senior vice-president. To economize, they furnished their offices with Newman's poolside furniture and a Ping-Pong table. Many of the furnishings are still used today.

From the beginning, Newman's Own defied industry tradition. Instead of spending hundreds of thousands of dollars on test marketing and research—which is customary in the food business—Newman invited friends over for a tasting. Everyone loved it, and that took care of test marketing. Today the company remains lean. Only ten employees work in the unpretentious headquarters, and Newman's Own goods are produced in fourteen North American factories. The company keeps tight control over product quality.

It was Newman's desire to produce healthful products, without preservatives and additives, that initially drove him to launch the company. In fact, the company has prospered despite the fact that the principals held no previous business experience. "There are three rules for running a business," Newman once told Hotchner, according to company lore. "Unfortunately, we don't know any of them."

But the company does know a market when it sees it. Many of the actor's favorite recipes, including those for lemonade, salsa, and pasta sauces, are now sold throughout the world. Its ingredients are natural, and its packages are as environmentally friendly as possible. Newman's image adorns the simple, homemade-looking product labels, which also include whimsical poems written by the actor himself.

Each year, Newman and the Hotchners pore through thousands of grant requests and, according to Hotchner, "simply give to the need-iest." Such recipients include a Sacred Heart nun in Florida who ran a school for the children of migrant farm workers. When her school bus broke down, she wrote Newman a letter and soon received a $26,000 check for a new one. Most impressive of all is the Hole In The Wall Gang Camp for children with cancer. Operated free of charge for the campers, it was opened with proceeds from salad-dressing and spaghetti sauce sales and now continues thanks to an endowment.

"There is always room for innovation and top-quality products," says Newman. "Our success is due to the fact that our products taste great and are of the highest quality, and one hundred percent of the profits are donated to charity."

Cultural Survival Enterprises

Operating out of Cambridge, Massachusetts, this company helps residents of the Amazon rain forest increase their incomes while working to save their home from destruction. Headed by Dr. Jason Clay—an anthropologist who also serves as research director of Cultural Survival Inc., a related nonprofit organization that was formed to protect the rights of indigenous people throughout the world—it is essentially a trading company that deals exclusively in rain-forest products.

The idea behind this for-profit firm is simple: Rain forests will have a better chance of staving off destruction if people who live there are provided with the means to simultaneously conserve their resources and make a decent living. (To earn enough to survive now, farmers and other producers usually must harvest more than is environmentally prudent.)

Clay's group helps these producers create cooperatives that offer their products at fair market prices, thus allowing them to earn more while harvesting less. It buys some of these products itself to sell to companies in the United States, which must then share their profits with the producers. And it introduces modern business strategies and new methods for using previously underutilized local products, such as the cashew fruit.

The organization's programs have proved financially sound, as has its efforts to raise the visibility of usable products harvested in the region. Ben & Jerry's and Patagonia are among the U.S. companies that have responded to its pleas by purchasing rain-forest products. The John D. and Catherine T. MacArthur Foundation, which dispenses grants on an annual basis, has also committed to providing loans that assist the activities of local producers.

Wynkoop Brewing Company

Alcohol and community development may seem an unlikely mix, but John Hickenlooper—the driving force behind this "brew pub" in Denver's historic Lower Downtown—has made a conscientious effort to change that. Since its 1988 opening as the first restaurant in Colorado that brewed and sold its own beer, his Wynkoop Brewing Company has become a commercial success as well as a model of social responsibility.

Hickenlooper, a geologist who found himself without a job in the mid-eighties, jumped on the brew-pub trend early after seeing the concept become popular in California. He and several partners raised the necessary funds, completely remodeled the lower two stories of a 72,000-square-foot warehouse built in 1899, and opened their doors just as Denver was emerging from a lengthy economic slump. Their effort was an instant hit, and the Wynkoop now serves as many as eleven hundred a day and employs eighty.

But Hickenlooper is not one to be satisfied with commercial success alone. At the same time he was raising funds for the restaurant, he was also developing a nonprofit organization called the Chinook Foundation. This pass-through fund has since been able to raise about $80,000 annually from a number of local individuals and then distribute it in small grants—usually from $1,500 to $3,000 each— to various community groups. Recipients are selected by a carefully chosen committee whose members generally have not worked together in the past, such as migrant laborers, gay activists, environmentalists, and minority artists.

Hickenlooper has also become a major player in the historic neighborhood known as LoDo in which his restaurant is now a prime anchor. He is on the board of the district organization that fights for preservation and zoning battles in this section that once was home to Bat Masterson and Buffalo Bill Cody. He provides beer for any local nonprofit organization that wants to sponsor a benefit. In 1991 he donated three hundred kegs. Recently he bought his landmark building, installed a jazz club in the basement, built a pool hall on the second floor, and converted the upper stories into residential lofts. (He moved there himself, of course, in 1992.)

Additionally, Hickenlooper and his partners have made the restaurant an excellent place to work—earning it a uniformly positive reputation among cooks, servers, and bartenders that is rare in its industry and producing a low turnover rate that is the envy of its competition. The Wynkoop, for instance, is one of the few restaurants that offers its employees a full-match health insurance plan, quarterly cash bonuses, and paid vacations. Everyone gets free bus passes and free meals when they work. And while it is open seven days a week, the brew pub closes on Super Bowl Sunday so that Hickenlooper and his partners can throw a big party for all employees and their families.

Sebastian International Inc.

Perhaps best known for introducing the popular hair-crimping iron in the mid-seventies, this beauty-products manufacturer has implemented a large-scale environmental program that includes the addition of numerous "environmentally friendly" items to its extensive product line. The company regularly donates corporate funds to several appropriate organizations. It has also installed motion detectors that turn on interior lighting only when an employee is actually in a room at its Woodland Hills, California, headquarters.

Under Pres. John Sebastian Cusenza, the company gives free shampoo to employees who carpool. It helps pay for a barge that provides medical services to Amazon tribes. Club UNITE, which stands for Unity Now Is a Tomorrow for Everyone, was recently established by Sebastian. The organization collects $10 donations from customers that UNITE passes along to one of several charities and in return these customers receive $15 worth of Sebastian International's products along with coupons good for another $65 worth of discounts. And it has implemented the Little Green children's environmental arts competition, which awards winners a $5,000 savings bond and a trip down the Amazon.

Company officials note that while the programs were being initiated and refined, Sebastian International doubled its sales.

The Body Shop and Aveda Corp.

Few products have come under fire in recent years like cosmetics. Feminists attack the very need for such items and the societal attitudes their use engenders; foes of animal testing publicly chastise manufacturers in the industry that have not yet developed a sensitivity to their cause. But at least two major suppliers—The Body Shop and Aveda Corp.—are showing that cosmetics can be developed and sold responsibly.

Founded in Brighton, England, in 1976, The Body Shop has helped set the standard for companies with a conscience. Under the direction of Anita Roddick, the firm's founder and group managing director, it has grown to six hundred outlets in forty countries. (Sixty-two shops are located throughout the United States, in Arizona, California, Connecticut, Colorado, Florida, Illinois, Maryland, Massachusetts, Michigan, Minnesota, Missouri, New Hampshire, New Jersey, New York, Ohio, Oregon, Texas, Virginia, Washington, Washington, D.C., and Wisconsin; a mail-order center is in Cedar Knolls, New Jersey.) Despite the tremendous growth, however, the company has never slacked off from Roddick's original concept.

"It made sense to me to find out what my customers wanted, then try to get it for them and sell them as much or as little as they felt like buying, without all the unnecessary, expensive packaging and hype that people associate with the cosmetic industry," she writes in her catalog. "I thought it was important that my business concern itself not just with skin and hair care preparations, but also with the community, the environment and the big wide world beyond cosmetics."

Along with about 250 potions and lotions for bathing, skin care, sun protection, hair treatment, perfuming, coloring, and just feeling good, The Body Shop's employees hand out pamphlets to their customers with titles like "Against Animal Testing" (the company voices its staunch opposition), "Reuse Refill Recycle" (a minimalist packaging philosophy is backed up by community action), and "What Is Natural?" (Beneficial and interesting ingredients are the claim to fame here.) The company additionally "does not promote idealized notions of beauty," it works for human rights issues around the world, and shop staff and corporate employees spend time on volunteer projects within their communities.

Aveda, based in Minneapolis, Minnesota, is also committed to "a more ethical approach to business and our life-style." Founded in 1978 by Horst Rechelbacher, a self-described environmental activist, the company promotes a variety of earth-friendly hair care, skin treatment, and other cosmetic products while striving toward engineering and community responsibility.

Among its activities, Aveda does not use animals for testing, uses ingredients derived from flowers and plants, and tries to ensure all such ingredients are organically grown; was the first American corporation to sign the Valdez Principles, which set ethical business standards on environmental matters; donates to organizations like the National Global ReLeaf Fund and the International Alliance for Sustainable Agriculture; accepts product containers from customers for recycling; and uses recycled, unbleached paper with soybean ink for all advertising, packaging, and stationery needs.

Like other conscientious companies, Aveda has also not ignored the business side of its business. The company has developed a comprehensive service and sales curriculum called SMART CARE that is designed to make its dealers more profitable.

Working Assets Long Distance

Imagine directing a portion of your residential phone bill to advocacy organizations like the Environmental Defense Fund, Amnesty International, Fund for a Free South Africa, and the National Coalition for the Homeless. This long-distance carrier makes such activity possible by donating 1 percent of all charges to nonprofit action groups that work for causes related to human rights, economic justice, and the environment.

Along with similar donations based on purchases made with the San Francisco–based company's Visa card and bookings arranged through its travel agency, regular dispersals are made to groups chosen each year by the customers themselves. (Ballots are mailed annually, so everyone gets to vote on which organizations will receive the funds.) Since 1986, this program has raised and distributed more than $1.3 million.

The company offers fiberoptic sound quality and rates that are comparable to those from competing carriers as well as special discounts for customers calling others who use its network. It is the only long-distance company preparing its bills with soybean ink on unbleached 100 percent postconsumer recycled paper, and it plants an equivalent amount of trees for every ton of paper that it uses.

In addition, customers are offered an opportunity to place discounted calls each month to specific corporate and political officials who are identified on every billing statement as being worthy of such targeted comments. Or they can opt to have the company send "a well-argued CitizenGram" in their name to these people, who have been targeted by a Citizen's Board comprised of the leaders of various progressive groups.

Aspen Skiing Company

Aspen may be best known as the ski resort for the rich and famous, but for more than a decade the former mining town in the heart of the Colorado Rockies has also been at the cutting edge of the environmental movement. It was the first ski area in the United States to recycle waste products, it pioneered the development of free mass transportation to cut pollution, and it has been an active proponent of wildlife-protection programs and innovative revegetation procedures.

The commitment began in the late seventies, when Aspen Skiing—the company that operates the ski runs at Aspen Mountain as well as at nearby Buttermilk and Snowmass—started its free bus system for both employees and guests. The program successfully removed a large number of passenger cars from the town's narrow streets throughout the winter months, which greatly diminished local automobile-generated air pollution. It also helped free up parking spaces for those who did use their cars. In the years that followed, many ski resorts around the country recognized the value of these efforts and implemented similar programs.

During 1989–90, Aspen also became the first ski area in the United States to initiate an on-mountain recycling program, which created a system for handling all the glass, aluminum, and cardboard that was discarded at its eleven mountainside restaurants. The program was then expanded to include the recycling of motor oil, computer and typewriter ribbons, and plastic toner containers, along with the purchase of a variety of recycled products, like paper for trail maps, brochures, business cards, letterheads, toilet paper, paper towels, and copy-machine paper. In 1991 the company also banned plastics and polystyrene—with the exception of plastic utensils—at the on-mountain restaurants and installed energy-efficient lighting and water-efficient bathroom fixtures at its base area and hotels.

Also in 1991, Aspen continued its support of recycling programs in the local community by donating approximately $100,000 in cash and in-kind services to local environmental organizations. It also began working with the Pitkin County Waste Recovery Center on an experimental program to compost all waste from its mountain eateries, which immediately cut Aspen Skiing's refuse collection so dramatically that now less than 10 percent of it goes into the county landfill. For these and other ongoing efforts, the Aspen Skiing Company received the Colorado Governor's 1991 Environmental Award.

In addition to originating revegetation procedures now followed by the highway department, mining industry, and skiing industry, the company has also joined with the county's Wildlife Task Force to initiate new habitat-protection standards. These combine tighter regulations with positive incentives, including neighborhood-conservation easements, tax breaks for initiating protective measures, and matching funds for preservation efforts. A city tax to raise funds for purchasing critical lands to be placed in public trust also resulted from the joint task force.

Consumers United Insurance Company

Because health-insurance companies have traditionally covered only traditional medical practices, this Washington, D.C., alternative has carved a successful niche for itself by also funding alternative health-care methods and practitioners. Its highly regarded Healthstar plan pays for treatment by homeopaths, midwives, acupuncturists, and the like in addition to funding treatment by medical doctors and other standard caregivers.

For nearly three decades, this employee-owned company has offered open-minded coverage in an industry typified by its rigidity and unwillingness to be flexible. Full reproductive care, maternity benefits, and preventive coverage, for example, are extended to all policyholders. The company also covers its clients' domestic partners regardless of their sex or marital status, and its rates are the same for men and women.

Along with these progressive major medical policies, Consumers United also offers term life insurance, Medicare supplements, and tax-deferred annuity plans.

Smith & Hawken

"At this time of year," begins a note from the owners of this popular mail-order firm in a recent Christmas catalog, "when the 'spirit of giving' can be rendered nearly meaningless by commercialization, it's fitting to turn our attention to the idea behind the phrase: appreciating what we have and sharing it with those we love. Because gifts we have long taken for granted—air, water, soil, natural and human diversity—are now endangered and need our attention, we try to create products that are restorative, natural, and beneficial to our society on many levels."

Such comments may spark cynical smirks when delivered by others, but their sincerity is beyond reproach when they come from Smith & Hawken. The firm, founded in 1979 by Dave Smith and Paul Hawken, offers high-quality clothing, gardening tools, plants and seeds, outdoor furniture, and housewares. From clothing produced without using chemicals to its organic coffee grown and harvested by a collective of Mexican farmers, it practices what it preaches.

Hawken, in fact, has been at the forefront of socially responsible corporate practices for several decades. His initial foray into the world of alternative business was a natural-foods company called Erewhon Trading Company, which he founded in Boston in the midsixties (and sold in 1973 when it was a nationwide effort grossing $25,000 a day). He also authored several well-received books, including *The Next Economy* and *Growing a Business*. Hawken recently left the company to write full time.

Today Smith & Hawken employs about 275 people in a series of old buildings in Santa Rosa and Mill Valley, California. Its products include recycled wrapping paper created by elementary school students and packaged by disabled workers; silk socks produced by former coca farmers in the Colombian Andes; clothing with buttons made from tagua nuts harvested from the Ecuadoran rain forest; and shirts, jeans, and naturally dyed wool sweaters from a cooperative in Oaxaca, Mexico.

Wherever possible, Smith & Hawken includes products in its catalog that generate income for their producers that would otherwise not be realized. It stresses natural alternatives to traditional items while retaining its emphasis on durability, quality, and reasonable prices. And it has been donating a portion of its pretax profits to environmental causes since the company opened its doors.

Tattered Cover Bookstore

Joyce Meskis is surely the envy of bibliophiles across the country. As owner of Denver's Tattered Cover Bookstore, often considered one of the best in the United States, she has the pleasurable task of tapping into her region's collective mind-set and in the process fills the shelves of her four-story, 50,000-square-foot store with volumes that run the gamut from the latest by Stephen King to a new collection by Colorado poets.

Meskis, who started her career as a bookseller in 1960, bought the Tattered Cover in 1974 when it was a "hole in the wall." By artfully combining superb service and an armchair ambience, it comfortably assembled a wide range of books from literary criticism and metaphysics to highly technical manuals and travel tomes. With a commitment to literacy and public service—her children's-books buyers regularly go to area schools to talk about books and read aloud, for example—the store outgrew two smaller sites before landing in its current home in Denver's ritzy Cherry Creek neighborhood.

Today the bookstore employs 320 and carries 400,000 volumes. It averages 2,500 transactions and 350 special orders each day.

While Meskis is regularly praised by the local and national media, she also gained recognition from her peers. She recently completed two one-year terms as president of the American Booksellers Association, a trade organization of eighty-two hundred members devoted to providing membership services, promoting the culture of the book, and protecting First Amendment rights.

But all of this isn't enough to keep the fifty-two-year-old Chicago native fully occupied. She is now also a partner in a redevelopment project that will convert old warehouses in Denver's historic Lower

Downtown neighborhood into offices, residential units, child-care facilities, and retail space—which will include a second bookstore.

The Amer-I-Can Program

At Jim Brown's spectacular home high above Hollywood, as many as seventy gang members from tough Los Angeles communities, like Watts, Compton, and Willowbrook, gather weekly to learn how to find a job, deal with their families, peacefully resolve conflicts, and, basically, function productively in society. This for-profit self-help program—founded and spearheaded by the charismatic fifty-six-year-old former pro football star and actor—combines the principles of self-determination and the tenets of capitalism with the twelve-step recovery plan of Alcoholics Anonymous. It has been so successful that other cities are asking Brown to set up shop within their borders.

After initially involving himself with another effort that taught self-management and self-control techniques, Brown decided to develop a program that became Amer-I-Can. He wrote the manual himself in late 1990, specifying the values of positive thinking, open communication, goal setting, family responsibility, and hard work. With an initial $250,000 grant from the California Department of Corrections, he took the program to prisoners and gang members. Since they respected him, they listened. More than two thousand inmates and eight hundred gang members from the L.A. area have since participated in the five-week, eighty-hour program, and a second year's allocation of $295,000 was provided.

The program's private, for-profit dimension has attracted attention and raised some eyebrows, as has its heavy reliance on the ex–Cleveland Browns running back and popular star of action movies like *The Dirty Dozen.* (Brown has reportedly placed about $300,000 of his own funds into the effort, for example, and he personally leads most of its sessions.) But his reputation and appeal have been the draw that lures many of society's toughest into the program, and the money proves to be as important as any other component: Each time a contract is secured, at least $500 of it is placed into special neighborhood funds that are dispersed to local "hardship cases" by a group of successful graduates from that area.

Notice of the program's success has spread quickly among municipalities around the country searching for their own solutions to the increasing problems presented by gangs and other purveyors of street crime. A little more than a year after its founding, officials from Ohio, Illinois, New York, and Nevada began discussions with Brown to develop local Amer-I-Can branches in their states.

Hi-Tec Sports USA Inc.

A promotional campaign initiated by this outdoor footwear company in 1992 is designed to raise money for preservation, protection, and restoration projects at national parks throughout the country. Operated in conjunction with the National Parks and Conservation Association, "Hi-Tec Posters for Parks" revolves around the sale of a limited-edition nature poster that is available through stores selling Hi-Tec hiking boots and any other outlet that wishes to carry it. The poster sells for $6.90, and all proceeds (minus production costs) go to the program.

The Modesto, California–based company is handling the development of these limited-edition posters and overseeing their distribution to dealers. It is paying for a series of four-color, full-page public-service ads appearing in several top consumer and trade outdoor magazines to promote the program. And it is supplying dealers with in-store promotional materials that can be used to generate additional sales to customers once they arrive.

This initial program ended at the conclusion of 1992, it was replaced by new posters and calendars to be offered throughout the following years. Hi-Tec anticipates that the effort will run on a continuing basis, with specific products offered to the public changing each year.

Gerry Baby Products Company

In an attempt to permit even the poorest families in America to obtain—and then utilize—child-safety automobile seats, this manufacturer is discounting the cost of its own products by nearly half for those who meet low-income requirements. Its program, called "Safe Kids Buckle Up," was launched early in 1992 in Washington, D.C., by Gerry president Larry Walker, former surgeon general C. Everett Koop, and acting U.S. transportation secretary James Busey.

Walker noted at the program's unveiling that car crashes remain the number-one killer of children in the United States, claiming 1,110 lives and injuring 95,000 under the age of nine each year. It is believed that the use of safety seats could cut those numbers in half, but statistics show they are used on only 50–80 percent of all automotive trips. "We want to be in a position to supply seats to everyone and not have inhibiting factors keep families from getting them," Walker said.

The program, which lowers the cost of Gerry's $80 car seats to $45 for eligible families, is being administered by child-safety organizations in one hundred cities around the nation. In addition, the Denver-based subsidiary of Huffy Corporation made an initial $100,000 donation to help kick off the campaign.

America Outdoors

Inspired by an independent cleanup effort along the Delaware River—which netted everything from tires to dynamite that thoughtless people had tossed into the water—a Knoxville, Tennessee–based trade group called America Outdoors organized the first annual National River Cleanup Week in May 1992. The results? Over 20,000 volunteers fanned out along 10,000 river miles, to pitch in on 250 separate projects that blanketed the United States.

David Brown, executive director of the group representing about 240 river outfitters, outdoor retailers, and watersport equipment manufacturers, says the idea was to create a cohesive nationwide effort that would draw maximum attention to the plight of America's rivers. He notes that in just one targeted waterway—the Ocoee River in southeastern Tennessee—some eight tons of garbage were removed by more than two hundred volunteers during the week, which is now planned as an annual event.

William McDonough Architects

By taking the tenets of the architect's creed a step further than many of his peers, New York–based William McDonough has landed on the cutting edge of socially responsible design. With his own firm supporting him, an impressive stack of newspaper and magazine clippings behind him, and some of the world's great buildings in his future, McDonough is using both his talents and his influence to push architectural projects in a more conscientious direction.

Since designing one of the first solar-heated homes built in Ireland while he was still a student at Yale, McDonough has strived to create beautiful and functional buildings that meet his environmental standards. That means windows that open, carpets that are nailed down (rather than glued), and walls that are coated with nontoxic finishes. His views have landed him on the front page of the *Wall Street Journal* as well as within every significant architectural publication in the United States. In addition, he is a much-in-demand speaker throughout the world.

Most significantly, perhaps, the company also secured a commission for him to design the seventy-story Warsaw Trade Center, which was planned as the tallest building in Eastern Europe before current events scuttled the project. His plans called for a twelve-story base made from recycled World War II rubble, a "skin" fashioned from recycled glass and aluminum, a twenty-story mesh tower that would glow from solar-powered batteries, the use of solid wood wherever possible (because plywood and particle board emit formaldehyde), and, of course, the inclusion of operating windows, nailed-down carpeting, and nontoxic wall finishes.

The proposal also called for development of a park of pavilions, galleries, and beer halls around the building's base that would have been created by local artists. But its most radical component would take shape miles away: McDonough had stipulated that a ten-square-mile forest be planted elsewhere in Poland, at a cost of $150,000, to compensate for the structure's destructive emission of carbon dioxide.

While this project has been effectively cancelled, McDonough is using many of the same concepts for a software development center that will begin construction in the south of France in 1993.

Such far-reaching plans are nothing new for the forty-three-year-old McDonough, who has designed everything from a highly regarded Manhattan restaurant (the Quilted Giraffe) to a musical stage set (for the band King Creole and the Coconuts) and a master-planned ranch (in Springdale, Utah). His most significant ecologically responsible project to date is the Environmental Defense Fund's New York headquarters, which opened in 1986 as a model of nontoxic design; McDonough's plans eliminated the sources of indoor air pollution, provided maximum ventilation, substituted beeswax for polyurethane on office floors, and utilized the other design components for which he has since become known.

Utne Reader

Adoption. The new unionism. Indian resistance. Americans and politics. Africa's invisible famine. Nature films. Naps. Creativity. Censorship. Baldness. These are but a few of the many topics covered in just three issues of a remarkable bimonthly magazine called the *Utne Reader*. Founded in 1984 by Eric Utne—who now serves as president and editor in chief—it assembles "the best of the alternative press" and presents it in a way that far extends the readership of articles promoting social responsibility, conscientious behavior, ethical business practices, and far-reaching thought in general.

Published in Minneapolis, Minnesota, *Utne's* editorial fare consists primarily of articles that originally appeared in small-circulation periodicals like *Business and Society Review* and *East Bay Express.* It also runs book excerpts and showcases such writers as Ken Kesey, Alice Walker, and Jeremy Rifkin. Material may be condensed from its original source and run alone or along with similarly themed pieces, or its contents might be extracted and combined with thoughts expressed in related articles and books. Reviews of magazines, books, records, and videos—as well as visually arresting graphics—complete the editorial picture.

But the magazine is sought after for its advertisements as well, since they provide enthusiastic readers with an all-too-rare window on the world of socially conscientious consumer products and services. Several companies showcased in this book (including Shorebank, Yakima, Aveda, Working Assets Long Distance, and Consumers United Insurance) are regular advertisers in the *Utne Reader.* Others range from Imagine Foods and Vitasoy to Quality Paperback Book Club and PBS Home Video. An array of ethical investment companies also promote themselves in each issue.

Additionally, the magazine has launched a Neighborhood Salon Association that puts readers in touch with others who share their social and political concerns. Some eighty-two hundred people responded to the magazine's initial invitation and formed more than five hundred "salons" in North America (including twenty-six in New York and thirty-three in the San Francisco area).

"Second only to my love for ideas is my love for getting together with other people to talk about ideas and to explore where that talk might lead," Eric Utne has written about the salons, although he might have been writing about his magazine as well. "We're extremely excited about this project. It might even help make the world a kinder and gentler place, one neighborhood at a time."

Artisan Maintenance

Mark Frederick believes in giving a chance to people whom others have passed by. His philosophy—manifested in employment practices at his Artisan Maintenance firm in Colorado—has proven both socially responsible and commercially viable since it was implemented when he started the company in 1985.

Frederick is president of this private, for-profit company that performs exterior maintenance for an assortment of clients in the Denver metropolitan area. (The work includes landscape upkeep, trash collection, and snow removal.) About one-quarter of his forty employees are physically or mentally disabled or residents of prison-system halfway houses. While he admits to being inspired to start the program because of the tax benefits it afforded him, he says he continued it because it worked, and he would not hesitate to recommend similar practices to others.

"They are a real dependable group of people," Frederick says of the members of his so-called Alternative Labor Program. "We sometimes have to do snow removal at four in the morning, and these folks show up on time all the time."

Tom's of Maine

In 1968, Tom and Kate Chappell moved from Philadelphia to Kennebunk, Maine, in search of a more simplified life-style. The couple used unprocessed foods and simple, unadulterated products. However, they were unable to find natural personal-care items for themselves and their children and decided to produce their own.

With a $5,000 loan from a friend, the couple began making products for home use that would not harm the environment. The first product, Clearlake, was the country's first nonphosphate liquid laundry detergent. The company encouraged its customers to recycle their empty containers by mailing them back, postage paid, to be refilled.

Soon the company branched into personal-care products and in 1975 introduced the first natural toothpaste with fluoride. As the company enters its third decade, it is a leader in the personal-care field, offering toothpaste, deodorant, mouthwash, flossing ribbon, shampoo, and shaving creams. The privately held company distributes these products to seven thousand health-food stores throughout the United States, Canada, and England and has a bicoastal presence in approximately twenty thousand food and drug stores. The company has experienced 25–35 percent growth each year.

Equally important is Tom's of Maine's commitment to its values. The company describes them as "respect for each other, our natural world, and our community."

This dedication is evident in every aspect of Tom's of Maine's business. For instance, 10 percent of its pretax income is donated to support nonprofit projects and groups devoted to the environment, human needs, and education. Its employees are encouraged to use 5 percent of their work time for volunteer activities. Some work at a local soup kitchen; others train mentally and physically challenged people.

A recent $25,000 grant from the company helped launch a curbside recycling program in the town of Kennebunk. In its first year, 70 percent of the town's residents participated.

Tom's of Maine makes all its products with the highest-quality natural and biodegradable ingredients. Its toothpaste is packaged in an aluminum tube that is recyclable, and its shampoo is packaged in recycled bottles. Tom's of Maine was the first in its industry to list all ingredients on the label, which also details their purpose and source.

Shaklee Corporation

Clare Hertel, public relations and promotions manager of the San Francisco–based Shaklee Corporation, recently faced a difficult situation. Her mother, who lives in Santa Fe, New Mexico, was seriously ill, and Clare wanted to be with her for an extended length of time. The thirty-year-old, then a four-year employee, had several choices: quit her job, take an unpaid leave of absence, or continue her work from New Mexico.

She submitted a proposal to her supervisor that recommended she work from an office in New Mexico for a four-month period. She outlined month-by-month projects and indicated that weekly updates would inform her supervisor of all activities.

Much to Clare's delight, Shaklee agreed to the arrangement. "When you consider the cost of training a new employee and the fact I was already well entrenched in my ongoing projects, it did make sense for the company," says Clare. Yet she believes the situation is unique. "I don't know of too many other companies that would have been so accommodating."

The Shaklee Corporation manufactures and distributes nutritional supplements and foods, personal-care products, household goods, and home water treatments. These products are sold directly to consumers by an independent nationwide sales force. Its manufacturing facility is in Norman, Oklahoma. This plant maintains rigid quality controls and utilizes modern production methods to develop its nutritional supplements. Shaklee products are safe for the environment and are not tested on animals. The company has been honored for its environmental conscience through the Family Circle Green Chip Award.

San Francisco Hat Company

Stephan Schinzinger and Sally Kellman are partners in two sister businesses that import and distribute products benefiting international environmental and labor causes. The San Francisco Hat Company, based in Berkeley, California, sells a fedora called the Rain Forest Hat made of palm-tree trimmings from Brazil; for every hat purchased, the manufacturer buys one acre of threatened rain-forest land. This is one of several hats the company sells to such retailers as Barney's New York, Nordstroms, I. Magnin, and the Nature Company. Their other business, the Tagua Button Company, imports buttons made of nuts from palm trees and last year sold a million pieces in the United States.

By providing a market for the trees' seed, the company is creating a reason to save the trees instead of cutting them down. In addition, it employs Brazilian residents who have established cottage industries producing both the hats and the buttons. The pair's work has been recognized by a UN delegation. With only four full-time employees in the United States, these two sister companies have achieved moderate sales increases for the past five years, with annual sales reaching $500,000.

Ohio Canoe Adventures

Ohio Canoe Adventures, a three-store specialty retailer based in a Cleveland suburb, is a family-owned business run like a big hobby, according to president Reece Fabbro. Since opening his first shop more than twenty-five years ago, he has conducted the business in an environmentally responsible manner. Among his programs is a popular wildlife refuge center, where, from a 100-foot deck outside the store's back door, customers can enjoy more than a hundred species of birds flying around four dozen birdhouses and seventy-five feeders.

Along with its boats, outdoor clothing, and other equipment, Ohio Canoe Adventures also sells a variety of products that help educate customers about the outdoors and environmental issues. In addition, Fabbro is launching a new corporation called Get Involved Inc. that will manufacture and distribute products that promote environmental awareness. All profits from this venture will be donated to Midwest environmental concerns. Fabbro and his thirty-five employees—many of them longtime associates who form a family-like work force—show how retailing can make a difference by further refusing to accept product shipments with excessive packaging materials.

Hanna Anderson Inc.

To prove that their children's clothing was of higher quality than any other brand on the market, Gun and Tom Denhark, the husband-and-wife owners of Hanna Anderson, Inc., issued a declaration in 1985: Any customer returning the company's clothing in good, used condition would receive a 20 percent credit off the original purchase price.

The program, called Hannadowns, started as a marketing promotion intended to demonstrate the long life of the company's high-quality Swedish-made clothing. Yet the result is that thousands of needy children are now wearing the returned items that Hanna Anderson donates to worthy recipients. In 1989 and 1990, for example, more than thirty thousand of these articles of children's clothing were donated to Portland, Oregon–area shelters for battered women.

Hanna Anderson is a mail-order company launched by its owners in 1984. Unhappy with the children's clothing she found in America, Gun sought 100 percent cotton, high-quality alternatives from her native Sweden. Soon the couple started selling by mail, and the company was an immediate success. More than 8 million catalogs are now distributed to homes throughout the United States. Sales in 1991 exceeded $34 million. The Portland-based company employs more than two hundred workers.

"The Hannadowns program is a real kick for all of us who work here," says marketing manager John Miller. "It shows that our product is high quality and helps out people in need. It's a win-win situation."

Julius Klein Cleaners

In January 1992, Alan Rappaport placed a sign in the window of his Julius Klein Cleaners. "Currently Unemployed?" it read. "We care. Let us help you look your best while interviewing for new opportunities. We will clean one suit or one dress per week FREE until you find employment. Call Alan. All arrangements will be kept strictly confidential. (Must present proof of current situation from N.Y. State Unemployment.)"

More than one hundred residents of the neighborhood around Third Avenue and Twenty-First Street in New York have taken Rappaport up on his offer. More importantly, as a board member of the Neighborhood Cleaners Association, Rappaport has motivated other cleaners throughout the tristate area to follow suit.

"I've been on both sides of the fence, and I know what it's like to be without a job," says Rappaport. "It's a great pleasure to help out."

The gesture has helped his Julius Klein Cleaners win additional customers as well. "People in the community thank us all the time, regardless of whether they need the complimentary service," says

Rappaport. "I've had customers give me donations to support the program."

Outdoor Industry Conservation Alliance

In 1988, Wally Smith, president of Recreational Equipment Inc. (REI), a national chain of outdoor stores based in Seattle, Washington, contacted the presidents of three other businesses in the outdoors industry with an idea. His thought: starting a coalition of businesses that would collectively donate funds to grass-roots environmental organizations.

Four years later and thirty-three members strong, the organization, the Outdoors Industry Conservation Alliance, has donated more than a half a million dollars to a variety of causes. Beneficiaries include the Oregon Rivers Council, a citizen-action effort that is working to keep the Northwest's free-flowing rivers undamned; the Green Mountain Club, a Vermont group that hopes to protect lands along the trail corridor in Northern Vermont; and the Western Ancient Forest Campaign, which hopes to save the last remaining ancient forests on the West Coast. These and dozens of other organizations receive grants ranging from $15,000 to $55,000.

What's especially unique about the organization is the united effort of a variety of businesses, many of which are direct competitors. An elected board selects which grants to approve and fund. All work is done by volunteers within the member companies, so that all of the money collected goes directly to the environmental groups. Yearly membership fees are $10,000 for companies with annual revenues of $10 million and more; $5,000 for businesses with annual revenues from $1 million to $10 million; and $1,000 for annual revenues of up to $1 million.

The group's ability to expand the number and size of its grants is due to the growth of the organization's membership. Because all member dues go toward project funding, these businesses provide an effective organization that represents the interests of outdoor users. No one Alliance member could have such an impact working independently.

"Our goal is to work with groups that can have an immediate impact on saving the environment," says Smith. "Working together as an industry, the results—free-flowing rivers, untouched wildlands, and backcountry trails—will be there for all our customers to enjoy for generations to come."

Toys for Special Children

"Play is work for children," explains Steven Kanor. "If a child doesn't play, he or she is not developing into a normal adult. And toys are critical for play."

This is the theory that motivated Kanor, a biomedical engineer, to design and adapt existing toys for handicapped children. Starting in his basement workshop in the early eighties, Kanor, the son of a toymaker, came upon the idea to develop sensitive switches that allow severely disabled children to produce movement in a toy. The switches are activated by a puff of air, the sound of a voice, or a gentle touch.

Toys for Special Children, based in Hartsdale, New York, is the company that resulted from Kanor's effort. Toys he adapted and sells through a mail-order catalog include a music box, activity centers, a walking dinosaur, and an authentic toy police car "complete with bump-and-go action, siren, and flashing lights."

Kanor is president of the twenty-person company that ships specially adapted toys and other equipment for the disabled all over the world. In a cluttered office filled with prototypes, Kanor says he feels he's doing what he enjoys. "I don't consider myself to be a role model. I just found a way that I can help out some other people. It's both a challenge and a joy," he says.

Glen Ellen Winery

Under a sprawling oak tree at tables covered with gingham table clothes, dozens of office workers, bottlers, vineyard farmers and shipping clerks of Sonoma, California-based Glen Ellen Winery share a noon-time meal. Helen Benziger, mother of five of the seven partners who own the winery, lights the candles on a cake, and the assembled workers sing Happy Birthday to the five employees with August birthdays.

The family-oriented celebration is just one of dozens of annual events demonstrating that the family-owned business considers its 300-plus employees as close as kin.

Since the Benziger family acquired the land in 1980, Glen Ellen Winery has grown from selling 6,500 cases in 1982, to 3.5 million cases in 1991. It is now the tenth-largest winery in the United States. The wine is sold throughout the United States and in twenty foreign countries.

Yet, while many wineries have adopted an institutionally oriented commercial face, Glen Ellen, despite its high volume sales, remains a family-oriented business. "We want to create a sense of the extended family to everyone we work with," says Barbara Wallace, the company's human resources director. "We don't have departments, but teams, and they are all self-directed."

The company emphasizes education and in the past two years has developed an in-house EdCenter that has adopted a "people teaching people" philosophy. Launched in 1991, Glen Ellen's EdCenter features classes on leadership, personal finances, understanding taxes, goal-setting, recycling, bicycle repair, computer skills, and even on pizza making taught both by Glen Ellen personnel and special outside instructors. Most important, says Wallace, are the language classes. "Most of our workers in the bottling plant are Hispanic," says Wallace, "and we felt the first priority was to help bridge the communication gap." Glen Ellen offers its workers not only ESL (English as a Second Language) classes, but also Spanish lessons for its English speaking personnel.

"Two years ago there was a real division as to where Spanish was spoken and where English was spoken. Now," says Wallace, "it's a combination of both."

Glen Ellen has invested more than $100,000 in its educational program. A dozen workers will take the classes that are held on the company's grounds or at the local elementary school. Since its establishment, the winery has extended the classes to its network of distributors and grape suppliers.

Wallace estimates the company spends 42 cents on every payroll dollar towards worker education and benefits. Why? "There is a growing Hispanic population in the Sonoma area," says Wallace.

Indeed, 33 percent of Sonoma county residents are Hispanic. "We looked at the untapped capabilities of our employees, and there was a genuine concern for our workers' welfare."

Glen Ellen Winery has been rewarded for the attention it gives its employees. It has a zero percent turnover rate, a coup in any work environment, and the EdCenter provides a vehicle to attract and retain employees. Most significantly, several former line workers have been promoted to front office jobs, and the bottling plant just went a full year without an accident.

Glen Ellen has also adopted an environmental program. It is one of the largest recyclers in Sonoma County and has sought more environmentally friendly packaging for its products. Its vineyard features integrated biological and chemical controls and uses beneficial insects and cover crops. Glen Ellen bottles its wines in recycled glass. The company recently wrote an environmental mission statement:

"To maximize our commitment to quality by striving to improve the environmental integrity of our products and to increase our efficiency towards environmentally responsible operation of our organization."

"We're dedicated to preserving the environment for ourselves and future generations," says Wallace. "And, most importantly, we want to positively influence everyone who works for, or works with, our company."

Tabra, Inc.

Flags from almost a dozen countries hang from the ceiling of Tabra, Inc., a jewelry company, as workers below meticulously string beads, position stones, and polish gleaming silver pieces. But the stars and stripes of Cambodia, Thailand, Laos, Vietnam, Samoa, India, Singapore, and the United States offer more than decoration in this brightly lit work-space. Rather, the hanging banners represent the many homelands of Tabra employees.

Eighty-five percent of the almost one hundred employees at Tabra are immigrants. They are from eleven different countries, with the highest percentage of workers from Laos, Cambodia, and Vietnam.

Incorporated in 1982, Tabra makes and sells high-quality jewelry to specialty shops, craft stores and art galleries throughout the United

States and in Japan. The exotic jewelry, which includes earrings, bracelets and belts, are based on ethnic designs, and are made with different combinations of metals, stones, and beads from throughout the world.

The company's founder and sole owner, Tabra Tunoa, travels to third world countries for several months of the year to find the unique stones and beads—and the inspiration for the designs—that make her line so distinctive. As her creations continue to express her own artistic and worldly style, Tabra says her work force is as much of a reflection of her business as the jewelry itself.

When it came time to expand her work force beyond herself in the early '70s, Tabra looked to Berkeley's local sidewalk peddler counterculture for workers. Unfortunately, her "hippie" coworkers created more problems than they solved.

Then, with the assistance of a local private industry council, Tabra hired her first foreign-born employee, a Vietnamese woman, whose skills and work ethic so impressed her that she wound up hiring a good many of her friends and relatives.

Since then, the company has been actively recruiting in the Bay Area's many ethnic communities. Such a patchwork of cultures offers plenty of awards, says Joyce Shearer, Tabra's human resources manager. Employees share their backgrounds and heritage with pot luck lunches, where they talk about the food from their native lands and bring family photos and maps from their homelands. The company also celebrates the holidays of the countries represented by its workers, such as the Loatian New Year celebration they had with twenty-five women dancing in their native dress.

The $4 million company also employs its own part-time language instructor that teaches an English class every morning to help overcome everyday challenges encountered in a multilingual work force.

Most importantly, Tabra provides a steady job and income for a segment of the population that needs help. More than half of Tabra employees were on welfare or unemployment when hired, says Shearer, and they are given job training, and an opportunity to grow, both within the company and into American society.

According to Tabra, hiring refugees makes her company superior. "People think Americans are the best, but our greatness is from the diverse cultures represented here."

14

Lessons of Conscientious Leadership

One of the best things about delving into the workings of today's companies with a conscience is the chance to meet the people behind the scenes. From visionary company founders like Yvon Chouinard of Patagonia to dedicated second-generation managers like Joan Shapiro of the Shorebank Corporation, the people who run these organizations are directly responsible for their deep commitment to both their communities and their bottom lines. They combine a social worker's sympathies with an entrepreneur's instincts, an inventor's street smarts with an M.B.A.'s business savvy. They are interesting to, and interested in, those around them. And fortunately for the rest of us, they are becoming the role models for successful corporate leadership in the nineties.

These people have put together a variety of businesses that operate in a variety of ways.

There are, not surprisingly, a great many common threads that run through all of these companies. Fourteen of them are listed and explained below. Businesses, large and small, that are thinking about joining their ranks would do well to study them and put their principles into practice.

- All of the companies were initially created and still continue to be led by farsighted people who visibly set their firms' moral tone and corporate course.

Without exception, every one of the organizations profiled in the preceding pages was the brainchild of one person or a few closely aligned individuals who remain actively in charge of their company's operation today. Also without exception, all of the founders have consciously set their firm's direction in terms of business practices, personnel matters, customer relations, and community involvement. These are people, in other words, who had a complete vision and were willing to personally work to see it realized.

Accordingly, all of the leaders know what it is like to roll up their sleeves and toil on the shop floor. For the most part, they started their companies with so little money that they were routinely called upon to work in product development, manufacturing, sales, delivery, and bookkeeping right from the start. They therefore learned their businesses from the ground up and are now listened to intently when they offer suggestions and advice to their staffs.

Now, however, the firms have grown large enough to allow these company heads to separate themselves from much of this gritty day-to-day activity. But business leaders we interviewed for this book choose not to. It isn't uncommon to see Ben & Jerry's Jerry Greenfield filling ice cream pint containers on the production line or Marilyn Hamilton of Quickie Designs enthusiastically discussing a technological innovation with a customer or Hass Hassan of Alfala's Markets behind the deli counter during the lunch rush. Similarly, most second-level managers in these firms willingly follow their bosses' examples and also spend a lot of time in the trenches.

These firms strive for social responsibility and manufacture products, with great pains to ensure they are used responsibly, or offer services that clearly help society. America Works, Greyston Bakery, and Shorebank may be the best examples of this: for-profit businesses that directly aid welfare recipients, the homeless, and low-income homeowners and businesspeople.

Others offer products that are unquestioningly helpful and healthy for those who buy them, for example, Quickie's wheelchairs, Celestial Seasonings tea and Alfalfa's groceries. Birkenstock sandals, Patagonia activewear, Grateful Dead music, Yakima racks, and Esprit clothing provide items that simply make people's lives better and more enjoyable. Even Ben & Jerry's, which made its reputation on fatty, superpremium ice cream, has rolled out low-fat frozen yogurt as America's tastes and nutritional desires change.

Positive product emphasis stems directly from the people who work in these companies. Everyone from management to line workers takes their social responsibilities very seriously. An ideal example is Celestial, whose employees rushed to buy back the company when it became linked with a cigarette manufacturer. Essentially, no one at the tea company wanted that association.

• Like all successful businesses, these companies stick to the basics and produce only top-quality goods or services once they have identified the right niche.

The leaders of every one of these firms subscribe to the same school of thought: Their commitment to corporate responsibility would have no impact if they were not also running a successful business, and they would not be running a successful business if they did not have a product or service that people were willing to buy.

Such public demand generally starts with an uncompromising commitment to quality, and this focus is obvious at every one of these companies. Ben & Jerry's carefully follows its ice cream to sales outlets around the world to ensure that customers get a product that meets their expectations. Patagonia repairs or replaces any of its garments that fail to match a buyer's demands. Quickie's wheelchairs are known as the best-designed and manufactured in the industry. Greyston cakes and pastries are prized in New York's top restaurants. America Works trains workers who can hold their own in the private sector.

All of this started with the identification of a specific niche that was, at the time, blatantly unfilled. Marilyn Hamilton, for instance, couldn't play tennis with existing wheelchairs, so she went out and had a superior product designed. Yvon Choiunard didn't like the climbing equipment available at the time, so he personally made his own on an anvil in his parents' backyard. Margot Fraser couldn't find sandals that felt good on her feet, so she began importing better models herself from overseas.

These initial forays into the development and delivery of high-quality products and services have never wavered, either. On occassion, these companies have made related decisions that had a negative impact on their bottom lines in the short term. But the enduring nature of these businesses and the fact that every one of their products and services remains heavily in demand in an almost cultlike fashion, shows that their long-term vision was correct.

• These companies have developed a public image that emphasizes their commitment to quality, and they often use nontraditional means to promote it and to speak directly to their customers on this and other matters.

Unlike companies that realize their environmental and social commitments late in life—and then spend $2 million to tell the public that they spent $1 million on some worthy cause—true companies with a conscience go about their twin pursuits of excellence and social responsibility rather quietly. Furthermore, at least two of the companies (Ben & Jerry's and The Grateful Dead) never advertise directly, while others that do so regularly (Patagonia, Esprit, and Alfalfa's) use their time and money to promote their philosophies as much as their products. And even those that lean toward more traditional ads (Yakima, Shorebank, Celestial, and Quickie) tend to create and run spots that emphasize the very principles that set them apart from their competitors.

What these companies do in terms of promotion is highly nontraditional. Some (Quickie, Ben & Jerry's, Patagonia, and Alfalfa's) regularly utilize event sponsorship to get their names before the public and tie their companies to various demographically matched activities. A few (Ben & Jerry's and Celestial) use their packaging to make a statement and rally support for favorite causes. And almost all rely extensively on the word-of-mouth testimonials that supporters are all too happy to give to their friends and acquaintances.

• These are companies that firmly believe in—and exclusively practice—the dual principles of self-management and decentralization.

Nowhere among these companies, for instance, will you find needless layers of bureaucracy or bloated management committees. There are no unnecessary vice-presidents. Orders do not come down to the assembly lines from lofty, insulated main offices in some far-off corporate headquarters.

Quickie's experience with its parent firm, Sunrise Medical, is possibly the best example. Sunrise, while it owns twenty-one companies and employs more than two thousand workers, operates out of a main office that is staffed with just eighteen people. Daily control of each of its divisions is truly in the hands of the leaders of those divisions. And when a new acquisition is made, new managers are almost never placed at its helm; instead, Sunrise encourages the existing management team to stay on and run the company in much the same manner as it did previously—with the additional help that Sunrise can provide through economies of scale and shared expertise.

Other responsible companies operate in a similar manner. The Grateful Dead has never had a true "manager," relying instead on band personnel to handle all of the duties typically performed by outsiders. And Alfalfa's puts its real power in the hands of store managers, who as "unit presidents" have the opportunity to shape their domains as they see fit—within, of course, the overall context of the company's basic ideology.

Additionally, all of the companies described within these pages practice an active policy of promotion from within. Since most of the managers have risen through the ranks, they usually believe in the same principles and tenets as the founders and are thus more likely to continue their companies' direction undeterred.

• The founders of these companies recognize that they are not perfect and have willingly brought in outside expertise when needed.

America Works is a perfect example of this. While it was moderately successful in the beginning under the management of its husband-and-wife founding team, the company eventually reached the point where it needed an additional perspective and added talent in order to grow. A retired manufacturing executive was invited to join the firm in 1987 as a third partner, and he brought needed capital to the company as well as a sense of formal business operation lacking in the founding entrepreneurs. By pulling in the reins, implementing rigid accounting procedures, and emphasizing the firm's past accomplishments, he helped America Works successfully expand into new markets.

Most of the other companies in these pages opted for similar changes. Shorebank, Quickie, and Ben & Jerry's all called in outside help when their founders recognized that they reached their limits in certain areas. They went out and found experts in these areas who were sympathetic to their philosophies and principles and unhesitatingly turned over responsibility and power to them. The results speak for themselves.

Such is not always the case, however. And the failures that occur usually stem from a fundamental judgment error on the part of the companies as much as on the part of those hired to help them.

Patagonia, for instance, totally missed the point when, in the late eighties, it brought in a new management team with hopes of moving the company forward. While this team was experienced and knowledgeable in both retailing and fashion matters, its members never fully understood the basic philosophy of the company's founder: that of creating an excellent, functional product that would, almost by definition, never appeal to a very wide circle of customers. After a disastrous attempt at mass expansion, which separated the company from its core constituency and threatened to displace it from its proven niche, the team was dismissed. Corporate control was returned to former managers who better understood the company's underlying mission.

The same can be said for Celestial's brief and very unhappy marriage with a corporate giant in the mid-eighties. Attempts by the new owner to place this very unique company in the same cookie-cutter mold in which it positioned all of its other subsidiaries negatively impacted morale and almost destroyed the tea maker's heart and soul. Fortunately, the Celestial executives who remained adamantly refused to give in to the pressure, and they eventually regained ownership of their firm and control of their destiny. Once again self-managed, the company is now solidly back on the track that led to its initial successes.

• These companies truly encourage each one of their employees to become part of a shared mission. They are offered stock options in the firm, encouraged to learn all they can about its operations and finances, and urged to take advantage of company-sponsored opportunities for growth in personal and business matters.

The gospel of full worker participation—sometimes known as "empowerment"—is heard more and more these days at large institutions like Ford, Goodyear, and General Electric. But it has been a hallmark of these twelve companies since day one.

Birkenstock and Yakima are among those with companywide

meetings at which everything from executive salaries to corporate donations are openly discussed. Quickie—and its parent, Sunrise—refers to every member of its work force as an "associate" in order to convey its heartful view of them as a partner in their common enterprise; like others, it also actively suggests that workers buy shares in the business. The Grateful Dead rewards longtime employees with positions of importance that sometimes stretch far beyond their central duties. Alfalfa's diligently trains prospective managers for newly created positions and then allows them to have almost free rein to run departments and even entire stores as they see fit.

Free or subsidized classes for employees—touching upon a wide range of subjects—are commonplace. Workers at these companies regularly have the opportunity to learn everything from checkbook balancing and CPR performance to contemporary management techniques and improved communications skills. Sophisticated educational seminars, such as Esprit's in-house lecture series, offer ideas and concepts that extend employees' knowledge about world matters and current affairs.

The result of these various activities is a work force that feels, justifiably, like an integral part of a company that cares for its well-being. This leads to decreased turnover and increased productivity and a more pleasant and satisfying work environment. After all, this was the reason that many of these company founders went into business for themselves in the first place.

• These companies always pay fairly on all levels and usually offer benefit packages that raise total compensation rates to heights far outdistancing the competition.

As executive pay became *the* corporate issue of the early nineties, leaders of these twelve companies remained beyond reproach. That's because their upper managers—from vice-presidents to owners—have never been the beneficiaries of exorbitant, if not undeserved, salaries. They are, in fact, usually underpaid in relation to their peers. But they are paid fairly and are usually eligible for regular bonuses and significant incentives tied to company performance. This latter practice is sometimes called "linked prosperity."

Lower-echelon workers at these businesses, on the other hand, tend to make more than their counterparts in comparable companies. Their pay scales are often relatively high to begin with, and benefits tend to be superior. (How many hourly workers in corporate America, for example, have access to on-site child care as do employees at Ben & Jerry's and Patagonia?) Bonuses, profit sharing, retirement programs, subsidized classes—all are regularly available to most of the full-time workers employed by these firms, which raises their compensation levels even more.

In addition, such generous benefit structures go hand in hand with the pleasant working environments to build loyalty and decrease costly turnover rates. There are incentives and opportunities for advancement regularly available to employees who perform their duties competitively at every level.

• These companies are strongly people oriented at every level, eschewing executive perks and often requiring that all employees be addressed by their first names.

Visitors to the firms profiled in the preceding pages are often surprised at the uniformly democratic nature of their operation. Reserved parking spaces are nonexistent. Titles are usually for outside use only, and telephone directories are sometimes alphabetized according to everyone's first name. On-site cafeterias regularly play host to company presidents and hourly wage earners, who often sit together at the same tables.

Despite the skepticism occasionally directed by outsiders toward such policies, these egalitarian attitudes do not ring false. Most company heads still honestly feel as if *they* are the hourly wage earners, and they refuse to act the way that they themselves never wanted their bosses to act. The result is a casual yet committed atmosphere in which artificial formality and class lines have no place.

The caring attitude that these firms display toward employees and their families is genuine, too. Owners and managers really feel empathy toward their work forces and consider them members of their own extended families. That's why it's easy to institute programs like on-site child care and substance-abuse treatment, which may decrease profits at the outset but generally more than make up for their start-up expenses through increased loyalty and productivity.

Management is also willing to go to great lengths, personally and professionally, to ensure that workers are safe and happy. One of the best examples occurred at Ben & Jerry's, where the plant manager learned of an employee's serious drug problem and not only convinced her to go into a rehab program but took care of her children over the weekend so that she could enter it immediately with peace of mind. That employee today has resumed her role as a productive member of the company and of society at large.

Other firms, like Greyston and America Works, also go the extra mile to make sure that everyone under their umbrella is achieving their potential in the workplace and in their outside lives.

• These companies constantly solicit input from their customers on all manner of subjects—ranging from product direction to corporate donations—and listen to what they are told.

Much as they treat their employees, these firms treat their customers as they themselves want to be treated. They always offer a first-rate product and excellent service. Advice on the use of their products is freely provided. Repairs, exchanges, and refunds are all cheerfully made.

Such action stems from an inherently benevolent attitude toward those who buy their products or use their services. These companies openly detest the word "consumer," which has, unfortunately, become all too common throughout the rest of corporate America. Companies profiled within these pages usually refuse to use it in any context, rejecting the very notion that it implies. Instead, they think of their customers as real people, and that view is manifested in myriad ways during their everyday dealings with the public.

Additionally, most of these companies think of their customers as almost an extension of their work forces, which in turn are considered part of their extended families. That's one reason why The Grateful Dead is happy to provide relatively low priced tickets through mail-order lotteries, why Patagonia is willing to make a free "Guide Line" available with technical assistance on its own products or any outdoor gear, and why Celestial Seasonings operates a toll-free number to provide environmental advice.

Conversely, the companies are happy to listen to suggestions and advice from their customers; many even set up toll-free phone lines to encourage such comments. And they always like to hear success stories and then relay them to employees and other customers through newsletters, catalogs, and other means.

• The founders and upper-level managers at these companies possess an extensive knowledge of current events and display a wide-ranging interest in affairs outside their corporate spheres.

Take an executive from any of these profiled companies to lunch and chances are they'll want to talk about far more than their own businesses. In fact, for many of them the topic of their corporation's operation is the last thing they want to discuss over a meal.

Instead, they're likely to share information on the local homeless situation, regional environmental issues, statewide educational policy, or national-defense matters. And they quickly prove that they are well read on the subjects and knowledgeable about their impact.

These corporate founders, one quickly discovers, have lives outside their corporations. As Grateful Dead cofounder Bob Weir noted, they live in this world with the rest of us. They read, they attend meetings, they pay attention to the society around them. And because they have a vehicle for social change at their fingertips—their companies—these interests regularly result in positive action.

Yakima and Patagonia, for instance, got involved in conservation issues because their founders, employees, and customers were all deeply concerned about the potential implications of current policies. Alfalfa's and Celestial became committed to pesticide and crop-management problems because they touch the companies' daily operations. Ben & Jerry's threw its support behind a dairy co-op and the concept of the family farm. Quickie was driven to start an organization for disabled youngsters. The Grateful Dead has funded school music programs.

But the social commitments of the companies in this book also extend far beyond parochial interests. Shorebank has an art gallery that displays the works of local minority artists. The Dead supports rain-forest preservation efforts. Patagonia gives money to Planned Parenthood. Ben & Jerry's helps fund programs promoting world peace. Esprit is deeply involved in ecological causes.

These and other programs show that socially responsible companies think about more than those issues that directly affect their bottom lines. They care about the entire world around them, and work daily to make it a better place in which to live.

• These companies do not hesitate to offer donations—either of cash or in-kind services—to organizations and people in need of help.

As recently as the mid-eighties, the average donation among American corporations was 2 percent of profits, and only two of the nation's top one thousand largest companies gave as much as 5 percent. Less than 30 percent of all U.S. firms, in fact, gave anything at all.

This follows the line espoused by economist Milton Friedman, who has long argued passionately in his books and essays against the very concept of corporate philanthropy. Such activity undermines the foundation of a free society, the nobel laureate contends, wherein company officials have only one duty: that of making as much money as possible. (For details, one need look no further than the title of Friedman's 1970 article in the *New York Times Magazine:* "The Social Responsibility of Business Is to Increase Profits.") Government, he adds, is the only entity that should work to cure social and environmental problems.

Of course, much of his philosophy was developed and articulated in the sixties, when it was still widely believed that government could—and would—strive to rid society of problems like racism, homelessness, environmental destruction, disease, and poverty. The ensuing decades, though, have been marked by a growing reluctance on the part of government to involve itself in such efforts as well as an increasing inability to fund measures in many of these areas even if it wanted to. Thus, it was only natural for businesspeople, particularly those steeped in the social consciousness of the sixties, to step in where government stepped out.

Companies such as those profiled in this book passionately argue that for-profit businesses—whether public or private corporations—with resources to respond to social ills have the moral obligation to fund needy causes. Furthermore, they note that government, even when it does respond, rarely looks toward the smaller grassroots organizations that these companies favor with their donations.

Additionally, many of these businesses spread their donations around in a democratic manner unforeseen by Friedman and his followers. The pertinent decisions, in other words, are often made by customers and employees along with corporate leaders. Ben & Jerry's, for instance, empowers an employee committee to select recipients for the thousands of dollars realized from its plant tour;

Patagonia makes the names of all its charitable recipients available to anyone—employee or customer—who wants them.

For most of these companies, the act of giving is deeply ingrained in the corporate culture. Money, services, and advice are regularly offered. In return, management, employees, and customers alike are justified in feeling that by simply associating with these companies they are helping to make the world a better place.

• These companies take an active role in the operations of their local communities, and their employees help them extend their influence wherever they do business.

This activity is different from the one described above in that it involves employees at all levels working personally for the betterment of the towns and cities—and surrounding regions—in which they live. It is regularly done on the employees' own time, often at their own initiative and with their employer's full support.

The people at Patagonia and Yakima, for example, are deeply involved in a variety of California's environmental issues that directly affect their lives. The Grateful Dead aids local fishing organizations that support programs enjoyed by several crew members. Employees at Birkenstock and Celestial help other businesses in their home communities develop recycling plans. Workers at Ben & Jerry's offer help to virtually any nonprofit group in their home state that requests it. Staffers at Quickie spend their weekends at athletic events for the disabled. Personal involvement in local affairs has been a hallmark of Shorebank's operation right from the start.

Universities around the country are jumping on this bandwagon, too, as their business schools begin requiring that students take "nontraditional" subjects like ethics and social responsibility. Furthermore, they are regularly mandating community service on top of coursework in these areas.

The personal involvement of the companies in this book is hardly new, and it often reaches far beyond their own cities and states. Shorebank officials travel to Bangladesh to help residents there start their own small businesses. Celestial employees personally help farmers all over the world implement sustainable agricultural practices and modern methods for increasing crop yields. Alfalfa's workers have taken a stand on international controversies like the tuna-dolphin issue and pesticide use.

• These companies deal as often as possible with like-minded businesses, and they encourage their employees to do the same.

A mutually beneficial cycle of commerce and assistance has developed among socially responsible companies, which regularly exchange goods and services and ideas. Not surprisingly, most of these firms also refuse to do any business at all with companies whose policies and principles run contrary to their own.

The most obvious example involves material sourcing, and Ben & Jerry's illustrates that as well as anyone. The company buys recycled products whenever it can, contracts with conscientious suppliers, if possible, for services like health insurance and credit cards, and prefers to deal with responsible vendors when purchasing the ingredients it uses in its ice cream and frozen yogurt. It has also stopped buying certain products when its employees, shareholders, or customers have pointed out valid reasons to suspend such an association. (A popular cookie is no longer an ingredient in one Ben & Jerry's flavor, for instance, at least in part because its manufacturer is a subsidiary of a cigarette maker.)

Additionally, employees at places like Celestial and Alfalfa's occasionally call on their counterparts at Ben & Jerry's for information on everything from recycling programs to personnel policies. Ben & Jerry's employees in turn buy clothing at a discount from Patagonia; the company recently increased its already substantial annual brownie sales account with Greyston Bakery; and it allows Alfalfa's to be the only supermarket in the country to dispense Ben & Jerry's ice cream by the scoop.

The above cyclical practices are growing in number, and when they are put into action, they increase business for everyone while helping conscientious companies take full advantage of the appropriate research and development already under way. (These relatively small companies, in other words, do not have to spend precious time and money reinventing the wheel.) In addition, such activities spark ideas that usually result in improved customer relations and increased community service.

Among other instances of this cyclical relationship: The Grateful Dead helps bands keep concert tickets out of the hands of scalpers and create special areas at concerts where fans can set up their home audiotaping gear, and Shorebank aids financial organizations and government entities that want to organize development banking institutions.

• These companies constantly look to the future but always pay attention to the past.

Forward-thinking business leaders avidly keep abreast of changing times and rarely have to be reminded of the lessons that history has to offer. The combination usually results in carefully thought out corporate and personal philosophies that can be easily adapted to shifting business and social trends.

Flexibility, and a willingness to refocus are two common traits among these firms. As the population ages, for example, Esprit increasingly turns to products that appeal to older customers. Changing nutritional habits spark the development of a line of frozen yogurts from Ben & Jerry's. The growing popularity of mountain bikes leads Yakima to boost its production of automobile roof racks designed to carry them. Quickie recognizes a need to expand from athletic-oriented wheelchairs alone to those for disabled kids and nonathletic adults, too.

At the same time, the recipients of these companies' largess also change when appropriate. Shorebank redirected its primary lending efforts from commercial to residential redevelopment when the latter proved more successful. Ben & Jerry's included peace programs in its social agenda when its founders realized the impact that supporting such causes could have. Patagonia added human-rights groups to its original roster of environmental beneficiaries. Greyston began developing residences for the area's homeless in addition to offering them jobs.

Most of this ever-changing activity grows directly out of the philosophies and principles espoused in mission statements that govern how almost all of these companies operate. These living, breathing documents are usually short on words, but they are consistently long on ideals. And while they never offer specifics, they always provide guidelines that tell every official and every employee exactly what is expected of them and their employer.

Most significantly, perhaps, these mission statements are subject to change. And they are changed, too, whenever the company recognizes a need to expand its direction, refocus its energies, or redefine its very existence.

For as was noted earlier, every company profiled in this book is essentially a collection of people: owners, managers, employees, customers, even neighbors who are affected by the firm's actions and reactions. Companies with a conscience recognize that fact and are always willing—and able—to make the alterations necessary to meet the current needs of the people they affect.

About the Authors

Mary Scott has worked with several companies developing and implementing social and environmental programs. She is also a journalist specializing in business. She lives in Berkeley, California.

Howard Rothman has been a small business owner, newspaper reporter, and magazine editor. He has contributed to nearly seventy publications and is the author of seven books. including *RX, Inc.: The Small Business Handbook for Building a Healthier Workforce.* He lives in Denver, Colorado.